Organizational Learning Contracts

ORGANIZATIONAL LEARNING CONTRACTS

New and Traditional Colleges

Paul S. Goodman

Richard M. Cyert Professor of Organizational Psychology
Carnegie Mellon University

OXFORD
UNIVERSITY PRESS

OXFORD
UNIVERSITY PRESS

Published in the United States of America by Oxford University Press, Inc.,
198 Madison Avenue, New York, NY, 10016
United States of America

Oxford University Press, Inc., publishes works that further Oxford University's
objective of excellence in research, scholarship, and education

Oxford is a registered trade mark of Oxford University Press
in the UK and in certain other countries

Library of Congress Cataloging-in-Publication Data

Goodman, Paul S.
 Organizational learning contracts : new and traditional colleges / Paul S. Goodman.
   p. cm.
 Includes bibliographical references and index.
 ISBN 978-0-19-973865-6 (hardcover : alk. paper)
 1. Learning contracts. 2. Education (Higher) I. Title.

 LB1029.L43G66 2011
 378.1'79—dc22   2010035773

To Denise
A Waterfall of Ideas

CONTENTS

PREFACE

Around 20 years ago, I received a call from the provost of Carnegie Mellon. He wanted to meet. Over the years we had other interactions, but what seemed strange to me was that he was coming to my office versus the more traditional way of setting up an appointment and visiting him.

The focus of this conversation was that the University had signed a memorandum of understanding with ITESM, a large private university in Mexico, and Paul Christiano wanted me to explore partnership opportunities with this university. This was the beginning of a more than 20-year exploration building global alliances for Carnegie Mellon. As discussed later in the book, these have taken many forms such as extending master's degree programs, particularly in information technology, to other countries and universities. There also has been the creation of educational networks composed of universities within or in different countries designed to help underserved educational populations with different forms of technology-enhanced learning. In other instances Carnegie Mellon has been a design partner in establishing new institutions of higher education. In most cases these educational innovations are still functioning. In the case of the original partner (ITESM) there have been a variety of initiatives in executive education, PhD education, and a joint master's program. These global activities have continued and been extended under the current provost, Mark Kamlet.

All of these global activities have paralleled my research agenda, which has focused on organizational change, organizational assessments, and team research, for some 40 years. For many years, these two paths of institution building and research were independent but complementary.

The book creates a convergence of these two paths in my life. It is inherent in the research focus of this book—creating new organizational learning contracts and assessing their impacts. It also is reflected in my choice of providing both a theory and practice component in the book. This practice component is reflected in the contributions of two individuals—Rick Miller and Steve Miller (not related)—who personally led the start up of two new colleges (chapters 7 and 8). I appreciate their collaboration. I drew on my personal experiences for the chapter on Design (chapter 9).

Writing is essentially an individual task. The responsibility for the design, implementation, and writing falls to me, with the exception of the two invited chapters.

At the same time, books are rarely the product of one person. My wife—Denise Rousseau, an organizational psychologist—read, critiqued, and edited all the chapters. In our marriage we have had this wonderful opportunity to provide critiques of each other's work in an open, thoughtful way, and at the same time, have an evolving wonderful marriage.

Gerard Beenen, then a doctoral student and now a professor at California State University, Fullerton, was an integral part of this book. He has played all the important roles including interviewing, data coding, data analysis, and writing, particularly chapter 4 on "Expectations." But more importantly, he has been the closest colleague to work through the big conceptual and more detailed part of writing a book.

Cathy Senderling has been the editor of this book. From year one in my career as an assistant professor, I always have believed in using independent editors. Cathy and I have worked together for a number of years. She has the qualities of being a good technical editor, but more importantly, she sees the big picture and has many important insights on structure.

Betty Cosnek has been my administrative assistant for 14 years. She always has been supportive and understanding. In respect to the book, she has managed the administrative parts of planning and implementing all the field work, as well as the creation of the manuscript. She is a good friend and valued colleague.

Others have contributed. Nora Balint is a relatively new member of our office. She did a great job on all the detailed aspects of building a book, such as problem solving, typing, references, ensuring tables are correct and in the right place. Nicole Jackson was one of our interviewers; she is working on her PhD. We had a big coding job to put the qualitative interview responses into some quantitative form. A group of students, led by Nicholas Yoder, helped in that task.

I appreciate the cooperation of our field sites. They were quite open, and we had access to students, faculty, and staff before and during our two-wave data collection. Following IRB protocol, we have not identified students, faculty, or sites.

This project was supported by NSF grant #0451310. We could not have done the research or book without this support. "Any opinions, findings, and conclusions or recommendations expressed in this material are those of the author(s) and do not necessarily reflect the views of the National Science Foundation."

PART ONE
Theory and Empirical Results

CHAPTER 1
Introduction

Imagine two very different universities, Alpha and Omega. Both recruit top-notch students and excellent faculty. Students spend about $250,000 to be educated at these private universities, both of which place graduates with large and small private- and public-sector employers or graduate programs at prestigious universities. But there the similarities end. Students at Alpha enter with a general idea of what the school will be like, while Omega students start school with very specific expectations about what they will learn and the means by which their learning will occur. Alpha's students mainly expect their school to provide them a challenging education and help them get a good job after graduation. Their instruction mostly consists of traditional methods such as lectures, labs, and some projects. These students are fairly satisfied with their education upon graduation. Students at Omega, on the other hand, expect a lot more than a challenging experience and a job. They expect to develop specific skills such as teamwork and qualitative and quantitative problem solving. They expect to develop these skills through specific forms of instruction including team-based projects that solve real-world problems, peer instruction, mentoring, participation in research projects, and some traditional methods. Omega students are highly satisfied with their learning experience upon graduation and remain very committed to their institution. Employers also are extremely satisfied with Omega's graduates because they are better prepared to solve real-world problems. Employers of Alpha's students, on the other hand, are satisfied with hiring Alpha's graduates because Alpha's selection process ensures most students have abilities that are well above average. Many employers of these graduates, however, spend significant time and resources on training them to solve real-world problems, since their education did not provide them such training—a problem rarely reported by employers of Omega's graduates. There is not a lot of transfer of learning between the learning experience of Alpha and the work setting.

This book develops and tests a framework for understanding, diagnosing, and evaluating differences across educational settings such as that described above, using a concept called an "organizational learning contract." An organizational learning contract (OLC) is a shared agreement among major parties in an educational institution regarding their roles and responsibilities with respect to learning. The relevant parties are students, faculty and staff, as well as alumni and external parties in some cases. The contract is "organizational" because it is initiated by the educational institution and represents a common or shared understanding among the parties about the learning process. In other words, the contract is between the institution and its members.

The contract we are talking about here is focused on learning. It spells out the actions each party should take, as well as defining what, how, when, and where learning unfolds in the institution. It is a collective psychological and normative contract, in that individual members collaborate in support of learning based upon their shared beliefs about how learning will take place. One finding from our research is that students, faculty, and staff in highly ranked traditional institutions have little understanding of any OLC, despite the large amount of time and resources invested in four years of college. Students and faculty in some of the newer institutions presented in the book have much clearer understandings about what, how, when, and where learning will occur.

Institutions have different organizational learning contracts. Some are very explicit while others are more implicit. Explicit means the institution uses many different socialization mechanisms to create a shared understanding about how learning will take place. Implicit means the opposite. Students, faculty, and staff have generic expectations, such as this college will require hard work, it will help me get a job, and so on. These expectations come from prior socialization experiences in high school and from family and friends, and not from the institution of higher education. Some contracts are quite specific as to what, how, when, and where learning will occur; others are more vague. Some contracts deal with many dimensions, while others are narrower.

INTELLECTUAL ORIGINS

The OLC concept has a number of intellectual origins. In the organizational psychology literature, there is an impressive stream of research (cf. Rousseau, 1995) on psychological contracts. These are psychological understandings between employers and individual employees about their roles and obligations. Failure to fulfill these understandings leads to violations and lower effectiveness (Zhao, Wayne, Glibkowski, & Bravo, 2007). It is important to note these psychological contracts are at the individual level. An OLC is at the institutional or college level. However, both rely on individual psychological beliefs and expectations in creating certain phenomena. In addition to the psychological contract research, there also is an educational literature on learning contracts. This parallels the literature on psychological contracts, as the contractual relationship is between a teacher and the student. The task is to build an individualized learning plan between the professor and student in a given course. Again, the OLC differs because it is an understanding initiated at the institutional level; specifically, all students are parties to the contract, and there is a shared understanding between students, faculty, and others about the basic elements of the OLC. All course and non-course learning experiences are part of the OLC.

Another relevant literature deals with organizational change (cf. Goodman, 1982; Goodman, 2001). The question is, how do OLCs come into being? To build psychological understanding among members of an institution requires careful consideration in the design, implementation, and institutionalization of the contract. One does not casually mention the contract in a recruiting visit and leave it at that. Rather, one has to embed the contract among all the relevant players and reinforce it through their practices in the institution. This is a difficult change challenge. Designing the basic elements of the contract is one phase. However, to make it operational one needs to go through the change phases of implementation and institutionalization.

There are other literatures that factor into the OLC concept. Interest in student expectations and satisfaction is related to the OLC (Kuh, Gonyea, & Williams, 2005). Unmet expectations within the OLC can result in student dissatisfaction (e.g., Braxton, Vesper, & Hossler, 1995). The role of student engagement and learning also has connections to OLC (Kuh et al., 2005). Organizational learning contracts can be specified in a way that enhances or detracts from student engagement and learning. Research on institutional image, culture, and mission (Kraatz & Zajac, 1996; Pike, Kuh, & Gonyea, 2003; Belanger, Mount, & Wilson, 2002) also parallels the formation of the OLC. Schools that have a salient identity, a shared set of values and beliefs, and a clearly defined mission may be more likely to have an explicit OLC. Note, however, that this is not necessarily the case. The OLC focuses only on learning, while an institution's image, culture, and mission may or may not be pertinent to specific beliefs about what competencies are to be learned, and how and in which environments these competencies will be learned. Thus, the OLC is both complementary to and distinct from psychological contracts, student expectations, and institutional attributes.

MY ROLE

My background and orientation toward research within and about organizations, rather than a specific focus on higher education policy or research, inform this book's design. I have done research primarily on organizational effectiveness, change, and workplace teams. My studies cross many sectors (e.g., factories, financial offices, mining, hospitals, etc.). I am not a "higher education person." However, as a field researcher, I study organizations to understand how they function by doing intensive studies rather than general surveys or experiments. Doing in-depth organizational studies in various industries provides me a range of perspectives for understanding organizational processes and assumptions that may be less accessible to higher education researchers and administrators.

My venture into the educational sector came about through my role in educational innovation in my university. For the last 20 years I have worked for the Provost of Carnegie Mellon University with a focus on building global educational alliances. Over these years, I have built educational networks (i.e., collaborations among multiple universities to provide education to underserved populations), developed specific global Ph.D. and Master's degree programs for the University, and participated in the design of new universities in Latin America and Asia. I have approached all these educational innovations from the perspective of organizational change and effectiveness. Many of these initiatives are still in operation. My first-hand engagement in these higher education changes provides insight into the issues surrounding the design and implementation of organizational learning contracts in universities.

CONTRIBUTIONS OF THE OLC

One requirement in introducing a new concept like the OLC is to address its contribution to theory and practice. OLCs can offer new perspectives to higher education and organizational researchers, as well as an opportunity for practitioners in the higher education field to sharpen their focus and enhance their educational programs.

CONTRIBUTIONS TO THEORY AND RESEARCH

Organizational learning contracts provide new insights into the literatures on learning, organizational change, organizational effectiveness, and psychological contracts. For example, we examine learning at the college level. We explore whether there is some understanding about learning outcomes and learning environments and how these understandings are learned and shared. This is very different from individual level studies on learning. Or we look at how the different learning environments contribute to personal models of learning. That is, what did the students learn about how to learn? In the change area, we explore, among other issues, the change mechanisms to create an OLC within the college community. We also examine the impacts of developed OLCs on various indicators of organizational effectiveness. In the literature on psychological contracts there is an emphasis on examining the consequences of violations or unmet expectations. In our study we will focus on the opposite case where expectations are met or exceeded.

Our main theoretical contribution will be in the development of the OLC. We want to explore how to operationalize this concept, identify differences across institutions, and assess its effectiveness. Answers to these issues will be relevant to researchers in the three literatures mentioned above as well as in higher education.

Contributions for Practice

This book will inform not only redesign in existing organizations but also the design of new organizations and institutions. If you are setting up a new educational institution, school, or organization, you need to think about how it will be different. You will be competing for students who might choose to go to established institutions. The challenge is to chart out the distinguishing features of your institution. In the context of OLC, an organization's leaders need to ask, "What features distinguish our contract from those of others?" Starting a new institution, in a sense, requires creation of a distinctive OLC.

At the same time, existing institutions are continuously facing a need to adapt to new challenges (e.g., financial constraints, new types of competitors). The environment of higher education is changing. Consequently, existing institutions must position themselves clearly in relation to alternative institutions. If two schools, for example, have equally strong reputations in undergraduate education, how can potential students determine which one may be a better fit for their goals and interests? The OLC provides a framework for helping institutions not only redesign themselves, but also position themselves relative to one another. Literatures on learning, organizational change, and design provide direction for the redesign process. The OLC also helps potential students, faculty, and administrators evaluate their interest in a particular institution. Whether it is a new or existing institution, OLC design is a critical process.

Another contribution is in the area of diagnosis and analysis. The OLC permits us to explore the intended outcomes from a college leader's or faculty's point of view and observe what actually occurs within that educational institution. Consider these two examples. I talked with a dean of a highly ranked educational institution about the college's OLC. We both agreed that having explicit learning outcomes should facilitate learning. The dean said the institution had eight 'metaskills' (e.g., quantitative analysis, team skills) students should acquire. These eight skills purportedly were well accepted by faculty, students, and staff. We subsequently went into this institution to do some systematic data collection. No student was familiar with all eight metaskills; in fact, we found that most had an incomplete understanding of only two or three. In point of fact, no real contract focused on learning outcomes existed. I went to another well-regarded school that claimed having its students do research was a defining characteristic of the institution. The school stated that doing research put students in a mentoring relationship and created a different learning environment. Follow-up assessments, however, indicated this school's students generally had no understanding that research was a learning opportunity available to them.

Both examples show the diagnostic value of the OLC. Properly executed, OLCs help educational institutions determine what has been promised and what has been realized with regard to learning. If there is a discrepancy between the promised contract and the contract in people's heads, then new processes need to be put in place. The question for the first institution, for example, was what mechanisms needed to be put in place to ensure the eight metaskills were a known part of everyone's contract and how could this understanding be sustained over time? This book will draw from the change literature to review key processes for implementation and institutionalization of the OLC.

Another example of the value of the OLC to practitioners is in the curriculum area. Organizational learning contracts should contain learning outcomes and learning environments. Learning outcomes represent the "what"—specifically, the knowledge, skills, and abilities you want the students to acquire. Learning environments refer to how, when, and where learning happens. Lecture, discussion, group projects, and peer teaching are all examples of learning environments. Mapping the relationship between learning environments and outcomes is fairly complex. Some environments work better or worse with different learning outcomes. For example, team skills are difficult to acquire via lecture; instead, group project work with feedback is probably more effective. The OLC provides a framework for designing and evaluating linkages between learning environments and outcomes.

One tool for mapping these linkages over a student's four-year educational period is to develop a matrix of learning environment by learning outcomes. Table 1.1 illustrates an outcome by course matrix for a business college. One can trace different learning environments by each learning outcome. Note the differences in learning approaches. This is an illustrative matrix compared to a more

Table 1.1. CURRICULUM MATRIX–INSTITUTE OF
MANAGEMENT–FIRST SEMESTER

Learning Outcomes	Learning Environments	
	Quarter 1	Quarter 2
Business Problem Solving	Lecture course in Economics	Case discussion course in Organizational Behavior
Collaborative Skills	Team Project on Economics	Team Skills Workshop
Global Multi-Cultural	Self-paced Language course	Self-paced Language course
Ethical	Great Books Discussion	Great Books Discussion
Leadership	Great Books Discussion	Leader Skills Workshop
Learning to Learn	Apprentice on Selected Country with mentor	Apprentice Assessment and Redesign–Curriculum with mentor

comprehensive matrix. The learning outcomes appear in the left column. Two quarters of data are shown. We inserted some, but not all of the learning experiences. In cell 1 there is a lecture course in economics. For collaborative skills there is a team project in economics. For global multi-cultural skills there is a self-paced language course. A discussion on Great Books contributes to ethical and leadership skills. Doing an apprenticeship with a professor on a selected country forces the student to think about how to learn. Since the problem is on another country, it enhances both 'learn to learn' and multicultural skills. In quarter 2, you see similar and different learning experiences for each of the outcomes.

This matrix would be extended for all four years. It is a visual way to show: (1) whether the learning outcomes are being reinforced, (2) whether different learning environments are being used, and (3) whether learning outcomes are being reinforced by different learning environments. The matrix can be used in building a new curriculum or reviewing a current one that needs to be revised.

Another diagnostic function of the OLC is to identify sources of satisfaction or dissatisfaction in educational institutions through assessment mechanisms. Most institutions are interested in this kind of data in order to build lifelong participants in their educational community. Satisfied students eventually become satisfied graduates. And satisfied alumni can become future employers, donors, contributors, and so on. The advantage of the OLC as a tool to accomplish these goals is that it contains highly specific expectations between the organization and its students about what will be learned and how. Therefore, the fundamental question over the ensuing four years is whether these expectations are being met, exceeded, or not met. All three categories are important for assessing some aspects of organizational satisfaction and effectiveness.

In summary, the specific expectations contained in the OLC can help inform research in a number of arenas, as well as helping institutions get better at designing, diagnosing, and redesigning the systems and processes that contribute to effective educational outcomes. All of these factors contribute to making the OLC an important tool for both theory and practice.

CURRENT TENSIONS AND THE OLC

Another way to think about this book is to look at the broader context in higher education. There are several reasons we should spend intellectual time and resources doing in-depth studies of this sector.

First, tertiary institutions are a critical part of the economic and social institutions of our society. In today's knowledge-based economy and society, universities, as engines of knowledge creation and transmission, become a more integral part of our daily lives (Duderstadt, 2000). Therefore, focusing on the distinctive roles of new tertiary institutions provides insights into how they may evolve and the implications of their evolution on existing institutions in particular, and society in general.

Second, although universities are major engines in our knowledge economy, there are forces working against their viability. These forces are driving the evolution and adaptation of new forms of higher education. The *financial* pressures are extreme for both public and private universities. Declines in public allocations, declining endowments, and increasing demands for student aid all place burdens on a university's economic viability (Rhodes, 2004). In addition, the *globalization of education* has paralleled the globalization of the economy. The emergence of educational gateways in locations like Singapore, which attract international universities, suggests we need to think globally when looking for new forms of higher education. It also increases the competitive environment for higher education. At the same time, *student demands* are changing. More students with diverse backgrounds want access to higher education, and their needs are more complicated (Zemsky & Duderstadt, 2004; Sax, Lindholm, Astin, Korn, Mahoney, 2001). The *information technology revolution* is further changing the structure and processes of the university (Goodman, 2001; Duderstadt, 2000). Newer forms of competition, such as the geographically distributed educational networks, represent alternatives to the more traditional forms of higher education. The growing role of multimedia technology is also changing how students learn. Finally, increasing pressures for *accountability* in institutional performance from public and private funders raise more questions about the role of the university (Rhodes, 2004). The implications of these forces or pressures include expanded and diverse providers of education, giving potential students more choices; fewer physical campuses; faculty operating independently of any one college or university; unbundling of the teaching, research and service functions; and so on (Levine, 2001). Whether all of these or other consequences occur is not the critical point. The basic idea is that several significant forces are threatening the viability of some educational institutions, while creating opportunities for new forms of institutions to emerge and evolve. The level of competition from traditional sources and new providers is becoming stronger over time. These external forces call for a redesign process in the field of higher education. The OLC and its components provide a framework for this redesign. Organizational learning contracts hold the potential to help new and existing institutions do more with less by focusing their energies and resources on the achievement of specific learning outcomes and new learning environments.

EMPIRICAL PERSPECTIVE

The general literature on higher education includes theoretical papers, qualitative pieces, and large-scale survey studies. Our strategy was to do an intensive longitudinal study of OLCs in three institutions. We collected data via one-on-one interviews from a sample of students over time. This strategy made sense given our focus to highlight the OLC. We wanted to see (1) how to measure the OLC; (2) what the differences are across institutions; (3) what the implications are for different contracts across institutions on student expectations, satisfaction and effectiveness; and (4) what we can learn about the practices of designing, diagnosing, implementing, and sustaining the OLC. These types of issues led us to do a more intensive study than a large sample study with a survey method. The latter type of study would not be able to answer these specific research questions. In addition, all our data have been coded, with appropriate checks for reliability, and quantitatively analyzed. This strengthens our ability to respond to the four research questions raised above.

Another unique feature of our empirical work is that we have selected two new institutions and one established or traditional institution as our sample. The new institutions had been in operation for around five years, while the traditional institution has been in operation for approximately 100 years. We examined both new and traditional institutions because we wanted to maximize the potential differences we might find in the institutions' OLCs. Our assumption was that new institutions might try to differentiate themselves through more explicit OLCs than an older, more established school.

All three institutions value both research and teaching and are not primarily focused on being high-quality teaching institutions. Additionally, all of these institutions have a physical location. That is, students are physically present rather than operating in a geographically distributed manner. Virtual universities (Cruz, 2001) are an interesting new form of higher education, but that is not our focus. Third, our institutions are autonomous. That is, the basic processes of designing the institution, implementation, and operation are done by each college. There may be ties to a larger institution, but independence is key.[1] Lastly, some of the colleges offer graduate degrees, others do not.

Given these similarities, the next question focuses on how the new and traditional institutions are different. Table 1.2 provides a general contrast between a new institution and a well-known traditional institution. Both organizations attract high-quality students and faculty. These specific differences in our sample will be explored in more detail in chapter 3.

Note that we are not arguing that these are the necessary or sufficient features of new forms of higher education. Different schools may have different combinations of features. But there are some basic structural differences between new and traditional institutions (Table 1.2). In the traditional institution, work is organized around departments, performance is defined in terms of research output with

1. There are examples of new colleges created by and within existing institutions (e.g., University of Michigan, George Mason), but these colleges are physically and organizationally highly interdependent with the larger institution (Duderstadt, 2000), and hence, would not be included in our sample.

Table 1.2. CONTRASTING NEW AND TRADITIONAL
INSTITUTIONS OF HIGHER EDUCATION

New	Traditional
Organization	
Interdisciplinary areas	Formal Departments
Interest groups	
Performance Criteria for Professors	
High-Quality teaching	High-Quality research papers
High-Quality research papers	High-Quality teaching
Patents	
Entrepreneurial startups	
Employment Policy	
No Tenure/Tenure	Tenure
Learning Environment	
Problem/project-based	Lecture with some problem/ project-based
Culture	
Continuous Innovation	High-Quality Work

expectations about high-quality teaching and the result of good faculty performance is tenure, a characteristic of most elite research institutions. The new institution differs with respect to its organizational form, performance criteria, and employment policy dimensions. In the process of teaching, the students in the new institution play very different roles. They are involved in the design of the curriculum and play active roles in teaching. Their learning environments focus on active learning and use a variety of learning approaches, such as group projects, peer teaching, and mentors to create explicit learning outcomes. Some of these features might also be present in the traditional institution, but their emphasis in the new institution is much stronger.

Another way to understand the new institutions in our study is to contrast them with a group of other new institutions that shares elements of the traditional institutions we studied. The key distinction is between new (in terms of age) and innovative (in terms of new ways to learn). Throughout the world, there have been new startups of institutions of higher education that in many ways are the same as the traditional organization we studied (see Table 1.2), in terms of their approach to learning. These startups have, to some degree, been reactions to existing public institutions, which essentially had "monopoly" positions discouraging innovation, with little faculty or student identification with these institutions. In contrast to the large public institutions, the new schools were smaller, more student-focused in terms of services and generally privately sponsored—but, like the traditional schools, these new schools were still organized by departments, and their approach to learning was the same as the large public universities (with the exception of smaller class sizes). That is, they looked pretty much like the traditional institutions in terms of learning, but were smaller in size and somewhat more student focused. This is quite different from the new institutions we studied. The new schools in this study have a completely different organizational structure than traditional schools and, more importantly, the students are involved in the key decision-making processes in the school. The differences between the new schools we studied and traditional schools go far beyond class-size reduction. The learning model in the new schools we studied is dramatically different. The students are involved in active learning, not just listening to lectures. Throughout their college years they are involved in mentoring, peer teaching, and project-based learning. Thus, there are fundamental differences between the new, innovative colleges we examined here and a new start-up that still shares many core elements with older, traditional schools.

PREVIEWING SOME CRITICAL ISSUES

Before we conclude this chapter, it is important to preview some of the critical issues inherent in this book, regarding the concept of OLCs.

The Change Dilemma

The OLC is about building a contract with members of an institution of higher education. It represents a shared understanding about who should do what, where, and how about learning. Explicit in this concept of OLC is change. Remember that we pointed out above the strong external forces that are challenging the viability of institutions of higher education, all of which represent initiators of change. At the same time there are equivalent counter-forces resisting change and attempting to maintain the "status quo." Since introducing and sustaining an OLC requires substantial organizational change, the fundamental question is whether it is likely to happen. Are the forces against change stronger than the net benefits of specific forms of OLCs?

Our basic response to this change dilemma is that new institutions will arise. These could be brand-new institutions or spin-offs from an existing institution (e.g., an honors college). Our expectations are that some of these will be in North America, but many more will be in other countries. One challenge when starting a new organization of any kind is differentiating what you plan to do from what is already being done. In the field of higher education, the OLC is one way to signal how your institution will be different. The other response to the change dilemma is that existing institutions could use parts of the OLC for diagnosis and redesign. For example, the dean mentioned earlier who claimed that his faculty, students, and staff understood the learning outcomes, could use the empirical data he received suggesting otherwise to initiate changes without building a brand-new learning contract. That is, parts of the OLC could help in diagnosis and redesign.

Levels of Analysis

Another fundamental question is whether the OLC is at the institutional or college level. Think of a university composed of different colleges. One college might be in engineering, another in fine arts, and still another in business. These are pretty different content or disciplinary areas. From our perspective, the OLC exists at the *college* level. The contract for a college of fine arts would be different from that of a college of computer science. In the next chapter, we will explore in more detail the issue of the OLC and levels of analysis. There are a variety of interesting issues, such as whether there can be both a college OLC and also some system-wide learning outcomes at a higher level of analysis (i.e., the university). How does an OLC work in a liberal arts college? Would the contract be the same for all the departments (e.g., chemistry vs. English)? We preview these issues here because we think they are important. The issues are further developed in the following chapters.

Generalizability

Two types of generalizability are relevant here. The first is whether the OLC is generalizable across disciplines. That is, can you build OLCs for a fine arts college and for a computer science college? Our position is that OLCs will work across disciplines, but there will be differences in the learning outcomes and learning environments. That is, designing and evaluating experiments in a science college probably would not be relevant in a fine arts college. The idea of stating outcomes and specifying the links between learning environments and learning outcomes would be the same for both colleges, but the content of learning environments and outcomes will be different.

The second generalizability question deals with what types of institutions of higher education would fit with the OLC construct. Our basic position, given the change dilemma mentioned above, is to focus on four-year, face-to-face institutions. The basic rationale is quite simple. Building a shared understanding about learning is a complicated change process. It requires multiple socialization processes, rich reinforcements, and on-going feedback. These conditions are more feasible to achieve at a regular four-year, face-to-face institution. In institutions that focus on distributed learning or primarily evening classes, it will be much harder to build an effective OLC. The socialization processes in the latter types of institutions are much more restrictive.

ORGANIZATION OF THE BOOK

This book is organized into two parts. The first section provides a theoretical perspective for organizing our thoughts on the concept of an OLC. We then present some empirical data contrasting new and traditional institutions. Specifically, we look at how expectations, learning environments, and selected effectiveness outcomes differ among these institutions. In part two, the practice section, we invite some of the designers and leaders of new institutions to reflect on what they have learned. These new innovative institutions have already passed the five-year mark. At least one class has graduated from each new institution, so there is a rich set of experiences to process. We ask the designers and leaders of the new institutions to reflect on their challenges and actions over the timeline, which begins with the conception of each new institution to its design, implementation, and transformation to its current state of equilibrium. These "lessons learned" should be valuable to people involved in starting new institutions, as well as those who are involved in redesigning existing institutions. Another chapter examines the role of a designer of these innovative institutions. A final chapter integrates the book's two parts with issues of theory and practice.

CHAPTER 2

Organizational Learning Contracts

This chapter delineates the concept of the organizational learning contract, the intellectual frame for our work. The learning contract represents the beliefs the respective parties hold regarding their duties, responsibilities, and expectations of each other in regard to learning. These beliefs are socially shared normative expectations about activities relevant to learning embedded in the organization. The key actors or participants in a learning contract in higher education include professors, students, administrators, alumni, and, sometimes, external constituencies.

Some of our research questions include:

- What is an organizational learning contract (OLC)?
- How does the nature of OLCs vary across institutions?
- How do the form and substance of the learning contract contribute to individual learning and organizational-level effectiveness?

DEFINITIONS

An organizational learning contract (OLC) is a shared agreement or understanding among the major parties in an educational institution regarding their respective roles and responsibilities with respect to learning. The fact that these understandings are shared is a structural property of the OLC. In other words, the relevant actors within the institution know the elements of the OLC, and everyone knows that others hold these same understandings or expectations. These understandings are at the institution level, independent of any individual. If a single student or professor leaves the institution, the contract is still intact. If a new person joins the institution, we should see socialization mechanisms in operation to ensure the newcomer develops an understanding of the contract elements. Of course, the extent to which these understandings are (or are not) shared among all parties shapes the strength and content of the OLC, a point discussed later in this chapter.

The understandings within an OLC represent beliefs or expectations about learning. Some understandings are quite general, such as "college will be challenging academically," or "I have to work much harder than in high school to get good grades." Others are more specific, such as "I need to be actively i nvolved in the design or redesign of this institution," or "I will be both a student and a teacher to my peers." Where the understandings are widely shared and more specific, they play an important role in guiding what behaviors members of the institution display.

The major parties to this contract include students and professors. Other players include administrators (e.g., deans, program heads, department heads) and staff (e.g., admissions counselors, student services staff). All of these individuals play some part in the learning process so, given our focus, they each should have expectations about their own roles as well as expectations about others' roles, such as teachers and students. They all are part of the organizational learning contract.

In some of the new tertiary institutions, alumni are seen as participants in the learning process. Their role is to come back to the institution in a lifelong learning role and some may come back as teachers. That is, alumni can be both learners and teachers. In some of these institutions, firms are also players in the learning process. By providing internships, they play an important role in the students' learning experiences. In some cases, firm personnel share their experiences in the classroom. Hence, they also hold an OLC.

There are at least two observations that arise from this enumeration of roles. First, there is considerable diversity across roles (e.g., student, professor, staff). Some roles, such as those of students and professors, impact learning in the classroom; others impact learning outside the classroom, such as staff or student activities coordinators. Some focus on intellectual skill acquisition, while others (e.g., advisors) deal with personal growth. Second, within a specific role, there may be substantial diversity. A professor in history may have very different views about learning attainment than a professor in math. Here, inherent differences across disciplines lead to different assumptions about what is to be learned and how learning comes about. This diversity between and within roles complicates the process of achieving shared expectations about the nature of the learning contract and shared understandings about whether the contract has been enacted. However, as will be discussed in the following sections, key elements of the OLC (e.g., learning outcomes) can transcend a specific course or discipline.

We used the broad term "educational institutions" in our initial definition of the OLC. The focus here, as previously noted, will be on tertiary institutions. Our primary interest is on four-year colleges that operate in face-to-face, rather than distributed, environments. These could range from colleges within large public or private universities to smaller, stand-alone liberal arts colleges. Educational institutions not included in this work are discussed in the section on "Design Issues" (p. 15 ff).

The last element in our definition is learning. We see this as a process by which people acquire new repertoires of behaviors. "Behaviors" are broadly understood to include values, attitudes, beliefs, knowledge, and specific skills, all of which influence behavior. The OLC, then, represents shared understandings about roles, responsibilities and activities that should or should not be enacted by the respective parties in the process of learning. They represent the what, how, who, when, and where about learning.

DIMENSIONS OF THE LEARNING CONTRACT

A learning contract represents a multi-dimensional space. In tertiary institutions, there are at least three major dimensions of a learning contract. First, there are learning outcomes. These are the results of the learning process, what we want to achieve. If someone graduates from an institution of higher education, what are the knowledge, skills, and abilities they should have acquired? Second, there are different learning environments (e.g., lectures, labs, apprenticeships) for learning. These are the ways in which learning takes place. Lastly, the learning outcomes and environments occur and are shaped by learning systems. These are the processes and mechanisms that implement, sustain, assess, and redesign the dimensions of the contract (see Figure 2.1).

We next examine each of these three dimensions in further detail.

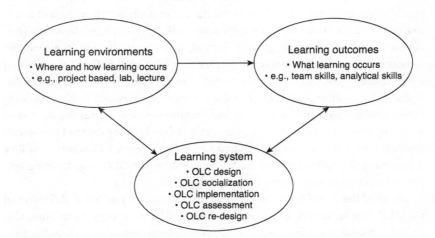

Figure 2.1: Dimensions of the Organizational Learning Contract (OLC)

Learning Outcomes

These represent the learning goals of the institution. Learning outcomes represent the knowledge, skills, and abilities to be acquired. Examples of learning outcomes from the institutions in our sample include quantitative skills, team or collaboration skills, or learning how to learn. Our goal is simply to provide examples of the concept of learning outcomes, not to suggest that these specific outcomes are the ideal set of outcomes for all schools. In each institution, the mix of outcomes will be different.

What are some key features of learning outcomes? First, they can be explicitly or not stated in the learning contract. In some institutions in our study, one can find discussions of targeted learning outcomes on the institution's website, during the recruiting of new students, in various presentations about the school, on course syllabi, and so on. These outcomes represent, at least in part, what the institution is attempting to do. They are explicit. It is possible for a set of outcomes to emerge *ex post*. That is, over time a set of outcomes emerges, which are understood to be the outputs of a particular institution. However, even in this scenario, we would expect some public forums to acknowledge these outcomes as part of the organization's identity. In this example the outcomes became explicit over time and we would expect to see differences in learning processes in the "before" and "after" conditions. If the outcomes are not stated, there will be no shared understanding and little guidance for what students should learn. That would be dictated by specific courses.

A second feature of OLC learning outcomes is the degree to which they are demonstrable. For example, an outcome that has appeared in a variety of educational institutions is the concept of collaborative skills. Given that a lot of work activities occur in a team context, acquiring collaborative skills can be seen as a desirable outcome. The issue is how you would know whether such a skill was acquired. The more you can be explicit about what collaborative skills are, the easier it will be to socialize people in that skill, reinforce that skill, develop a shared understanding of that skill and measure it. Some examples of subskills within the collaboration concept might include managing time in a group, making group strategies explicit, and resolving points of conflict. For any of these subskills, one can identify metrics. For example, the metrics for managing time in a group can draw upon a rich literature on the timing and pacing of groups, alternative measurement procedures, and some normative rules about how pacing can lead to effective or ineffective group performance (Gersick, 1988; 1989).

What one wants to avoid is general or abstract statements of outcomes that do not have clear, demonstrable indicators. Presenting an outcome such as improving "global awareness" is too general. If one can move to a more specific enunciation of that outcome, such as the ability to speak and read another language, the outcome then becomes demonstrable and measurable. In any institution, there will be a limited number of important learning outcomes. The outcomes of greatest importance should be stated at a level where one can identify specific operational and trainable subskills. Note, however, that there also is a danger in being too specific by listing so many subskills that faculty and students cannot identify, let alone focus on, the most important. This makes the OLC unmanageable and undermines its goals. People's attention is limited. The focus should be on a small number of very key outcomes with measurable subskills.

A third feature of OLC learning outcomes is they are linked to specific learning experiences. That is, the contract is that (a) the student will have a new set of collaboration skills, and (b) these skills are linked to the specific student's learning experiences in the institution. From a causal perspective, the learning of collaborative skills is linked to identified learning environments (e.g., project-based learning) and not due to other exogenous factors such as students' natural maturation. An important qualification is that the learning experiences or environments can be tied to courses, a curriculum, or non-course learning opportunities within the institution; there is significant design flexibility within the OLC framework.

The rationale for including learning outcomes as part of the OLC is quite straightforward. If you know what you are to learn and how to determine when you have learned it via measurable indicators of your success, it focuses your attention on these dimensions over the four years and facilitates learning (Anderson, 2000). If I know that I will be evaluated on whether I develop collaborative skills, I focus my attention on learning activities that will facilitate collaborative skills. As long as the learning environments connect to the outcomes, learning should occur.

Learning Environments

In addition to outcomes, the learning contract deals with learning environments. These refer to how learning takes place. There are some basic assumptions underlying these environments. Some of these may include:

- The student is primarily a passive or active learner.
- The professor is primarily a provider of information or a mentor and co-learner.
- The focus is on absorbing teaching material or developing problem-solving skills.
- The knowledge presented is primarily explicit or both explicit and tacit.

One of the popular environments is the lecture. We all have images of entering the large lecture hall with the professor poised to present a class. The assumptions underlying this model include: the student is primarily a passive learner, the professor is a provider of information, the focus is on absorbing the lecture material, and the information is primarily explicit. This learning model is prevalent throughout the world.

However, there are many other learning environments. Table 2.1 describes different models, their focus, and rationale. For example, learning on your own puts students in a semi-structured position where they have to search and acquire information on their own. This contrasts with a lecture, where one is provided the information and must encode the information and then be able to apply it in some later situation. Developing learning on your own is a metaskill, which has broad implications for learning after college. Another environment is peer-based instruction, in which the student becomes the teacher. Here, the task is to take a body of information and decide how to effectively organize it and present it to others. This is another powerful process for learning.

One characteristic of the new forms of higher education institutions is a greater emphasis on the alternative models in Table 2.1. They are not emphasizing these forms of learning simply to distinguish themselves from more traditional institutions. The fundamental assumption is these more active forms of learning facilitate learning and transfer of learning to new situations (Barnett & Ceci, 2002).

Table 2.1. ALTERNATIVE LEARNING MODELS

Learning Environment	Focus	Underlying Rationale
On your own	Learning how to learn	Learning is a life-based rather than just a school-based activity and students need to learn to do it on their own.
As an apprentice	Learning from and observing how experts solve problems—tacit knowledge	Higher-order thinking and problem-solving skills grow out of direct experience.
In a team	Acquiring collaborative skills	Group settings force new forms of learning. Effective groups are critical for many work and non-work activities.
In a studio	An alternative to the traditional classroom with an emphasis on learning content by doing. It represents a combination of mini lecture, lab, and discussion within a classroom format.	Students learn more and more deeply when involved in "guided practice" with timely and constructive feedback that enables them to continually evolve their understanding and/ or skills.
In an internship	Learning how to apply knowledge and skills in a real-world setting	Learning is enhanced when it takes place in the context of a compelling situation.
As a peer-based instructor	Learning by teaching others	Students are forced to organize information, connect it to prior knowledge of their peers, provide examples, etc.—activities that enhance information processing and thus integration into existing knowledge structures.

The models in Table 2.1 contrast with the more traditional forms of learning such as lecture, discussion, and laboratory sessions.

Another way to characterize learning environments is how explicitly the mix of environments is stated. In some of the new institutions in our study, they state the mix of learning environments in a very specific way through multiple socialization mechanisms. That is, both before the students come to the college and when they are in residence, they are explicitly told about and participate in the different learning environments. Therefore, we would expect to see clear expectations about project-based learning, peer teaching, mentoring, and so forth in the OLCs of these institutions. It is not that peer-based learning, for example, will be absent from other institutions. But the socialization process for this form of learning environment will be less explicit. Also, the frequency of employing peer-based learning or other related environments will be less in these other institutions.

Organizational Systems

The third part of the OLC is a series of organizational systems that are responsible for the socialization, assessment, and redesign of the learning contract. These are embedded at the institutional level and are likely to be enacted by staff (e.g., admissions for recruiting), faculty, and administrators. They represent structural mechanisms of the organization, independent of any individual.

Socialization

Above, we mentioned that one key feature of the learning contract is its level of explicitness. The learning outcomes and learning environments need to be well understood. But how does this happen? The answer is that it can happen in several ways. First, there are many socialization mechanisms within an organization that can be used to ensure the OLC becomes and remains a shared understanding. These efforts may have started during the recruiting process, before students become members of the institution. They may be in the form of recruiting materials, visits by recruiters, or visits to the new campus. Upon acceptance, the socialization process continues in orientation and throughout the four-year period. The design of the curriculum is another approach to socialize or reinforce the contract. Curriculum committees reinforce outcomes by building course matrices (like the one shown in chapter 1) over the four years to visualize how learning outcomes are acquired over time and across courses using different learning environments. This is an independent way to determine which courses and learning environments are reinforcing the learning outcomes. In addition, a variety of system components can support the OLC during the four-year period. These may come in the form of out-of-class activities that support the contract, grading on both course activities and learning outcomes, or having students monitor their own progress on learning outcomes. The key idea is that there is a series of activities, both pre-college and during college, designed to create a shared understanding of the OLC.

Other organizational mechanisms can be used to reinforce a shared understanding of the learning contract. In most higher education institutions, relevant effectiveness indicators typically come from administrators or the board of the institution, rather than from faculty or students. The decision about how and when to evaluate a faculty member's performance is a related element. The elements of the evaluation process signal the relative importance of teaching, research and innovation to the institution. We would expect an institution's faculty evaluation and reward system to support specific elements of its learning contract. If the institution's effectiveness indicators focus primarily on research outputs and less on the quality of the undergraduate experience, for example, we would not expect to see learning environments requiring high levels of labor investment on the part of the teacher (e.g., studios, apprenticeships). Similarly, the culture of the institution is another mechanism for shaping the learning contract. If the learning contract focuses on certain explicit outcomes, such as teamwork or communication skills, we would expect a culture that focuses and reinforces attitudes and beliefs about the importance of these skills.

Assessment

Another key system component that can shape the organization's learning environments and outcomes is an assessment of the state of learning. Are the learning outcomes being realized? Is the stated mix of learning outcomes and environments being deployed? We would expect organizations with strong OLCs to have multiple forms of assessment. These could come from course performance, student evaluations, or assessments from external constituencies (e.g., business partners). In the case of the professor's assessment, course performance would be divided into assessments of how well the professor is meeting course goals and meeting learning outcomes relevant for this particular course. In a more traditional institution, student course evaluations would be a major assessment mechanism. In this case, the evaluation is as much about the nature of the course as it is about specific outcomes.

The basic role of assessment is to determine whether there is a discrepancy between desired states and actual states. Let's take the outcome "lifelong learning." An assessment of this outcome would require identifying subskills such as the ability to search for information. We would look at antecedents such as the number of times the student practiced search activities on a project and received feedback. Changes in the quality and speed of search would identify possible skill changes. If there are discrepancies (i.e., actual states are lower than desired states), this would motivate a redesign process.

Redesign

After ensuring the OLC is explicitly understood and assessing the state of learning in the institution, the third task of the organizational system is to correct discrepancies between desired and actual states in the learning contract by initiating redesign activities. In some institutions, this is done by the senior administration or a curriculum committee led by faculty. Also, there may be student involvement. Our experience is that in the newer innovative institutions, students are more involved in the total redesign effort than in traditional institutions.

The basic task over time is to (1) identify any discrepancies between the expected contract dimensions and the enacted dimensions; (2) to understand the source of the discrepancy; and (3) to reintroduce, as appropriate, a mix of socialization mechanisms, structural changes in the institution, and assessment and redesign processes in order to remove the discrepancies and maintain the contract over time.

In all of this, alignment is a key theme. Alignment means the three components of the OLC—the outcomes, learning environment, and system mechanisms—complement one another to some degree. If we wanted to enhance the outcome of "lifelong learning," for example, we would not adopt the lecture method as the dominant learning environment. Other environments, such as apprenticeships, teams, studios, and peer instruction, would be more aligned with this outcome. If we wanted to emphasize an apprentice-mentor model, which is very labor intensive, we need to design a congruent performance evaluation system for the mentor or professor. If the organizational context is characterized by an autocratic culture with centralized decision making, then it will be difficult to build collaborative learning environments and to expect collaborative skills as a viable learning outcome.

SOME DESIGN ISSUES

At this point the reader should have a basic idea of the OLC and its three major components: outcomes, learning environments, and organizational systems. In this section we want to clarify some basic design issues: the level of analysis, the generalizability of contracts, and how to differentiate across contract types.

Level of Analysis

One fundamental question is about selecting the level of analysis. A typical university operates at the university, college, department, and perhaps center or institute levels. We have been clear that the OLC is at the organizational level, but which part of an organization is the appropriate level? A university represents tremendous diversity in disciplines. The learning activities and experiences in an engineering or science college are quite different from learning in a fine arts college.

Our view is that one should build the OLC at the college level, not primarily at the university level. We suggest this for two primary reasons. First, there are inherent differences in what is to be learned and how skills are to be learned. Much of the learning for the science college occurs in the lab. That is not true for the people teaching or learning fine arts such as music. The second reason deals with the implementation and evolution of the contract, meaning how the learning outcomes and learning environments become understood and shared by the faculty, students, and staff. As pointed out above, this represents a big investment in socializing the parties to the contract. In addition, it means providing students and faculty with assessment and feedback on their progress along the learning outcomes. Also, there need to be some system mechanisms for redesigning the contract as warranted. All of these activities—socialization, assessment/feedback, and redesign—are much easier to do in a college with homogeneous interests. Also, a college is simply a smaller unit than a university. A college's smaller size and greater homogeneity should enhance the ability to implement these three processes.

While we argue that the OLC should be at the college level, there could be room for some metaskills in the OLC. One could see a university articulating a small number of these skills that it believes should be common to the OLCs across its colleges. Writing and presentation, problem-solving, or global awareness skills are possible examples. The university might take the position that regardless of your college concentration, developing and improving your writing and presentation skills is essential for any graduate of the institution. These specific skills might be enacted in a different context for the chemistry or history major. But improvement of these skills could be a consistent, university-level position. It would be emphasized in pre-college recruiting materials, orientation, and through workshops during the four years. Of course, there needs to be a link between the college and university. Both units need to embrace these metaskill sets for any learning to occur.

Alignment between the university's culture, goals, etc., and the college's OLC is critical, not just for the creation of the metaskills mentioned above. If a college within a university wants to redesign its OLC to represent a more explicit set of learning outcomes and a more diverse set of learning environments, it needs some level of independence to do this redesign work. The college also needs to be sure that the university's reward system is compatible with its newly designed OLC.

The liberal arts college represents a different setting. Such schools are often much smaller than even colleges within a university. Also, their focus is on creating a special undergraduate learning experience. The level of analysis at a liberal arts college follows the same principles as presented above, but the balance between metaskills and disciplinary skills is different. Remember, the contract is about learning. Acquiring the skills to design and evaluate an experiment in chemistry is still different from doing literary analysis. That is, both what one should learn (learning outcomes) and how one should learn (learning environments) will be different.

These differences need to be reflected in the OLC. At the same time, the liberal arts college has a unique position in the educational marketplace. There are likely to be values and skills these institutions want to impart, quite independent of the student- or faculty-specific disciplinary orientation. This could take the form of expecting all students to develop skills that help them "learn to learn," so they will have good skills for enhancing their learning in a variety of topics, independent of college and well after their college years have ended.

In summary, our position is that in a university the college is the appropriate level of analysis for initiating and sustaining an OLC. At the same time, we acknowledge there might be a few university-level learning outcomes. At a smaller liberal arts college, there would be more balance between department- and college-level learning outcomes. Regardless of the institution's size, there need to be learning environments to complement the meta- and disciplinary-specified skills across the institution.

Generalizability

A second issue is the generalizability of the OLC. Earlier, we said our focus is on four-year, face-to-face institutions. We do not think the OLC would work in typical distributed environments, meaning schools where students primarily learn in multiple locations (e.g., home, work) using different forms of technology to receive information from a central source. They are primarily not spending time in a common location with other students. The key idea of the OLC is building a shared understanding about roles and responsibilities concerning learning. This shared understanding comes about through extensive socialization attempts, assessment and feedback on learning outcomes and redesign of the OLC to sustain it over time. Delivering these processes in a distributed environment is much more difficult. There is no sense of community; students are not co-located and may be learning at different times. Building an effective OLC in a face-to-face, four-year institution is very challenging. Trying to build an OLC in a distributed environment is much more difficult.

There are many other kinds of institutions of higher education. For example, some universities primarily operate in the evening, providing education to working adults. While this is a face-to-face environment, the time spent at the institution is only a few hours per week. Given that these students are focused on work, families, and education, it seems like a difficult environment to build an OLC. In the four-year, face-to-face environment, the students' focus and attention is primarily on the college experience. In the latter setting, multiple socialization assessment/feedback and systematic design efforts are much easier to implement. This is not the case when students are not fully engaged in the institution.

Community colleges are another example of post-secondary educational institutions. Here, the underlying principles are the same. If students, time-wise and in terms of focus of attention, are fully engaged in the institution over multiple years, then the opportunity to create an OLC is viable. If, on the other hand, they are only marginally involved in the community college, opportunities to create an OLC are fewer. The environment in some individual degree programs within a broader community college setting (i.e., programs that lead to a professional degree such as nursing) may lend itself to development of an OLC, but community college environments, with shorter-term students and a substantial percentage of students with families and jobs that take away focus from the institution, would likely not support an OLC.

Inherent in this discussion is that creating significant change in existing higher educational institutions is very difficult. Despite the many external forces (e.g., technological, economic) challenging the viability of these institutions, there are equivalent forces offsetting these external pressures and pushing for the "status quo." Given that instituting an OLC is a major change, we want to focus on institutions where the possibility of change is more likely. The four-year, face-to-face environment—where there can be many socialization, assessment, and redesign efforts—seems to provide at least the minimum conditions for building an OLC.

Another form of generalizability deals with content or disciplinary areas. Is an OLC more likely to be implemented in colleges with technical orientations than more humanities-based orientations? Our position should be clear on this point. An OLC can be initiated in any disciplinary area because one should be able to explicitly state learning outcomes and environments no matter what the major. Regardless of the curriculum content, one needs effective socialization, assessment, and redesign mechanisms. One also needs to be cognizant of the change dilemma mentioned above.

Differences among Organizational Learning Contracts

All institutions of higher learning have some sort of an OLC. However, the form and content of these contracts differ (often greatly) depending on the institution. Table 2.2 describes different forms the OLC may take. In a "weak" contract setting, the level of shared understanding is limited among the key actors. Some students or some professors might know about some of the contract dimensions. But the contract, as we have defined it, is not widely shared among the relevant actors or enacted.

In contrast, the expectations within the OLC tend to be very specific in strong contract environments. An example would be stating team skills as a learning outcome. This is a specific outcome. It is quite different from saying that "your academic experience will be very challenging" and "hard work is necessary." These are very general expectations that are likely acquired prior to college. Friends, family and secondary school environments could impart these general expectations.

Table 2.2. ATTRIBUTES OF WEAK VS. STRONG CONTRACTS

	Weak OLC	Strong OLC
Shared Expectations	Limited/Diffuse/General	Extensive/Specific
Socialization Mechanisms	Informal	Formal/Explicit
Assessment/Feedback	Diffuse/Vague Standards	Explicit Standards
Mechanisms	Diffuse Monitoring	Focused Monitoring
	Feedback and Diffuse Rewards	Feedback and Explicit Rewards
Redesign Mechanisms	Informal/Unspecified	Formal/Multiple, Specific Methods
	Periodic/Irregular	Continual/Regular

Team skills, on the other hand, are unique to a college. The goal of developing team skills is embedded in recruiting materials and made explicit during orientations. From day one, classes utilize learning environments that reinforce team skills (e.g., project-based learning). Secondarily, non-course experiences reinforce this outcome. Also, mechanisms are in place to assess progress and implement redesign activities. All the relevant players are engaged in enhancing this specific outcome. It is, to some extent, self-designing.

There are many reasons why some institutions have general rather than specific contract dimensions. First, we have said creating an explicit OLC with specific outcomes, environments, and system mechanisms is a difficult, challenging task, given the inertia in many institutions of higher education. Second, building a strong OLC is based on assumptions about how people learn and what facilitates learning. For example, stating specific learning outcomes is based on an assumption and evidence in learning theory that this facilitates focus of attention and learning in respect to that outcome. Not all institutions understand, support or believe in that connection between stating specific learning outcomes as a means to facilitate learning. Another reason is that many institutions of higher education either have an outstanding reputation (e.g., Harvard, MIT) or the financial structure to provide quality, lower-cost education (i.e., public universities). In these cases, the institutional reputation or financial structure will attract the very best students. On the other hand, start-up institutions have a different challenge. They want to attract high-quality students, but they have no reputation and, in most cases, are not accredited. They want good students and faculty, but they have no "track record." One way they can distinguish themselves is by creating an explicit and different contract from that of their established competitors. One important design aspect of the research conducted for this book was the inclusion of new as well as traditional institutions. Our assumption was that this would create differences in OLC design and implementation. To be clear, we are not arguing that traditional and new institutions correspond directly to the weak vs. strong contract dimensions. But we do think new institutions, given their dilemma of attracting good people without an established reputation, may use the OLC as a way of differentiating themselves.

Being more specific about what people will learn (learning outcomes) and how people will learn (learning environments) is one effective way to distinguish their institution from others.

The forms of an OLC can be differentiated in other ways. For example, we have discussed the role of socialization in developing a shared understanding with respect to learning. In strong OLCs, there are many mechanisms. They can be found pre-college through the four years and even, perhaps, after graduation. The opposite is true in a weak OLC environment, in which there are generally few internal mechanisms.

Earlier, we discussed the assessment/feedback process as being essential for bringing about learning and the transfer of learning. To accomplish assessment and feedback, one needs specific learning outcomes, followed by standards to measure development of that outcome, a monitoring/measurement process, followed by feedback and some reinforcement. If we select an outcome such as "learning to learn," we first need to define its dimensions. One subskill could be learning how to search and to evaluate sources of information. The next step would be to articulate operational standards for effective searching and evaluation. Monitoring mechanisms, such as professor or self-evaluations, would then be put into place in different learning experiences to assess this particular subskill. For example, evaluations of a project could provide assessment on the quality of search activities. The standard could be derived from past student performance in a similar class and project. The process would conclude with providing the student, professor, and/or administrator information about the development of this skill, at least at the course or college levels. It also would be necessary for the individual to acquire feedback on his or her performance and ways for improvement. Again, the strong OLC environments will have many explicit mechanisms over multiple learning environments to monitor and provide feedback across multiple levels of analysis.

The last dimension that differentiates strong vs. weak contracts is redesign. Introducing and sustaining an OLC is a continuous process over time. Some learning outcomes will show development, others not. Why does this happen? Is the problem in the learning environments or in systems such as socialization or assessment? Part of the redesign process is to identify discrepancies between the stated contract and reality, note the discrepancies, and initiate change. Strong contract environments have many formal mechanisms (e.g., curriculum reviews, information technology systems measuring outcomes) designed to show discrepancies and initiate changes. Note that the redesign process in a strong environment is explicit, occurs with multiple mechanisms over time, and includes many of the relevant players (e.g., students, faculty, and administrators). In a weak OLC contract this redesign is not explicit and happens informally and in a periodic fashion.

Another way OLCs can differ is in terms of content. Different institutions might select different mixes of learning outcomes, which in turn should lead to a different mix of learning environments. The mix of system mechanisms (e.g., socialization, assessment) also may vary. Importantly, there is not some "optimal" content. Rather, the content of an OLC represents the choice of the institution and is influenced by the institution's comparative advantage and disciplinary focus. At best, we can point out examples of learning outcomes and the learning environments (Table 2.1). Note that when we discuss the institutions in our empirical work we will capture their learning outcomes, environments, and system mechanisms.

Before we explore some of the consequences of an OLC, it is probably important to acknowledge there are variations in the strength of an OLC. It is not necessarily strong versus weak. For example, there could be an outcome that is very important to the institution and it is stated very explicitly and supported by the appropriate mechanisms. At the same time, the rest of that institution's contract may be very diffuse and have no supporting mechanisms. There are many possible combinations within the strong versus weak contract continuum.

ORGANIZATIONAL CONTRACT CONSEQUENCES

We have identified the major components of the contract and discussed processes that lead to the development and sustainability of the OLC, as well as variations in types of OLCs. We next turn to the potential set of consequences that may occur when the OLC becomes operational.

Violations

One of the simplest consequences of the contracting process is a violation. Violations are discrepancies between the contract expectations and actual practice. A violation can involve any dimension of the learning contract and any actor. Students may expect a high-quality lecture/discussion course, yet experience the opposite. Professors may expect the opportunity to choose any of the learning models in Table 2.1, but find their choice restricted. An alumnus may be promised learning opportunities after graduation, but the quality of instruction is lower than expected. In each example, we posit that expectations were clear and shared by others in their respective roles, but these expectations were not realized in practice.

A fairly extensive literature (Rousseau, 1995) suggests that discrepancies between one's expectations and actual experience can lead to dissatisfaction and forms of withdrawal behavior (e.g., lower commitment to and identification with the organization, lower retention and graduation rates). In some cases, these discrepancies will make some activities seem less desirable than others. Consequently, unmet expectations would contribute to lower motivation and performance levels. They also detract from creating a long-term relationship with the students. Most universities want to maintain ties with their students after graduation.

Intersender Conflict

In any institution, there is an interconnected set of roles. The professor, student, advisor, teaching assistant, dean, and so on are all linked together. In this case, let's assume expectations are in conflict for a single course. The professor wants the students to be more actively involved in a studio or team-based learning model. Due to past experiences with this professor or via experiences with other professors who articulated but did not follow through on this view of learning, the students are divided. There may be other players, such as advisors or teaching assistants, who downplay these learning models. In any case, there are conflicting expectations. Let's move to a curriculum level. To build any of the skills such as collaborative skills or learning-to-learn skills, the focus is more on the curriculum level than on any single course. It is unlikely any single course would be able to build these as long-term skills. It can happen in an integrated curriculum over a number of courses and out-of-class activities. However, let's think about a curriculum where some courses reinforce collaborative skills, while other courses emphasize competition or individual-level skills. At the curriculum level, there are mixed signals about building the desired metaskills. In a similar vein, a faculty member is encouraged to explore new learning models such as studios, apprenticeships, or peer-based instruction. Colleagues may have rejected these time-intensive models in order to allocate more time to research or personal activities. These are all situations where there are clear expectations, but they are in conflict.

There is a general literature on intersender role conflict (Jackson & Schuler, 1985; Kahn, Wolfe, Quinn, Snoek, & Rosenthal, 1964; Tubre & Collins, 2000). The basic findings are that intersender conflict results in stress and dissatisfaction. The levels of stress are probably greater when there is conflict within a course versus the curriculum. A course is more defined in terms of relevant actors, time and place. Also, the more central the conflict is to performance in the course, the greater the levels of stress. For example, if team-based learning represented 75 percent of the course yet it was an object of conflicting expectations, the level of stress and dissatisfaction would be great. High levels of stress, in turn, can decrease learning and performance.

Contract Ambiguity

Ambiguity is another potential consequence in the formation of a learning contract. Any of the three elements of the learning contract may be ambiguous. Learning outcomes are often not explicitly stated. The socialization mechanisms or reinforcement mechanisms are often absent rather than explicit, or provide mixed signals. Most institutions do not explicitly state an OLC as a matter of admission or employment, nor do they provide explicit training in learning outcomes or alternative learning models. Hence, there is a great deal of ambiguity about learning processes other than the most traditional practices.

As with intersender role conflict, ambiguity can have negative consequences in terms of stress and dissatisfaction (Jackson et al., 1985; Kahn et al., 1964; Tubre & Collins, 2000). In the context of the learning contract, however, this is probably not the case. People have prior beliefs about learning and are more likely to move to a fallback position. Over a 12-year period, students have observed a particular learning model. Upon entering college, it is reasonable for them to expect some variant of that model where the "teacher teaches" and the "student learns." The new professor similarly has gone through a 22-year period, observing others teach, and is likely to adopt one or more of these models. A professor exposed to the different models in Table 2.1 may show a greater proclivity to use different models, compared to someone observing a single model of education. The basic result of ambiguity about outcomes or learning environments is that people can revert to more familiar outcomes or models.

Alignment Conflicts

Let's assume contract expectations are clear and shared. Another possible consequence of the learning contract is lack of alignment among the contract dimensions and the broader organizational context. For example, there is a shared understanding about the need for building collaboration skills. There is a set of learning experiences designed to enhance collaboration skills. But, the culture of the institution and its organizational structure are autocratic and hierarchical. Or the organizational reward system does not support high faculty engagement with students in learning environments requiring high involvement.

When learning outcomes, environments, the organizational systems, and organizational context are not aligned, this should over time negatively impact achievement of the learning outcomes and jeopardize the long-term viability of the learning experience. In the above example, where there is lack of alignment, we would expect the development of lifelong learning or collaborative skills to be impaired.

It is important to note that lack of alignment is not necessarily tied to our earlier distinction between weak and strong OLCs. In weak OLCs, there are a few general expectations (e.g., "you need to work harder in college"). It is possible that the student expectations are not met. However, since there are fewer, more general expectations, it might be harder to violate these expectations. For the strong OLC environments, there are many, more specific expectations, so on one hand, it may be easier to create violations or unmet expectations. In these settings, violations also may be more adverse and serious. On the other hand, institutions that build strong OLCs are cognizant of the contract and the consequences of not meeting these expectations. Therefore, in general, we would predict any of the above negative consequences would occur with similar regularity for both weak and strong OLCs.

Met or Exceeded Expectations

All of the above consequences are negative in nature. Violations, conflict, and misalignment all lead to stress, dissatisfaction, or a learning contract with mixed signals. Another possibility is that expectations can be met or exceeded. The students are told they will be involved in active-based learning. In reality, the level of project- or problem-based learning is met or is much greater than the students initially expected. Or, students were told they would be involved in the design of the college or curriculum, and their expectations were met or exceeded.

In most cases, when expectations are met or exceeded, we should expect substantial positive effects. If, for example, student expectations about involvement in the design of the college or curriculum are exceeded, we would expect positive feelings generated by the extra level of involvement. Met or exceeded expectations should lead to positive feelings about specific objects (e.g., a particular instructor or course), but also generalize to positive feelings about learning and the institution.

An Aligned Institution

Using a similar argument, an aligned system should have positive effects on attitudes on learning. An aligned system is where learning outcomes, learning environments, organizational systems, and the context (e.g., culture) of the institution are both congruent and self-reinforcing. In this setting, we would expect learning outcomes to be acknowledged and to improve. There should be positive views of different learning environments and positive views of the institution. That is, with met or exceeded expectations in an aligned institution we would expect individuals to learn in a more effective way and the relevant parties to have positive views of the quality of education, quality of students and faculty, and to identify positively with the focal institution. In addition, we would particularly expect the new strong-OLC institutions with met expectations and alignment to attract, over time, high-quality students and faculty. Also, we would expect, in institutions with primarily met or exceeded expectations, alignment, and a strong OLC, to be able to demonstrate a successful transfer of OLC learning outcomes to other work environments.

SUMMARY

We have outlined the major elements of the OLC—outcomes, learning environments, and organizational systems. All three elements drive the learning process. Outcomes signal the competencies the institution wants to create. Different outcomes require different learning environments. And, lastly, an OLC cannot be created without organizational systems. They represent the mechanisms for making the contract explicit, assessing its implementation, and facilitating its sustainability over time.

We also argued that all institutions of higher learning have an OLC of some kind. The critical distinction is whether the OLC is weak or strong. In strong OLCs, we expect the relevant actors (e.g., students, faculty, and administrators) to report more specific expectations. These expectations will be created by the institution's socialization mechanisms. We also expect in institutions with strong OLCs that the relevant people will be more knowledgeable about learning outcomes, learning environments, and the socialization, assessment, and redesign mechanisms that exist. At the same time, we need to acknowledge that the actual experiences during the four years are critical determinants of effectiveness for the institution and the individuals. If there is alignment between the OLC and the organizational context, and expectations are met or exceeded, students will be satisfied and more engaged in learning and institutional effectiveness will be higher. The opposite also is true. In the case of weak OLCs, the patterns are the same. If students had a few general expectations such as "this will be academically challenging" over the next four years and it was, then the students are likely to be satisfied. If it was not academically challenging, then we would expect more dissatisfaction at the individual and institutional levels.

In those cases where expectations and actual experiences match in both the weak and strong OLCs, the strong OLC environment should have an advantage over the weak one on dimensions such as learning and other effectiveness indicators. The rationale is that in the strong environments there are clearer understandings about what to learn (learning outcomes) and how to learn (diverse and properly matched learning environments). These understandings should be translated into higher levels of engagement and learning of specific outcomes. One of our research goals is to be able to distinguish empirically between strong and weak OLCs. Another goal is to trace out the implications of these differences on effectiveness for the student and institution.

CHAPTER 3
Research Plan

This chapter outlines our research strategy. We review the rationale for our approach, features of the sample, and the nature of our measures, including the coding process and the form of our analysis. All of these factors are designed to answer the basic three questions of this book: (1) How can we measure and operationalize the OLC, (2) can we identify differences across institutions in dimensions of their learning contracts, and (3) how do differences in OLCs affect indicators of individual and institutional effectiveness?

Information on student experiences and outcomes as well as institutional effectiveness criteria can be gathered in many ways. Some studies have adopted a primarily qualitative approach, in which student interview transcripts (Light, 2001) or qualitative observations are used to illustrate points about student or institutional factors. Others have done large-sample survey studies of student engagement and learning (e.g., Braxton, Vesper, & Hossler, 1995; Kuh, Gonyea, & Williams, 2005; Pike & Kuh, 2005). This type of strategy permits more quantitative analysis of the survey data, and the large national samples used in the cited studies addresses the question of generalizability. There are a variety of other empirical studies using different designs, sampling measurement, and forms of analysis. We explore some of these studies, as well as our results, in more detail in chapters 4 through 6.

Our research strategy was to do an intensive longitudinal interview study at a few institutions. We chose the interview approach because it was difficult to know *ex ante* what might be in the students' OLCs. Some responses will be unique to a particular institution. A semi-structured interview lets you ask the same questions in the same order across institutions, but at the same time it permits tapping both similar and dissimilar knowledge across institutions. We adopted a longitudinal design to track how consistent the OLC is over time.

Our selection of just a few institutions was guided by two factors. First, we wanted to include new institutions in order to ensure we had differences in the

OLCs across institutions. New institutions are rare entities. They are entering a competitive marketplace. Many excellent colleges and institutions with strong reputations already exist. These high reputations serve to attract high-quality students, faculty, and administrators. The challenge faced by new institutions is that they want high-quality students, faculty, and administrators, but they have no reputation. One strategy for these new institutions is to differentiate themselves from their competitors on something other than reputation or past history. We believe that building a distinctive OLC is one way for these new schools to compete. This is congruent with our research questions of being able to identify differences among OLCs and their consequences.

The other reason for a small sample was simply a matter of costs. Our interviews were time-demanding. It was difficult to schedule and complete four interviews per day per interviewer. Therefore, we needed multiple interviewers. All the interviews were one-on-one and were conducted by the same interviewers at two different times, or waves, approximately a year apart for each college. The expenses included training interviewers and conducting each interview. The institutions we chose are in different locations, which increased travel costs. Once the interviews were completed they needed to be transcribed and then coded by a different group of research assistants. Given all of these costs and the limited number of new institutions from which to choose, we limited our sample to three comparable institutions.

SAMPLE JUSTIFICATION AND POTENTIAL LIMITATIONS

We selected three colleges (referred to herein as A, B, and C) that valued teaching and research, were four-year institutions, and met in a face-to-face environment. They offered undergraduate degrees with a technical professional focus. The colleges featured comparable disciplinary areas, settings, faculty, and students. Note that we did not consider any of the new distributed institutions of higher education. We think these are very different learning settings and attract very different kinds of faculty and students than institutions with face-to-face learning environments.

One strategic decision was to select some new institutions as well as a traditional institution. A new institution is one that has only recently graduated its first class of students. The two new institutions in our study graduated their first class in 2007. In addition to being new, these institutions were focused on new ways to build an OLC. On the other hand, the traditional institution is a highly ranked college and has been around for 100 years. The main reason for looking at both new and traditional institutions is that one of our key issues is to explore differences in OLC and their implications on institutional effectiveness. The design of the study also will permit us to identify similarities among institutions. Despite some differences in the OLC each institution has developed, we hoped to identify some common understandings or shared experiences.

Of course, we are cognizant of the limitations of this design. First, given the small sample size, how generalizable are the results? Can we take results from this study and apply them to other, similar institutions of higher learning? On one hand, in terms of specific findings, the answer to this is probably no. For example, if we found that the explicit OLCs designed around collaborative skills in one of our institutions led to the transfer of these skills to a work environment, that finding would be consistent with our overall theoretical perspective. But generalizing this finding to other institutions that differed in size, source of funding, culture, or other aspects should be done with caution. On the other hand, there are some metaprinciples regarding OLCs and institutional change in this specific finding that could be adopted by other institutions. For example, lessons learned could include how this institution made the contract explicit, what socialization practices were used pre-college and during college, what kinds of learning environments were used, what types of assessment and redesign methods were utilized, etc. Our argument is not that the specific socialization methods or the particular learning environment used should be copied by other institutions. However, we do believe that the underlying processes used (e.g., socialization) need to be enacted even though they might not be exactly the same, in order to achieve this finding of explicit contracts on collaboration skills leading to transfer outside the college environment. Our basic argument is that the specific findings may not be generalizable given the small sample size, but the metaprinciples underlying these findings should provide a useful guide for both future research and institutional design.

Another limitation in using three institutions is that it is very difficult to sample three institutions that are exactly alike. This creates problems in interpreting similarities or differences across the three institutions. We try to address this issue, particularly in chapter 6, but it is a possible limitation.

The following sections provide more detailed information on the institutions and the student sample.

INSTITUTIONAL FEATURES

For both Colleges A and B, the inaugural graduating class of 2007 started in the fall of 2003. They are truly new institutions. College A was launched through the initiative of a private foundation. The foundation's trustees intended to create a small, standalone undergraduate school that provides a high-quality education. Students can complete their degrees by taking courses in College A, with the option of courses in other nearby high-quality institutions with which College A has established alliances. Its main source of funding is an endowment established through the private foundation that launched the college.

College B was funded by the government as an undergraduate college in a larger new university that also offers undergraduate, graduate, and professional programs. Its main sources of funding are the government, an endowment, and some student tuition and fees. College B's leadership was given free rein to design the school. The university-level leadership was not part of the design or implementation of the new school. By being a part of a larger institution, the existing infrastructure such as financial procedures, reporting procedures, admission procedures, etc., were designed and operated by the larger institution. But all the basic decisions about the OLC, faculty, hiring, and so forth were done independently by College B.

College C is an established traditional college contained within a mid-sized university that offers undergraduate, graduate, and professional programs in business, humanities, social sciences, and applied and natural sciences. It was founded more than 100 years ago and has a well-established reputation for producing high-quality research and providing high-quality undergraduate and graduate education. It also relies on government and industry research grants, an endowment and student tuition as funding sources.

ORGANIZATIONAL FEATURES

Faculty in different technical disciplines in College A are grouped together under one interdisciplinary department. They are rewarded for high-quality teaching, research productivity, and other innovative outcomes such as patented inventions and entrepreneurial activities. College A does not grant faculty tenure. It offers an initial probationary contract followed by longer-term, renewable contracts. College B has a traditional faculty employment policy that includes an initial probationary contract with the possibility of tenure based on research productivity and teaching quality. Faculty members tend to be informally grouped by interest areas, not formal departments. Both Colleges A and B ask students to participate in curriculum design and delivery. For example, students help faculty select course content, and may deliver in-class presentations or provide peer tutoring. The learning environments in College A and B include a lot of project-based learning in which students solve real-world problems, mostly as members of student teams.

College C has a more traditional organization structure, with faculty residing in different departments based on their technical disciplines. They are rewarded for research productivity and quality teaching outcomes. The college's employment policy includes a traditional tenure system based on these outcomes. Faculty members have sole responsibility for curriculum design and execution. Course content is delivered using mostly traditional lectures with some project-based learning activities for students.

Some of the differences in the educational orientation between schools are shown in Table 3.1. Students are more involved in designing the learning environments in the new schools. Also, the learning environment is more of an active-based learning environment in Colleges A and B than in the traditional school.

Table 3.1. EDUCATIONAL FEATURES OF NEW
AND TRADITIONAL COLLEGES

	New Colleges (A and B)	Traditional College (C)
Institutional Accreditation	Must be obtained	Already obtained
Institutional Reputation	Not yet established	Well established
Curriculum Design Process	Faculty and students	Faculty
Teaching Responsibility	Faculty and students	Faculty
Teaching Environment	Problem/project-based learning with some lecture	Lecture with some problem/project-based learning
Learning Assessment	Targeted competencies assessed across courses Student portfolios to document competency development	Traditional course-specific grading system

ORGANIZATIONAL LEARNING CONTRACTS (OUTCOMES, ENVIRONMENTS, SYSTEMS)

The designers of Colleges A and B intended to have explicit learning outcomes. College A has nine learning outcomes and B has eight. The two colleges' learning outcomes are specific to each school. They do, however, have common areas such as quantitative data analysis, team skills, and communication skills. College C's learning outcomes are similar to those in College A.

Both A and B use a variety of in-class and out-of-class learning environments to help students achieve these outcomes. Examples of in-class environments include lectures, hands-on projects, design and fabrication studios, interdisciplinary learning, and team-based assignments. Out-of-class environments include extracurricular activities, research projects, consulting projects, small business startups, and internships. For example, College A expects students to engage in skill-based activities (e.g., creating art, playing a musical instrument) not directly related to their course of study. College C focuses more on in-class learning environments. Although College C students are encouraged to participate in some extracurricular activities, they are more focused on achieving course grades.

Colleges A and B have several distinct learning system features. First, they have explicit socialization practices intended to establish and reinforce students' OLC for learning. For example, College A requires applicants to participate in an on-campus interview process. This process includes completing a project-based assignment in a team that includes other applicants. This helps assess applicants' fit with the college and gives applicants a realistic preview of what to expect as students. Colleges A and B courses focus on the learning outcomes defined by each college. For example, College B identifies learning outcomes and sub-outcomes for each course. College A also sponsors special events in which students showcase projects they have worked on during the year and identify the specific learning outcomes they achieved on those projects. College B uses a sophisticated information system to track each student's learning progress for each specific outcome. Finally, Colleges A and B both solicit feedback from students to improve the curriculum. Typically this is done through faculty/student teams versus the traditional student survey format. All these learning system features are used from the first year through graduation. They are part of the OLC.

College C has fewer explicit and consistent learning system features. On-campus interviews are not required for admission, though applicants can visit campus on their own initiative. There is no explicit process for linking learning outcomes to course content. One system feature distinct to the university at large is an explicit emphasis on interdisciplinary learning and research. This emphasis is communicated to applicants and students through a variety of channels including marketing materials and extracurricular activities sponsored by the college and university. Student feedback is gathered through course evaluations and limited student participation on departmental committees. College C does not solicit improvement feedback from students to the same extent as Colleges A and B.

FACULTY AND STUDENT RECRUITMENT

During their respective start-up phases, Colleges A and B recruited faculty from major research universities. Faculty hires were based on academic credentials, research records, teaching achievements and enthusiasm for and experience in building an institution. College A also focused on hiring faculty with well-rounded interests and accomplishments. For example, some faculty are accomplished artists or musicians as well as scientists. College C recruits faculty primarily based on their research records and teaching potential. Nearly all faculty in the three colleges have doctorates from U.S. universities.

The populations for each college include a range of domestic and foreign students. College A recruited students domestically due to legal constraints associated with foreign students in the new college. An initial pilot class was extensively involved in the design and founding of the college. They participated in its design for one full year before starting formal classes. Most of College B's students are domestic, with some smaller portion coming from foreign countries. The initial group of students also participated in the college's design, though to a lesser extent than in College A. College C has domestic students as well as a diverse multinational student population. Students did not participate in designing the college since it was already established.

OTHER FEATURES (LOCATION, NON-CLASSROOM ACTIVITIES, SPORTS ACTIVITIES)

College A is located in a suburb of a large metropolitan region within close driving distance of several high-quality universities and colleges. One of these institutions is within walking distance. College B and C are in urban environments with easy access to public transportation and proximity to other universities and colleges.

All three colleges have a variety of social and special-interest clubs that students can join. Colleges A and B do not participate in collegiate athletics, but students can participate in intramural sporting activities (e.g., soccer). College C has a limited collegiate athletic program.

SAMPLE

We conducted our wave-one interviews with students from the three colleges between November 2005 and February 2006. We then did wave-two interviews over the same period (November 2006 through February 2007) one year later. Our sample of students included freshmen (Class of 2009) and juniors (Class of 2007). The number of students interviewed in wave one were 56, 33, and 54 for Colleges A, B, and C, respectively. The following year we contacted the same respondents at each college for a second-year follow-up and added some new students. The total wave two numbers were 61, 32, and 46 for Colleges A, B, and C respectively. Across the colleges, 89%, 79%, and 80% of the respondents, respectively, were interviewed during both time periods. (See Table 3.2.) We oversampled slightly in year two since it was difficult to anticipate the number of repeat students we could expect to reach in year two. In the final analysis, a majority of the students were interviewed in both the first and second years. At the end of each interview session in year two, we asked the student to fill out a survey. This was done at the end of the interview to ensure we would get 100% response rates for the survey from our year two interviewees (there was no survey in year one).

Table 3.2. TOTAL PARTICIPANTS BY SCHOOL

	College A	College B	College C
Wave 1 Total	56	33	54
Wave 2 Total	61	32	46
Participants in Both Wave 1 and 2	50	26	43
Retention	89%	79%	80%

INSTRUMENTS

The primary data collection instrument was a semi-structured interview (see Appendix 1). Altogether there were 12 questions with subparts in the year one interview and 17 questions in the year two interview. The content of interviews in years one and two were nearly identical, with a few exceptions. The year two interview added questions asking students to describe their approach to learning and to elaborate on summer internship experiences (if applicable). Common topics included student expectations of their college, how they acquired these expectations, whether expectations were met, the students' role in decision-making, critical incidents, and so on. These were driven by our conceptualization of the OLC. Some representative questions included:

- When you came to (name of college) there was a "contract." This college was going to provide you a set of educational experiences and there were a set of activities and responsibilities you were going to do. We want to explore both of these expectations. Thinking about (college) now, what are the educational expectations or promises of what (college) is going to do for you educationally?

- In any relationship expectations can be met, exceeded or not met. Let's review the expectations you specified.
  Expectation. You mentioned (expectation "x").
  Would you say this expectation has been: (Note: tense might change)
  -Not Met_____
  -Met_____
  -Exceeded_____
  Probe: Why did you select this answer?
  Probe: If unmet, how do you feel about that?

- Let's switch the question around. We have discussed your expectations of what _____ is going to do for you educationally. Let's ask the other question: What does (college) expect of you as a student?

  Probe: Anything else?

- Personal Model of Learning

You're in your _____ year at (college). There is a strong emphasis here on learning and how people learn. We want to explore how you think about effective learning. How would *you explain your approach to effective learning to a new student* at (college)?

The interviews were conducted by three individuals (two PhD students and the author). There was extensive one-on-one training to ensure comparability in interviewer actions. As a field researcher for more than 40 years and an instructor in field methods, I have had extensive experience in interviewing and interview training.

Average interview time was one hour. Of course, there were variations by student. The interviewers took extensive, real-time notes in each interview. Time was allotted between interviews to review the transcripts to ensure each interview was accurately recorded in the notes. All interviews then were transcribed.

Developing a coding system for each question was the next challenge (see Appendix 2). This was guided by our conceptualization of the OLC.

The principal investigator read all interview transcripts and derived coding categories for each question based on the OLC and participant responses (cf. Miles & Huberman, 1994). Interview transcriptions were then reread until no new categories could be identified. The resulting coding schemes for each question are organized by category with subcodes within each category. For example, when asking students, "What do you expect your college will do for you?" the responses are organized by five categories: (For each category we note the number of codes, and the number of the category)

(1) "Education" (9 category "10" codes);
(2) "Professors" (2 category "20" codes);
(3) "Students" (3 category "30" codes);
(4) "Institution" (9 category "40" codes); and
(5) "Environment" (3 category "50" codes). Some examples of category "10" codes are "Challenging academic environment, hard work, high quality education" (code 11), "Project based work, teams, learning from others" (code 13) and "Interdisciplinary learning environment" (code 15).

Or we would take a question such as, "How did you learn about this expectation?" The list of expectations was generated by a prior question (see above). The coding system then reflected possible sources for learning about the specific expectation being discussed. Some examples include: from the college's recruiting materials, website, or on-campus visit; or from one's family or a secondary school counselor. The first set of examples is tied to a specific college; the latter examples come from precollege experiences. We expected the new versus traditional colleges to differ on these learning sources (see chapter 4).

The interview transcripts were coded after a period of training. Some transcripts were coded by two individuals to ensure reliability. Average inter-rater agreement across a selected set of questions was 89%.

In addition to the formal instruments, we visited Colleges A and B. We have done this since their inceptions. We used these visits to interview the leaders, administrators, faculty, and students about the institution (e.g., how it was organized) and to gather individual-level beliefs from the students about topics such as why students applied, their initial expectations, relationships with faculty, etc. From faculty and administrators we inquired about topics such as the initial planning period for the college, challenges in year one, views about culture of this institution, their motivation for joining the institution, etc. In addition, we reviewed each college's recruiting materials, website, write-ups by members of each college about the institution, and other available materials. Finally, we collected stories about each college. A similar approach was used for College C in terms of talking to members about the institution as well as their own beliefs and reviewing institutional materials.

In addition to the interviews in the second wave of data collection, we gave students a survey which they completed before leaving. All students interviewed in wave 2 completed the survey. The survey included a number of areas, with multiple Likert-type items. Areas covered culture of the institution, teaching environment, student services (e.g., placement), identification with the institution, and so on. We used the ordinal values of the response categories to analyze the data (Appendix 3).

COMPARISONS AMONG INSTITUTIONS: ALTERNATIVE EXPLANATIONS

We identified a number of similarities and differences across the institutions we studied, leading to some theoretical bases for our analysis. One basic theme is that we expect differences in the three colleges' OLCs, which should have implications for how students represent their contracts to the interviewers; this, in turn, should affect the effectiveness indicators used across the institutions. One problem with this position is that we have a small sample study and cannot control for a variety of factors that might suggest alternative explanations. Two significant factors could be the quality of students across institutions and the quality of faculty. If one college dominates with higher-quality students and/or faculty, that might account for some of the differences reported in the following chapters, quite independent of the structural factors that define the colleges' OLCs.

Because independent data were available for these two areas, and these elements are significant in an academic institution, we proceeded as follows: To measure student quality, we collected SAT scores. These data were available for Colleges A and C but were not available for College B, because College B does not require students to take the SAT for acceptance. We will thus treat College B separately. SAT scores are composed of three dimensions—math, critical reading, and writing. One can score up to 800 points for each section, for a potential total of 2,400. We were able to get data for classes entering in the years 2005 through 2008. The writing dimension was added in 2006. Therefore, the total potential scores for 2005 will be different from the other three years. Note that this four-year time period covers the time when both of our study samples were at their respective schools.

Initially, one might expect that College C students would have higher SAT scores since it is an established, highly ranked institution. In fact, College A had the highest SAT scores over this four-year period. While the differences are statistically significant, they do not seem practically significant. Both Colleges A and C are attracting students in the mid to high 90th percentile. These are very good scores, and the differences between the 94th, 96th, or 99th percentiles are unlikely to explain differences in OLCs. Both colleges are attracting the best. See Table 6.1 and our discussion about these findings.

In terms of the quality of faculty, we assessed for all three colleges where the faculty obtained their PhDs. University rankings are an approximate indicator of quality. We used two rankings from *U.S. News and World Report* (2010). These rankings involved (1) the top 130 U.S. universities, and (2) the top international universities, which includes U.S. universities. Most faculty members across all three colleges earned their PhDs from U.S. universities. If we look at mean rankings, Colleges A and C have faculty from similarly ranked schools and both are more highly ranked than College B. See Table 6.2 and our discussion about these findings. The smaller number of faculty in Colleges A and B makes the comparisons across colleges more difficult as variation may have had more of an effect on rankings.

Overall, Colleges A and C seem comparable, with College B slightly below the other two on the student and faculty quality measures. (There were some SAT scores for College B students.) However, the magnitude of the differences does not support the alternative explanation of student or faculty differences explaining the results of this study.

ANALYSIS

The analysis was first done at the college level. We examined similarities and differences between colleges on topics such as expectations of the college; whether expectations had been exceeded, met or not met; personal models of learning and so on. If relevant, we did contrasts by students from the class of 2007 to the class of 2009. We did this, for example, on the question about expectations of the college. In addition, we did comparisons of wave one and wave two data. We present both quantitative and qualitative data.

DISCUSSION

We elected to do an intensive, longitudinal study of a few institutions. This strategy was influenced by the newness of the OLC concept and, to some extent, the unique nature of OLCs. By "unique," we are referring to variation both between the colleges and between individuals. First, there is not a common or optimal OLC at the college level. We expect to see variation across all institutions. Second, a key component of the OLC is a shared understanding of the OLC. But in reality there is inherent variation in the degree to which an understanding can be shared among students and faculty. Given these qualifications about variation at the college and individual levels, we still expect to see college effects. That is, if we examined how students learned about OLCs, institutions with stronger OLCs should use more college-initiated socialization mechanisms. Also, these expectations should be more specific than those of an institution with a weaker OLC.

To meet the challenge of operationalizing the OLC concept, we used multiple methods (i.e., interviews and surveys) to identify similarities and differences across institutions. We selected both new and traditional institutions for our sample. The assumption was that new institutions would try to differentiate their OLC from those in existing institutions. To collect data on effectiveness, we adopted an input-process-outcome model (see chapter 6 discussion section) and used multiple methods (e.g., objective and subjective) to assess multiple indicators of effectiveness. To reflect temporal issues, we sampled students from different classes and collected data over at least a two-year period.

We will explore both the strength and limitations of the study's methodology as we review the findings for the following three chapters. These chapters explore, respectively, our findings on expectations, learning, and effectiveness.

CHAPTER 4

Student Expectations for New and Traditional Colleges

This chapter explores student expectations about their institution and their institution's expectations about them. Expectations are beliefs about what the institution will do for them as well as how, where, and when the institution will do it and, conversely, what they will do for their institution. The OLC specifically represents a set of shared expectations about learning, which is the focus of this chapter.

The existing literature on student expectations is informative for our analysis. One critical finding focuses on whether expectations are realistic, while others focus on the match between expectations and actual experiences. Matches between expectations and experiences are important because they are positively associated with student satisfaction, engagement, personal development, and higher retention and graduation rates (e.g., Ewell & Jones, 1993; Kuh, 1999, 2001, 2005; Yorges, Bloom, DiFonzo, & Chando, 2005).

Here, we build on this literature and provide a different perspective. We contrast student expectations or, to be more specific, students' OLCs, in new and existing institutions. One distinguishing feature of new, innovative institutions of higher education is an explicit effort to create a contract with students about what the college will do for them and what they must contribute to the college. These new institutions take a more proactive role, both before and during their students' college experiences, to reinforce these expectations. This orientation is a matter of survival. To exist, new institutions must paint a compelling picture of why good students should go to their institution. This fundamental driver should lead the new institutions to a more differentiated set of expectations when compared to traditional institutions.

We examine these differences through the lens of the OLC. We begin by examining prior studies on college student expectations, with attention to their relevance for the OLC construct. Second, we develop five predictions regarding differences in organizational learning contracts for new vs. traditional colleges. Third, we test these hypotheses using longitudinal data collected from two new schools and one traditional college. Finally, we discuss the results and implications of this investigation of our expectations.

SOCIOLOGICAL, ORGANIZATIONAL, AND PSYCHOLOGICAL PERSPECTIVES ON STUDENT EXPECTATIONS

Though research on student expectations is limited (Kuh, Gonyea, & Williams, 2005), sociological, organizational, and psychological models of student retention and success usually include student expectations as one input (among others). Each of these three perspectives views expectations as perceptual filters through which students interpret their college experiences (Howard, 2005; Miller, Kuh, Paine, & Associates, 2006). The greater the degree of alignment between expectations and experiences, the more engaged students will be in their educational process, and the more committed to their institutions.

Sociological Perspective

The sociological perspective emphasizes how a student's background (e.g., family upbringing, socioeconomic status) interacts with the institutional environment (e.g., academic and social norms) to influence his or her expectations, experiences, and withdrawal behaviors. Tinto's (1993) student departure model is a prominent approach. According to the model, students' expectations are based on their backgrounds (e.g., socioeconomic status) and prior encounters with the institutional environment. These expectations, in turn, influence their academic and social intentions and goals (Tinto, 1993: 54f). Students whose expectations match their educational experiences perceive a higher degree of fit with the institution, resulting in academic and social integration. Academic integration means a student adopts norms expected in an academic environment (e.g., attending class, earning passing grades). Social integration entails genial relationships with peers and faculty. Academic and social integration strengthen students' institutional fit, resulting in stronger institutional commitment and retention.

Apart from Tinto's model, other socioeconomic factors by themselves, such as student demographics and background (e.g., parental education), do not appear to exert a strong influence on students' expectations before they enter college (e.g., Olsen, Kuh, Schilling, Connolly, Simmons, & Vesper, 1998; Kuh et al., 2005). This suggests colleges should be able to influence what students expect of their college experience (Miller et al., 2006). It also is consistent with our idea that learning contracts are initiated by the school.

Organizational Perspective

This perspective focuses more exclusively on how institutional attributes (e.g., size, resources, processes, mission) influence students' expectations. Bean's (1983) approach has been prominent, emphasizing how the institutional environment either confirms or refutes students' prior beliefs (including their expectations) about college. Students experience a higher degree of fit when their expectations are met. A higher degree of fit strengthens their institutional commitment and increases their retention in school.

Apart from Bean's model, other studies find organizational features such as frequent communication with students, fair policies, and student participation in institutional decisions are positively related to students' social integration, commitment, and intention to remain at the school (Berger & Braxton, 1998; Braxton & Brier, 1989). Shared institutional values also are positively related to student learning and personal development (Kuh, 1995). Other evidence suggests institutional features may be classified by typologies of student engagement that are indicative of shared beliefs (Pike & Kuh, 2005). Though not explicitly measured in all of these studies, shared expectations that are met are one mechanism that links organizational features to student success (Helland, Stallings, & Braxton, 2001–2002). For example, students who expect to participate in institutional decisions will view such engagement as normative. Their institutional commitment will depend in part on whether their expectations are met. These findings are consistent with our idea that OLCs should exert greater influence to the extent that the parties have a shared understanding of contract provisions.

Common to these studies is a focus on how a school might influence students' expectations after they have enrolled. This has led Kuh and colleagues to propose that studies are needed to understand "what forms of anticipatory socialization are most effective in helping establish high expectations for college on the part of new students" (Kuh et al., 2005: 61). That is, we need to understand how schools can influence students' expectations *before* they enroll (Kuh, 1995; Kuh et al., 2005; Kuh, Lyons, Miller, & Trow, 2003; Longden, 2006; Pike & Kuh, 2005). The OLC provides a framework for understanding how schools can exert such influence. Anecdotally, we know such influence is possible since schools with strong identities (e.g., West Point) elicit expectations about the educational experience even before a student enrolls (Lipsky, 2003).

Psychological Perspective

This perspective focuses on how students' beliefs about their abilities and the desirability of expected outcomes influence their expectations and success outcomes. Prominent theories include self-efficacy (Bandura, 1997), expectancy-value (Vroom, 1964) and achievement motivation (Dweck & Legett, 1988).

Expectations are beliefs that guide students' intentions and influence their pursuit of some activities and avoidance of others (Howard, 2005; Kuh, 1999). Beliefs can be positively or negatively oriented. For example, students who believe they can be effective in student government will be more likely to participate if they view this as a positive thing. Such students would be more likely to have higher expectations for student government participation—that participation will be a rewarding experience, that the student government will be run effectively, and that their participation can make a difference. Students who view such involvement negatively will avoid participation even if they believe they can be successful. Such students would be more likely to have lower expectations for student government participation—that participation will be waste of their time, that participation won't make any difference on campus. An implication of this is that students with higher expectations may be able to achieve more successful outcomes. Recent research does show student abilities, aspirations, and positive orientations toward college are positively associated with higher student expectations and better learning outcomes (Kuh et al., 2005). Yet, higher expectations also may be more difficult to meet. The work literature shows that when employees' expectations for their employer are not met, they are less satisfied, less committed to the organization, and more intent on quitting (Zhao, Wayne, Glibkowski, & Bravo, 2007). These relationships also should apply to students' expectations for their colleges (Howard, 2005). When students have high expectations for college and their expectations are not met, they are likely to be less engaged in and less satisfied with their educational experiences. In the same vein, we expect that organizational learning contract breaches will be detrimental to student satisfaction, commitment, engagement, and retention. Thus, schools should encourage high expectations while providing the necessary conditions to ensure those expectations are met (Kuh et al., 2005). From a learning contract perspective, schools need to initiate what students should expect. They also need to provide experiences that meet or exceed expectations to ensure contract provisions are met.

Summary Implications of Sociological, Organizational, and Psychological Perspectives

Sociological perspectives suggest student demographic factors appear to have little influence on student expectations. This means schools should be able to use learning contracts to initiate such expectations. Organizational perspectives also suggest schools can influence expectations, though research is needed on how schools can be more proactive by influencing expectations before enrollment—an idea captured by the learning contract. Psychological perspectives emphasize the importance of setting high expectations and ensuring schools provide educational experiences that align expectations and experiences. We propose the OLC as an organizational-level mechanism for creating, influencing, and fulfilling students' expectations.

ORGANIZATIONAL LEARNING CONTRACTS IN NEW AND TRADITIONAL COLLEGES

This section compares and contrasts the new and traditional colleges that are the focus of our study. Table 4.1 summarizes predicted differences between the new and traditional colleges, in which the new colleges are expected to have stronger OLCs and the traditional school is expected to have a weaker OLC.

Creation of Student Expectations

Colleges A and B have no alumni networks or established reputation to attract applicants. Consequently, they need to communicate why applicants should expect an educational experience that will be distinctively different (and in some ways, superior) to that of other established colleges. Without a compelling proposition, the new schools will have difficulty persuading high-quality applicants to enroll. Anticipatory socialization is a tactic they can use to communicate the roles and responsibilities of potential students (Feldman, 1981). For example, unique marketing materials and school-initiated campus visits can provide applicants a preview of what to expect as students. These experiences should provide students a more widely shared, specific, and distinctive set of expectations for the new schools. In contrast, College C's established reputation ensures a steady stream of highly qualified applicants. College C has little incentive to proactively communicate what students should expect. Applicants will rely more on their own experiences than

Table 4.1. ORGANIZATIONAL LEARNING CONTRACT (OLC) DIFFERENCES BETWEEN NEW AND TRADITIONAL COLLEGES

Predicted Differences	New Colleges (A and B)	Traditional College (C)
Overall Differences in Typical Student Expectations	More distinctive, less diffuse	Less distinctive, more diffuse
	More widely shared	Less widely shared
	More consistent over time	Less consistent over time
	Freshman myth less likely	Freshman myth more likely
OLC Dimensions		
Learning Outcomes	More awareness	Less awareness
	Better common understanding	Worse common understanding
	Better free recall of targeted competencies	Worse free recall of targeted competencies
Learning Environments	More alternative environments (e.g., interdisciplinary and project-based learning)	More traditional environments (e.g., access to good teachers)
Learning System	More processes to reinforce the learning contract	Fewer processes to reinforce the learning contract

on school-initiated activities to form general impressions about the college. For example, potential students may use college rankings that provide little detailed information about each college (cf., Ehrenberg, 2005). This means College C could display organizational learning contracts that are more diffuse and generic. For example, prospective students may expect to have good teachers or to be challenged academically—expectations that most college students have in general. Also, College C's complex and multifaceted set of relationships, programs, purposes and goals will make it difficult for undergraduate students to discern a simple, common representation of what they should reasonably expect (Win & Miller, 2005). This means that any specific expectations found at College C should be shared by a smaller percentage of students than will be the case with the new institutions.

Existence and Understanding of Learning Outcomes, Environments, and Systems

The new schools, with stronger contracts, use a competency-based portfolio to assess learning progress. This is a feature of their learning contracts. A larger percentage of students in the new schools should know that these specific learning outcomes exist, should be able to recall more of these outcomes, and should be able to understand their meaning. While College C also has a set of learning outcomes that are part of the professional accreditation standards for its program, given the reliance on its existing reputation and a more diffuse learning contract, a smaller percentage of students in College C should know these learning outcomes exist and should be able to recall them and understand their meaning. Also, the new schools will have active-based learning environments and explicit system processes (e.g., recruiting, grading on learning outcomes, and meeting class goals) to reinforce the organizational learning contract.

Contract Violations

In which type of institution will contract violations be more prevalent? Opposing arguments can be made about contract violations in the new and traditional colleges. "The freshman myth" is pertinent to these arguments (Stern, 1966). This is a commonly observed phenomenon in which college freshmen have unrealistically high expectations that are not met (e.g., Baker, McNeil, & Siryk, 1985; Darlaston-Jones, Pike, Cohen, Young, Haunold, & Drew, 2003, Kuh 1999; Kuh et al., 2005; Olsen et al. 1998). For example, freshmen typically expect college to be more academically challenging than they actually find it to be. Put another way, aspects of their learning contracts are violated. There are two rationales why Colleges A and B may have more such violations than College C. First, errors and unforeseen circumstances that accompany institutional startup may make it difficult for A and B to provide the promised experience to their students. For example, resource constraints may hinder their ability to deliver the experiences promised to applicants (cf. Desrochers, New Directors for Higher Education, Fall 2007 issue on the founding of UC Merced). Second, if A and B's students have higher and more specific expectations than their College C counterparts as predicted, they also will likely have more contract violations. For example, they may expect an innovative curriculum. Yet because the school seeks legitimization through the accreditation process, the school may need to conform to more traditional educational forms. So, one perspective is that new institutions will have more violations due to the startup process and to external environmental pressure to become like a traditional institution.

An alternative argument can be made that Colleges A and B will have fewer contract violations. This view is based on the rationale that failing to live up to students' expectations is very risky for A and B. Students with unmet expectations will be less satisfied and less committed to their school and have weaker intentions to re-enroll (Howard, 2005; Zhao et al., 2007). Dissatisfied students can tarnish the school's image, making it more difficult to attract well-qualified applicants. Thus, the new institutions are under tremendous pressure to deliver on their promises to ensure their students have satisfactory experiences. Satisfied students will be more likely to re-enroll, to graduate, and to create positive success stories for the school. We favor this argument over the opposite perspective for two reasons. First, Colleges A and B were well-funded ventures that did not encounter substantial resource constraints during startup. Second, the pressure to operate more like a traditional institution was mitigated by the fact that both A and B adopted innovative learning environments and specific learning outcomes. It still may be possible that over a longer period of time (e.g., a decade), A and B become more like the traditional colleges. This, however, is a different argument. Our argument pertains to the initial startup period that includes the graduation of at least the first few classes.

If Colleges A and B have more specific organizational learning contracts with fewer violations than College C, this has implications for the consistency of the contracts over time as well as between students. Colleges A and B's contracts should be more consistent from year to year, and more likely to be shared by upper and lower classmen. For example, freshmen who expect team-based learning during their first year should have the same expectation a year later. This is because there should be greater matching between expectations and experiences for students in Colleges A and B than in College C. And freshmen and juniors alike should expect team-based learning. This should lead to more commonly held understandings among students in A and B than in C.

To summarize, we made five predictions about organizational learning contract differences between Colleges A and B, and College C. First, A and B should be more likely to initiate their contracts with their students. That is, student expectations should be more likely to come from school-initiated sources. Second, A and B should have more specific and distinctive contracts (i.e., less diffuse) that are more widely shared by students. Third, these differences should be evident for all three contract dimensions (outcomes, environments, and systems). Fourth, A and B should have fewer contract violations. Fifth, A and B's contracts should be more consistent over time and should be consistent across both upper and lower classes.

Data to support or reject these five predictions came from one-on-one interviews conducted at two time periods approximately one year apart. See chapter 3 for more information.

RESULTS

Differences in the Source of Student Expectations

As we discussed above, a key feature of the organizational learning contract is that it is initiated by the school. Students may develop expectations from a variety of sources. Information sources initiated by the school can include materials produced by the college (e.g., brochures, websites), school-initiated visits to campus or outreach to high-school campuses. Sources that are not initiated by the school may include prior experiences of one's family or peers, information from high school counselors, and college review guides. We predicted Colleges A and B would be more proactive than College C at initiating what students should expect for their educational experiences. To test this, we asked students at each school, "How did you learn about your expectations for college?" This question was linked to the specific expectations they generated. Figure 4.1 compares the percent of student expectations by school originating from school-initiated sources and other sources. As predicted, Colleges A (65%) and B (50%) had higher percentages of school-initiated

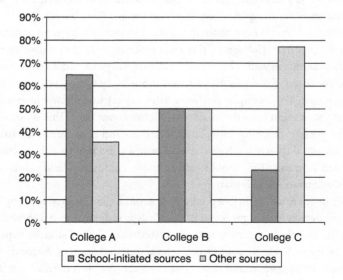

Figure 4.1: Percent of expectations sources by College

expectations than did College C (23%). This shows the expectations of students at Colleges A and B were more likely to be initiated by the schools. For example, Colleges A and B's students relied mostly on materials provided by their schools (A: 34%; B: 33%) to develop their expectations. College A's students also relied on school-initiated campus visits (25%). College C's students relied more on their prior beliefs about college (22%) than students at either College A (5%) or College B (7%).

Differences in Contract Specificity, Distinctiveness, and Strength

We predicted Colleges A and B would have contracts that are more specific and distinctive to their institutions, as well as more commonly shared by students. For example, students at Colleges A and B should expect to encounter alternative learning environments. College C's students should have more diffuse, general expectations. We also want to distinguish what students expect from their college and what they believe the college expects of them. For this reason, we asked freshmen and juniors the following questions at time 1 (fall of 2005) and time 2 (about one year later): "What do you expect from your college?" and "What does your college expect of you?" Asking students to freely recall their expectations, rather than giving them a list to choose from, reduced the likelihood the same expectation would come to mind for many students. Based on this, if at least 20% of students recalled a particular expectation, we considered this an adequate threshold to be a part of the school's contract. Tables 4.2 and 4.3 show what students expected of their schools at times 1 and 2, respectively. Expectations that were generic (i.e., that students in any college may have) are distinguished from those that included specific contract dimensions. Expectations included in each school's contract, based on our 20% threshold, are in bold.

For Tables 4.2 and 4.3, the differences are most apparent between Colleges A and C. First, especially in time 1, College A had more expectations per student (3.6) than C (2.1). Second, College A had more expectations that met the threshold to be considered a part of its contract than College C at both time 1 (A: 7; C: 3) and time 2 (A: 7; C: 5). This means College A's learning contract is more explicit and complex. Third, a higher percent of College A's students recalled the same expectations, indicating more widespread understanding about what is in their contract. Fourth, College A's expectations were more distinctive and focused on alternative learning environments. College C's expectations were less distinctive and more generic. For example, at time 1, College C's expectations included "academic challenge," "good professors," and "make me marketable" (i.e., prepare me for employment). These are expectations that students at any school might have. One exception for time 1 is "interdisciplinary learning" (shared by 19% of students), which is a stated value of the university in which College C resides. In contrast, only one of the seven expectations for College A was generic—"academic challenge." The others refer to five distinctive learning environments (e.g., project-based learning, learning-by-doing)

Table 4.2. PERCENTAGE OF STUDENTS RECALLING
EXPECTATIONS BY COLLEGE (TIME 1)

What expectations do you have for your school?	College A	College B	College C
Generic expectations			
Academic challenge	71%	21%	70%
Good professors	18%	6%	21%
Make me marketable	7%	36%	28%
Learning environment expectations			
Interdisciplinary	45%	48%	19%
Project-based learning	38%	12%	0%
Learning by doing	30%	18%	7%
Close professor contact	30%	3%	5%
Small classes	20%	21%	7%
Innovative approaches to learning	14%	18%	5%
Learning outcomes expectations			
Soft skills emphasis	11%	6%	12%
Learning systems expectations			
Provide feedback to improve school	20%	6%	0%
Strong support system	18%	0%	9%

and one learning system component ("feedback and change"). Thus, College A had a more distinctive set of expectations in its learning contract. Even for "academic challenge," it is possible College A students were referring to the demanding alternative learning environments students expected. "Academic challenge" at College C probably refers to the expectation that college will be more difficult than high school. Differences between Colleges B and C were less pronounced, though still important. For example, a higher percentage of College B's students expected alternative learning environments at both time 1 and time 2 (growing from 36% to 52%) compared to College C (20% to 31%). This was especially true at time 2. A higher percentage of students in College B also expected interdisciplinary learning at both times 1 (B: 48% C: 19%) and 2 (B: 52%; C: 14%).

The number of shared expectations and percentage of students sharing the same expectations also appear to increase with time. This is most apparent for College C and least apparent for College A. At College C, in addition to the same three generic expectations observed at time 1, we note the addition of three specific expectations ("project-based learning," "learning by doing" and "soft skills") to the college's learning contract at time 2. This likely occurred because in years 3 and 4 (the students' junior and senior years) the required curriculum for College C includes more project-based courses. We return to this point in our results for prediction 5 (page 63 ff.). It is sufficient to say here that College C students, and to some extent College B students, may have developed more expectations over time

Table 4.3. PERCENTAGE OF STUDENTS RECALLING
EXPECTATIONS BY COLLEGE (TIME 2)

What expectations do you have for your school?	College A	College B	College C
Generic expectations			
Academic challenge	95%	27%	89%
Make me marketable	31%	58%	57%
Good professors	10%	0%	37%
Other (accreditation)	10%	0%	0%
Networking with others	3%	12%	0%
High quality students	3%	0%	14%
Learning environment expectations			
Learning by doing	63%	36%	31%
Project-based learning	59%	36%	20%
Interdisciplinary	46%	52%	14%
Close professor contact	32%	15%	0%
Innovative approaches to learning	19%	12%	0%
Out-of-class learning	14%	24%	9%
Flexible curriculum	3%	3%	11%
Small classes	3%	18%	0%
Learning outcomes expectations			
Soft skills	34%	36%	31%
Learning systems expectations			
Strong support system	19%	0%	9%
Provide feedback to improve the school	15%	6%	0%

as they accumulated experiences with their institutions. In contrast, College A's learning contract did not change much from year 1 to 2. This shows most of its students' expectations were developed earlier (e.g., before starting school) and is consistent with the prediction 1 results (that new colleges are more likely to initiate the content of student expectations). Overall, the results in Tables 4.2 and 4.3 generally support prediction 2, especially for the comparison of Colleges A and C. To the extent that the differences are not as clear when comparing Colleges B and C, we note that College B's students differ from those in College A in an important way: College A's students spend a high percentage of their time in the college, which greatly influences their OLC expectations. In College B, students spend a large percent of their time outside of the college taking courses in other colleges in their university. These other colleges are not guided by the OLC of College B. Hence, the learning environment in College A is stronger, resulting in a more specific and widely held set of learning expectations.

Tables 4.4 and 4.5 show similar results for what students believed their schools expect of them. For example, at time 1 (Table 4.4), Colleges A and B had more

Table 4.4. PERCENTAGE OF STUDENTS RECALLING WHAT
COLLEGES EXPECTED OF THEM (TIME 1 DATA)

What does your school expect of you?	College A	College B	College C
Work hard	86%	33%	17%
Help improve school	55%	21%	6%
Uphold honor code	46%	15%	15%
Positively represent school	34%	33%	24%
Perform well outside school	23%	21%	9%
Community service	21%	3%	6%
Help build community	14%	12%	9%
Balance school and non-school activities	14%	6%	22%
Motivation to learn	9%	24%	2%
Leadership/communication skills	4%	24%	4%
Innovate	4%	3%	2%
Interdisciplinary learning	2%	18%	0%
Give back time/$ to school	2%	6%	7%

expectations per student (A: 3.4; B: 4.4; C: 1.9), more expectations in their contracts (A: 7; B: 4; C: 2) and a higher percentage of students who shared contract
expectations (A: 21–86%; B: 21–33%; C: 22–24%). This shows more agreement
on a wider variety of expectations for the new colleges. Though these expectations
were more difficult to classify as generic or distinctive to the college, meaningful
differences emerged between schools. For example, College A's students widely
agreed (86%) they were expected to "work hard," as did 33% of College B's students.
That is a pretty generic belief, although it was one held by only 17% of students in

Table 4.5. PERCENTAGE OF STUDENTS RECALLING WHAT
COLLEGES EXPECTED OF THEM (TIME 2 DATA)

What does your school expect of you?	College A	College B	College C
Work hard	71%	69%	78%
Help build community	59%	31%	33%
Uphold honor code	54%	13%	28%
Help improve school	39%	19%	0%
Positively represent school	29%	44%	30%
Perform well outside school	23%	28%	17%
Motivation to learn	20%	9%	7%
Innovate	13%	9%	2%
Interdisciplinary learning	13%	6%	15%
Balance school and non-school activities	11%	13%	0%
Give back time/$ to school	11%	6%	11%
Leadership/communication skills	9%	9%	9%
Community service	2%	6%	2%

College C. "Uphold the honor code" (46%) and "Community service" (21%) were distinctive to College A's contract. "Performing well outside of school" and "Help improve the school" were in both A's and B's contracts, but not in C's. This could reflect students' awareness that since their college does not have an established reputation its success depends at least in part on their own efforts. There again appeared to be a time effect here, with more and different expectations for time 2 more evident for College C than for A and B. For example, College C students were more likely to be expected to "Build community" and "Uphold the honor code" in time 2 than time 1. These results also support prediction 2, which states colleges with stronger OLCs will have more shared, specific expectations that are consistent over time.

Differences in Learning Outcomes

We predicted students in the new colleges would share more of the three learning contract dimensions (outcomes, environments, and systems). For learning outcomes, this means students at the new colleges should be more likely to recall specific learning outcomes they expect to develop while in school. To directly assess the learning outcome dimension, we asked students in each college if there was a list of learning outcomes they were expected to acquire during their education. We then asked them to freely recall as many outcomes as they could and to define each outcome. Figure 4.2 shows the percent of students at time 1 who believed there were specific competencies they were expected to learn. As the figure shows, 91% of College A's students and 55% of College B's students believed there was such a list, compared to 22% of College C's students. Time 2 results were the same. There was a much higher awareness of such a list at Colleges A and B than C.

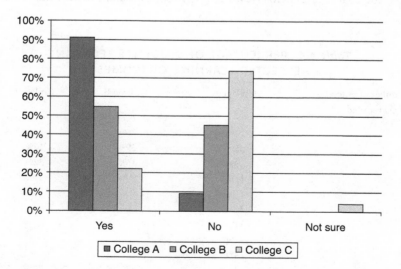

Figure 4.2: Student Responses to Question: Is there a list of competencies you are expected to learn?

Table 4.6 displays the percentage of students who freely and accurately recalled specific outcomes at time 1. We know College A expects its students to acquire nine learning outcomes, while B and C each expect eight outcomes. A higher percentage of the College A students accurately recalled the listed competencies. For example, 45% of College A's students recalled at least five of their nine expected competencies, compared to 0% of College C's students. Again, time 2 is the same. Prediction 3 is thus supported for learning outcomes.

Differences in Learning Environments

We reasoned that alternative learning environments would be more prevalent in College A's and B's contracts. Tables 4.2 and 4.3 show contract expectations for each college. A higher percentage of students in Colleges A and B expected alternative learning environments. For example, at time 1 (cf. Table 4.2), five of seven of College A's contract expectations pertained to alternative learning environments ("project-based learning": 38%; "learning by doing": 30%; "interdisciplinary learning": 45%; "small classes": 20%; "close professor contact": 30%), and two of College B's contract expectations pertained to alternative learning environments. Yet none of College C's contract expectations pertained to learning environments. "Interdisciplinary learning," a distinctive feature of College C, was just below the learning contract threshold (19%) at time 1. The same pattern was true for time 2, with the following exception: At time 2, College C's students were more apt to mention "project-based learning" (20%) and "learning by doing" (31%). Again, this suggests an effect of time on College C. Students were more exposed to and became more aware of these environments between times 1 and 2. These results support prediction 3 for more alternative learning environments in the newer institutions.

Table 4.6. PERCENTAGE OF STUDENTS RECALLING EXPECTED LEARNING OUTCOMES

Number of outcomes freely recalled	College A	College B	College C
0	20%	36%	26%
1	5%	39%	17%
2	9%	15%	32%
3	11%	9%	19%
4	11%		7%
5	20%		
6	14%		
7	7%		
8	4%		

Note: Rounding leads to percentage totals not adding up to 100.

Learning Systems Differences

Learning systems are organizational mechanisms that initiate, sustain, and facilitate the redesign of organizational learning contracts. We predicted this dimension would be more evident in the new colleges in two respects. First, Colleges A and B should be more likely to engage in activities that initiate expectations with their students. The reported results supported this prediction: A higher percent of students' expectations in Colleges A and B were initiated by the colleges even before the students had enrolled. Second, in response to the questions about what students expected of their colleges and what they thought their colleges expected of them (cf. Tables 4.2 and 4.3), we predicted a higher percentage of students in the new schools with stronger OLCs would freely recall learning system components. "Provide feedback to improve the school" was part of College A's contract at time 1 (20%) but not time 2 (10%) (cf. Tables 4.2 and 4.3). This expectation was not mentioned at all by College C's students. The same theme is in Tables 4.4 and 4.5, as "Help improve the school" appeared in College A's contract at time 1 (55%) and time 2 (39%). This also was part of school B's contract at time 1 (21%) and just below the threshold at time 2 (19%). It was not part of College C's contract at either time. These interview data provide some support for the existence of system differences across the schools.

Another way to look at system differences is to look at some structural differences between the institutions. As indicated earlier, Colleges A and B were more active in building recruiting materials and initiating more elaborate recruiting activities. In addition, students in these two colleges had to distinguish between achievements in learning outcomes and achievements in courses. In both Colleges A and B, students saw non-classroom learning experiences as important for developing outcomes. Also, each college offered its students ways to showcase their development in these outcomes outside of the classroom. All of these structural mechanisms are ways to socialize and to assess student progress on contract dimensions.

Differences in Meeting Expectations

We developed two potential opposing arguments about contract violations. One argument was that the new schools would have more violations due to the errors that happen during startups. However, we favored an alternative argument that the new schools would have fewer violations because the risk of failure as a consequence of such errors is too high. For example, if violations lead to unsatisfied students, the new schools will have difficulty recruiting a high-quality applicant pool for the next year. We asked students if each expectation they recalled was exceeded, met, or not met. Tables 4.7 and 4.8 display the answer to this for times 1 and 2. Expectations were shared by at least 20% of students.

For all expectations, the results show little difference between schools in each category, with one exception. A higher percentage of expectations were *exceeded* for the new colleges at time 1 (A: 39%; B: 36%) than for College C (23%). Though consistent with our prediction, we also expected to find differences in expectations that were *violated*.

A closer analysis of the data revealed College A's exceeded expectations were concentrated on three of the seven expectations that met the contract threshold (academic challenge, learning by doing, close professor contact). Violations concentrated on two of the seven contract expectations (interdisciplinary learning, feedback to improve the school). By comparison, the percentage of College C's violations was about the same for the three expectations in its contract.

These results are interesting in several respects. First, the literature on workplace expectations focuses on unmet expectations, not exceeded ones (Rousseau, 1995). Yet, we find College A's and B's students were more likely to report exceeded contract expectations. Second, it shows that the violations that did occur (especially for College A) concentrated on only a few expectations. This is consistent with both our preferred argument (i.e., it will simply be too risky for the new colleges to have dissatisfied students) and, to some extent, the counterargument (new colleges will be prone to execution errors) regarding contract violations—at least for College A. The fact that College A had a number of exceeded expectations suggests this school is focused on reducing its risk of having dissatisfied students. At the same time, the fact that two expectations were not met shows the school had at least some execution errors. One also should note that College A had more expectations in its contract, which increased the probability that some would be unmet. While College B had fewer contract expectations, most were met or exceeded. There was no significant number of unmet expectations, which supports the idea that for new colleges to survive over time, they have to remove or minimize the risks of student dissatisfaction. Third, the lack of differences in violated contract expectations needs to be considered in light of differences between the schools. College C has a long history of socializing new students and an established set of organizational processes for doing so, which might account for its lack of contract violations. Yet the students at College C also had relatively fewer expectations of their school, and the expectations they did have were generic and not unlike the expectations we might find for most students in any college. In contrast, Colleges A and B had no history of socializing students and had to develop a new set of organizational processes for doing so.

Table 4.7. PERCENTAGE OF STUDENTS RECALLING CONTRACT EXPECTATIONS (EXCEEDED, MET, AND NOT MET) BY COLLEGE (TIME 1)

To what extent have your expectations been exceeded, met, or not met?	College A	College B	College C
Exceeded	39%	36%	23%
Met	46%	53%	59%
Not met	15%	12%	18%

Table 4.8. PERCENTAGE OF STUDENTS RECALLING
CONTRACT EXPECTATIONS (EXCEEDED, MET, AND NOT MET)
BY COLLEGE (TIME 2)

To what extent have your expectations been exceeded, met, or not met?	College A	College B	College C
Exceeded	34%	39%	32%
Met	54%	52%	60%
Not met	12%	10%	8%

Yet their students had a greater number of more widely shared, distinctive and specific expectations, which increased the chances that some would be violated. Thus, given the lack of differences between the new and traditional colleges on this measure, some evidence suggests Colleges A and B focused on providing experiences that matched student expectations. These schools' level of experience was not comparable to that of College C, but these two new schools met or exceeded their students' expectations nonetheless.

Consistency in Expectations

An implication of the prior results is new schools should display greater consistency in learning contracts in two respects. First, students in the classes of 2007 and 2009 who were interviewed at the same time should be more likely to report common expectations in Colleges A and B than in College C. This would show contract continuity for two samples of students who enrolled in each school two years apart from one another. Second, when the same students from both classes were interviewed at times 1 and 2, those from the new schools should be more likely to share the same expectations in year 2 that they shared in year 1. This would indicate contract continuity for the same student sample year over year.

Tables 4.9 and 4.10 compare the classes of 2007 and 2009 at times 1 and 2. The results show that students in the classes of 2007 and 2009 in College A had virtually the same expectations. For example, in year 2, the class of 2007 students had seven contract expectations and the class of 2009 students had eight expectations, six of which were held in common. By comparison, College C's classes of 2007 and 2009 each had five expectations, three of which were held in common. College B's classes had three expectations in common. Thus, College A's upper and lower classmen had more expectations in common than their College C counterparts. The pattern for College B appears to be more similar to that of College C than College A. As we mentioned previously, students in College A operate in a focused learning environment, while students in College B split their time between their college and other parts of their university that do not advocate the same OLC found in College B. This makes College B appear more like the traditional institution in some respects.

Table 4.9. CLASSES OF '07 AND '09 CONSISTENCY IN CONTRACT EXPECTATIONS BY COLLEGE (TIME 1)

	'07	'09	'07	'09	'07	'09
What do you expect from your college?	A	A	B	B	C	C
Academic challenge	69	74	20	22	68	71
Make me marketable	•	•	•	56	26	29
Good professors	•	22	•	—	•	33
Good facilities	•	•	—	•	—	•
Learning by doing	28	33	•	28	•	•
Project-based learning	59	15	•	•	—	—
Interdisciplinary	62	26	60	39	21	•
Close professor contact	34	26	•	—	•	—
Innovative	•	•	20	•	—	•
Flexible curriculum	—	•	—	•	•	•
Small classes	24	•	•	28	•	•
Soft skills emphasis	•	•	•	•	•	•
Strong support system	•	•	—	—	•	•
Feedback and change	21	•	•	—	—	—

Note:— = percentages < 5; • = percentages 5 < x < 20.

Table 4.11 compares colleges at time 1 and 2 with matched sample data—we include those who responded to our interview question at both times 1 and 2 in the analysis. The results also show greater consistency from year to year in the learning contract content for College A than for College C. The same is true when comparing Colleges B and C, though to a lesser extent. College A's organizational learning contract had six expectations at time 1 and seven at time 2, and five of these expectations were recalled in both years. School B's contract had five expectations at time 1 and seven at time 2, with four recalled in both years. College C's contract had two expectations at time 1 and six in time 2, two of which were recalled in both years. This shows College C students developed more expectations with experience and their contracts were more likely to change over time (e.g., to become more complex). Thus, Colleges A and B were more likely to help establish what students should expect before they enrolled. Further, these expectations are fairly consistent from year 1 to 2. These results support prediction 5.

DISCUSSION

This study generally supported our idea that an organizational learning contract exists between an institution and its students as well as our five predictions about how new and traditional colleges should exhibit different kinds of learning contracts.

Table 4.10. CLASSES OF '07 AND '09 CONSISTENCY IN CONTRACT EXPECTATIONS BY COLLEGE (TIME 2)

	'07	'09	'07	'09	'07	'09
What do you expect from your college?	A	A	B	B	C	C
Academic challenge	75	91	•	39	81	95
Make me marketable	34	20	47	67	56	58
Good professors	•	•	—	—	•	53
Other (accreditation)	•	•	—	—	—	—
Networking with others	—	•	•	•	—	—
High quality students	—	•	—	—	•	21
Diverse students	—	—	—	•	—	•
Good facilities	—	—	—	•	—	•
Learning by doing	53	57	•	56	44	21
Project-based learning	53	51	33	39	38	•
Interdisciplinary	44	37	20	78	•	•
Close professor contact	28	29	20	•	—	—
Innovative	•	•	—	•	—	—
Out-of-class learning	•	•	•	33	•	—
Flexible curriculum	—	—	—	•	—	21
Small classes	•	—	20	•	—	—
Soft skills emphasis	28	31	•	61	56	•
Strong support system	•	26	—	—	•	•
Feedback and change	•	•	—	•	—	—

Note:— = percentages < 5; • = percentages 5 < x < 20.

As predicted, the new schools, with stronger contracts, were more proactive at initiating organizational learning contracts with their students. This was supported by the higher percentage of expectations that were initiated by the new schools as compared to the traditional one. It also shows that schools can influence student expectations before they enroll by using anticipatory socialization tactics. Consistent with this idea that schools initiate contract expectations before students enroll, time appeared to have more of an effect on College C's contract than either of the new colleges. Our year 1 samples included entering freshmen (class of 2009) and already enrolled juniors (class of 2007). For College C, new students had fewer, less explicit, and more generic shared expectations than those starting their third year. This indicates that the juniors we interviewed developed more specific expectations over time, while freshmen came in with general expectations based on their pre-college experiences. A similar effect was observed over time. College C's contract started out in time 1 with two generic expectations, and four more specific expectations were added in year 2 as students accumulated more experience. In contrast,

Table 4.11. YEAR 1 AND 2 CONSISTENCY IN LEARNING CONTRACT EXPECTATIONS BY COLLEGE

	Yr. 1	Yr. 2	Yr. 1	Yr. 2	Yr. 1	Yr. 2
What do you expect from your college?	A	A	B	B	C	C
Academic challenge	74	100	24	28	74	91
Make me marketable	•	30	48	72	29	59
Good professors	•	•	—	—	•	38
Other (accreditation)	—	•	—	—	—	—
High quality students	•	—	—	—	•	•
Good facilities and resources	•	—	•	—	—	•
Learning by doing	30	50	20	44	•	32
Project-based learning	38	58	•	32	—	21
Interdisciplinary	42	44	40	52	•	•
Close professor contact	28	38	—	•	•	0
Innovative	•	•	•	•	3	—
Out-of-class learning	•	•	—	32	—	•
Flexible curriculum	•	—	•	—	•	•
Small classes	•	—	24	•	•	—
Soft skills emphasis	•	28	—	44	•	32
Strong support system	•	•	—	—	•	•
Feedback and change	22	•	—	•	0	0

Notes: Using matched sample Year 1 and Year 2; — = percentages < 5; • = percentages 5 < x < 20.

College A's entering freshmen and returning juniors shared nearly identical expectations in year 1 and their expectations were stable between years 1 and 2.

There also was evidence that Colleges A and B had more complex contracts with expectations that were distinctive to their institutions, especially in regards to alternative learning environments. College C had expectations that one might expect to find at any college. In fact, for the year 1 sample, the three most widely shared expectations at College C were general beliefs that one would find in almost any college (academic challenge, good professors, make me marketable). There was some support for our opposing arguments about contract violations. Though the new colleges did not have a lower percentage of unmet expectations in general, they did have a higher percentage of exceeded expectations in time 1. This suggests that at least for time 1, Colleges A and B might have worked extra hard to provide experiences that were consistent with what they had told students they should expect. A closer look at the data focusing only on expectations that rose to the level of being part of the contract (i.e., met the 20% threshold) showed that College A's violations were concentrated on two expectations (interdisciplinary learning and providing feedback to improve the school). There were probably execution errors in meeting both these expectations. In the first case, College A depended on other institutions to provide interdisciplinary courses, complicating the delivery of this expectation. In the second case, the class of 2007 students who participated in starting the school may have helped set very high expectations about the administration's responsiveness to their feedback. As the school moved from its launch to the execution phase, it may have become more difficult to accommodate student input, resulting in perceptions of violation. There are some other data on student involvement in decision-making that support this finding (see chapter 6 for more discussion about student involvement). On the flip side, College A (see Table 4.7) did especially well at exceeding three contract expectations in year 1 (academic challenge, learning by doing, close professor contact). The administration appeared to work hard to ensure at least some student experiences were consistent with what they were told to expect. This supports the argument that the new schools would be vigilant at preventing errors because of the risks of failure (e.g., difficulty recruiting students).

It is important to consider whether differences in learning contracts between the new and traditional colleges may be due to other systematic differences between the schools. Counter to this possibility, we found the greatest differences between Colleges A and C. Yet students at these colleges also were the most similar to one another on some important dimensions. They were more likely to apply to and to be accepted by both institutions, had similar proportions of males vs. females, and had comparable SAT scores (see chapter 6, p. 5 ff).

The methodology in this study has several limitations. First, using the free recall method to identify student expectations has some disadvantages. It is possible students did not recall a particular expectation simply because it did not come to mind during the interview. Also, individual differences could lead some students to share more information than others. For example, students who are more sociable or extroverted might have been more apt to share information with the interviewers. However, we did find consistency in expectations in Colleges A and B, suggesting that the methodology did not cause significant problems.

A second limitation is the criterion we used to determine if an expectation should be included in each school's organizational learning contract. If at least 20% of students in each college sample mentioned a particular expectation, we included it in the contract. Though this is a somewhat arbitrary threshold, we believe it is reasonable given the fact that each expectation was freely recalled, without prompting by an interviewer or a questionnaire item. And in most cases, a higher percentage of students shared contract expectations. For example, at time 2, 17 out of 19 total contract expectations for all three colleges were shared by greater than 31% of students.

A third limitation is that we did not measure how specific contract expectations that are met or exceeded might translate into other positive outcomes, such as engagement or learning. The workplace literature shows employees whose expectations for their employers are not met are less satisfied with and less committed to their employers and are more likely to intend to quit their jobs (Zhao et al., 2007).

This also should be true for students whose expectations for their colleges are not met (Howard, 2005). However, a clear finding across all three schools is that there were relatively few unmet expectations. We did measure students' organizational commitment at time 2. On a scale of 1 to 5 (with 1 indicating stronger commitment and 5 weaker commitment), College A's students ($n = 60, M = 1.40, S = 0.51$) were more committed to their organizations than those in College C ($n = 43, M = 2.27, S = 0.88$), and the difference was significant ($p <0.0001$). The same was true when comparing College B's students ($n = 32, M = 1.93, S = 0.63$) to those in College C ($p <0.05$).[1] In addition, we measured student attachment at time 2 (Table 6.9). Here, students in College A, and to some extent College B, reported strong attachments to their institutions.

Another issue is that our data are about student expectations. But the contract is about expectations for all the players (e.g., faculty, staff). The time and expenses incurred in interviewing precluded extending our sample. We did informal interviews with some faculty and staff during the time of the study. That data collection is supportive of what we have reported here and in other chapters.

Limitations aside, this chapter makes several contributions to the research on student expectations. The main contribution is the strong evidence it provides for organizational learning contracts. We argued and found support for the idea that students' expectations can be categorized by three learning experience dimensions: the learning outcomes they expect to achieve, the environments in which they expect to achieve these outcomes, and the mechanisms by which the contract provisions will be initiated and sustained. We found students at the new colleges had expectations that were more distinctive to their institutions, more likely to include these three dimensions, and more widely shared. This chapter and Chapters 5 and 6 support the basic features of the organizational learning contract specified in Table 4.1.

Another contribution of this chapter is its demonstration that schools can successfully initiate student expectations earlier in the educational process—even before the students enroll in the school—and can provide environments that match those expectations. Prior research has focused on how schools might affect expectations after students enroll. We found the new colleges were more likely to influence students' expectations before they enrolled. This shows how anticipatory socialization can have a positive impact on student expectations.

A third contribution is this chapter's comparison of the organizational learning contracts of new and existing colleges. Prior research on student expectations focused on existing, traditionally oriented colleges. A new innovative college is an ideal setting to study learning contracts because students need to have a clear sense of what to expect that is different from a traditional college. In our study, the new colleges had more distinctive learning contracts than the traditional college.

---

1. Results of independent samples means comparison, 1-tailed tests not assuming equal variances.

CHAPTER 5
Learning

I n this chapter, we explore differences in learning between students with strong versus weak OLCs. In the prior chapter, we reported on students' expectations. In this chapter, we explore their learning experiences as well as some of the consequences of these experiences. Specifically, we examine the learning environments they used, their beliefs about how learning environments affect learning outcomes, critical incidents they have experienced during their time in college and the impacts of these incidents with respect to learning, what they have learned about learning, and the learning climate at their institutions. Understanding these learning issues is fundamental to understanding the OLC in general, as well as its differences across schools with different characteristics.

LITERATURE

In each of this book's empirical chapters, we link our work with the broader literature on learning in institutions of higher education. Our goal is not to do a comprehensive review; rather, it is to acknowledge prior work and connect it to our story. Our selection strategy in this review was to (1) reflect diversity in variables, methods, and level of analysis, and (2) identify studies relevant to our focus on the OLC. Prior research has examined a broad range of variables and methods that impact learning. Some studies looked at institutional variables, such as size, resource allocation practices, and control systems. Others considered organizational factors such as climate or culture (Berger & Braxton, 1998). Curriculum design, teaching practices, and student characteristics also have been examined.

One trend in the literature is to move toward a more systemic view of how students learn. The National Study of Student Learning (Pascarella, Edison, Hagedorn, & Terenzini, 1996) and the National Survey of Student Engagement (Kuh, 2001) are in this tradition. These studies build more comprehensive models that include a range of factors, from institutional attributes to student characteristics, as a way to investigate the multiple factors affecting student learning. For example, Lambert, Terenzini, and Lattuca (2007) examined the impact of pre-college student characteristics, institutional program characteristics, faculty activities, student experiences, etc. on two student skills—design proficiency and group competencies. The model in this research is that institutional, student, program, and teaching characteristics affect student experiences, which in turn affect learning. We selected the Lambert study because it drew its data from colleges that emphasized professional technical skills. This study suggested that pre-college experiences and institutional characteristics explain only a small portion of the variance in both competencies (i.e., design and group skills). Program and faculty characteristics were more important predictors of learning. Program characteristics studied by Lambert et al. (2007) included an emphasis on teaching in personnel decisions, communication, and project skills. Faculty characteristics focused more on active learning principles and less on traditional pedagogy.

Another study in this systemic tradition (Kuh, Gonyea, & Williams, 2005) looks at institutional, demographic, program, and faculty characteristics in a more diverse sample of undergraduates. Consistent with the findings of other studies, institutional and demographic variables were not strong predictors of academic competence in the Kuh et al. study (2005). Student perceptions of the support they received from faculty, administration, and peers were a strong predictor of academic competence. Also, students who were cognitively and academically engaged reported higher scores on academic competence. Colleges that emphasized hard work and more time studying had higher student academic engagement.

The contributions of the systemic approach are twofold. First, it focuses on multiple levels of influence (e.g., individual to institutional) on learning. Second, this approach postulates a mediating model where the independent variables (e.g., program characteristics, teaching practices) affect student engagement or experiences, which, in turn, affect learning. The systemic studies tend to have similar methods, using large samples with surveys as the primary measurement tool. The dependent variables in many of the studies are self-reports of skill or competency acquisitions.

In addition to studies using the systemic approach, some qualitative interview-based studies capture students' experiences and learning in greater detail. A study by Light (2001) listed a number of findings about how students learn. These include the importance of working with others: Doing homework with others facilitates learning; activities outside of the classroom, especially in residential settings, were critical, as were mentored internships. More assignments that provided more frequent feedback were preferred over fewer assignments that provided less frequent feedback. These and other findings mirror some of our study's findings.

Our study differs from these prior studies in a number of ways. First, we want to compare institutions with strong versus weak OLCs. We want to see how these institutions differ in their learning environments, if they make any connection of learning environments with learning outcomes, and the extent to which they feature personal approaches to learning that support the contract. Second, our methodology relies primarily on in-depth, face-to-face, one-on-one interviews rather than the survey methods used in the systemic studies. The advantage of a personal interview is that it permits respondents to generate personally relevant ideas as opposed to responses primed by questions in a questionnaire. We coded all of the interview data and conducted quantitative analyses on similarities and differences between institutions. Lastly, we did an intensive study of three institutions using multiple methods as opposed to a large sample study using a single method or a purely qualitative study.

Although our focus is different, there are thematic connections with the literature. In the new innovative institutions in our study, teaching is emphasized in personnel decisions and there is a movement away from traditional pedagogies. Active-based learning, communication, and project-based learning, as well as strong support systems between faculty and students are themes both in the literature and in our study.

This chapter is organized around a series of topics. We first wanted to compare the learning environments in Colleges A, B, and C. How are they different? Then, we gave the respondents a mapping task. We wanted to know, given a learning environment, how it impacted the set of learning outcomes. The students had to connect environments to selected outcomes. The third issue focused on critical incidents. We asked students to describe incidents at school that shaped how they thought about themselves or the college. When we coded the incidents, a large percentage was about learning. This enabled us to explore similarities and differences across colleges. Next, we asked students to articulate their personal model about learning. That is, we asked them if a new student came to their college, what they would tell the new student about being an effective learner. Lastly, in the second wave of interviews, we had students complete a survey about their college's culture, focus on continuous improvement, and decision making, as well as some questions on learning.

Given this type of data, we expect or predict that institutions with strong OLCs should operate in more and different types of learning environments and should also emphasize active learning. When students map learning environments to learning outcomes, it will be difficult to compare across institutions because learning outcomes vary by institution. However, we expect to see a more complex mapping of learning environments to learning outcomes in the new institutions, simply because of the greater emphasis on the OLC in these institutions. In the critical incident question, we expect to find a relatively high percentage of incidents about learning across all institutions. These incidents should be about personal and skill development. In the section on personal models of learning, we expect a stronger focus on learning from peers and project work in the stronger OLC institutions. The rationale is that there are more frequent project-based classes and a stronger culture for working together in the new institutions. Lastly, given the above observations, we expect attitudes about the learning climate to be stronger and more positive in the institutions with stronger OLCs. This hypothesis is reinforced by the finding, reported in chapter 4, that most expectations were exceeded or met.

LEARNING ENVIRONMENTS

During our interviews at both time 1 and time 2, we gave the students a list of 10 possible learning environments and asked them to allocate their learning time across the environments. That is, they were to think of the total time they spent in learning activities, which included classroom and non-classroom time. Then, they were to allocate the percent of time spent in lectures, labs, group work, and so on. Figure 5.1 displays the results. Most of the learning environments are fairly easily defined. Peer teaching means the student spent time teaching others, formally or informally. Mentoring means working with a professor on various issues. Internships represent work opportunities within or outside the institution. A studio mirrors the studio in Architecture. In traditional (non-architecture) courses, the studio unfolds as a combination of mini lectures, laboratory tasks, and discussion (Wilson, 2001). Figure 5.1 displays the results. A and B are the new innovative institutions with stronger OLCs, while C is a well-known traditional institution.

As Figure 5.1 shows, there is a greater emphasis on the lecture method in the traditional school (34% vs. 23% or 27%). Group or project-based learning was

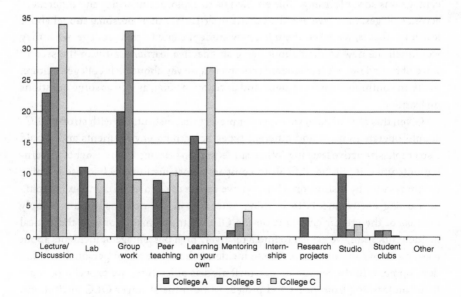

Figure 5.1: Learning Environments—Wave 1 % of Total Learning Time

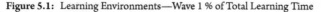

more prevalent in the two new institutions. Learning on your own was greater in the traditional institution, consistent with the lower percentage of group work in this school. In the newer institutions, there was more time spent working together, either in formal groups or informal learning assignments. Another insight from Figure 5.1 is that students in the new institutions spent time in all of the environments. In the traditional institution, there were three categories with no endorsements. This reflects greater variety in learning environments in the newer institutions.

Because we collected data from freshmen (Class of 2009) and juniors (Class of 2007) at time 1, a reasonable question is whether there are differences between these two classes. For new institution A, the percentages of time spent in the various types of learning environments were basically the same, except for lecture/discussion. Juniors spent proportionally more time (28%) in this environment than freshmen (18%). This difference probably reflects the initial major emphasis on group work for freshmen, while upper classmen take more electives with greater variation in teaching methods, including the use of lectures. Group work is important for all four years, but it starts off the initial educational experience. This initial heavier focus on group work is another way to socialize students in the active learning mode that is inherent in the institution's learning contract. For the second new institution (B), the percentage of allocations is roughly the same across freshmen and juniors. For the traditional institution, most of the allocations are the same, with the exception of the lecture method. Here, freshmen experience a much higher level of lecture methods (40%) vs. juniors (27%). This difference reflects the structure of many traditional institutions. The lecture format dominates many introductory courses. Then, as one moves to the junior and senior years, there are more seminars or project work. This would account for the greater percentage of lecture time for freshmen. This difference also reflects the importance of early experiences. In the newer institutions they start out with multiple environments with a greater emphasis on group learning, while in the more traditional institution the lecture/discussion method is initially emphasized.

Data for time 2 were collected one year later. The freshmen are now sophomores and the juniors are seniors. We asked the same question about allocating 100% of their time across all learning time, both in and out of the classroom. The results (see Figure 5.2) were in the same order of magnitude as in Figure 5.1. Lecture represents a greater percentage of total learning time in the traditional institution (C). Group work, on average, is higher in the newer institutions. More time is allocated to working on your own in the traditional institution.

Figures 5.1 and 5.2 show there is congruency between espoused theories and theories in action for the new institutions. It is one thing for the new schools to assert that their institutions will be different. The real issue is whether they are different in practice. There appear to be differences in the learning environments, at least through the eyes of the students in the new institutions. Institutions with stronger OLCs use more diverse, active-based learning environments.

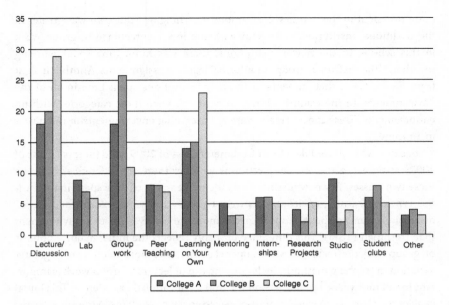

Figure 5.2: Learning Environments—Wave 2% of Total Learning Time

LEARNING ENVIRONMENTS—LEARNING OUTCOMES

We asked students to map the relationship between the different learning environments and learning outcomes. The students had a matrix of learning environments by learning outcomes. Their task was to specify which environments led to changes in specific learning outcomes. For each institution, the learning environments were the same, but the outcomes varied because each institution had its own unique combination of categories. We placed no constraints on the mapping process. A student could relate a learning environment to any, all, or none of the learning outcomes. We present the summary data in a matrix of environments by outcomes, with the percentage of mentions in each cell for time 2. To simplify examination of the table, we entered all percentages in excess of 40% and used a "•" to indicate percentages between 20–40%. Blank cells had very low or no endorsements.

We present each institution separately because the outcomes differ. For new institution A (Table 5.1), quantitative skills were most tied to the lecture. Qualitative skills were related to many learning environments, but the linkage was less strong. For diagnosis as an outcome, group discussion, lab, and group projects were the strongest contributors, but the absolute percentages were between 20–40%. Team skills, not surprisingly, were most closely tied to group projects and the studio, while student experiences in campus clubs also contributed. Lifelong learning, which refers to the skill to learn on your own over time, seemed to be most affected by learning on your own and group projects. Changes in communication skills were most tied to group project work and peer teaching. The opportunity to teach others

Table 5.1. CONNECTIONS BETWEEN LEARNING ENVIRONMENTS AND LEARNING OUTCOMES

College A

	Quantitative	Qualitative	Diagnosis	Team	Lifelong Learning	Communication	Context	Design	Opportunities
Lecture	57%				•	•	41%	•	•
Lab work	•	•	•						
Group discussion		•	•	•		•			
Group project work			•	50%		70%			•
Peer teaching		•				55%		•	
Learning on your own	•	•			70%	•			
Mentoring						•	•		•
Internships				•		•	•		50%
Studio		•		•				41%	
Student clubs				•		•	•		•
Other									
Count	44	44	44	44	44	44	44	44	44

Note: • = percentages between 20–40, blank = percentages between 0–19.

was a strong way to sharpen communication skills. Understanding contextual differences in problems was affected most by the lecture method. Design, as an outcome, was affected by a studio environment. For opportunity, which referred to skills in identifying and implementing new business and technological opportunities, the internship was the most important influence.

We examined whether there were noticeable differences between the two classes. There did not seem to be major differences in the relationships between the mapping of learning environments to changes in learning outcomes between the classes of 2009 and 2007. The relationships mentioned above characterized both groups. Team-based work seemed to be related to more learning outcomes than any other environment. This is consistent with the group focus in this institution. For students in the class of 2009, the lecture was a more important mechanism for learning. This result may seem surprising, given the earlier finding that showed less emphasis on the lecture method in this institution. But one must pay attention to the wording of the question. We are asking for their map or beliefs on how lecture contributes to changes in learning outcomes, not about the frequency of use of this method. For these individuals, the majority of their high-school instruction before coming to institution A was in the lecture format. They are only one year into a new environment. So we might be capturing prior beliefs about high school, which is less true for the students in the class of 2007, who are further removed from high school.

Another way to look at the data is to ask whether any of the outcomes are associated with multiple environments. For this part of the analysis, we relaxed the strength of the tie between environment and outcome to those where at least 20% of the respondents endorsed some linkage. The most noticeable connection is between the outcome of communication skills and the multiple environments of group work, peer teaching, group discussion, mentoring, and internships. The outcomes of qualitative reasoning and lifelong learning also were affected by multiple environments.

The findings for Colleges B and C are shown in Tables 5.2 and 5.3. As mentioned, all of the colleges have a different set of outcomes, while the learning environments are the same for all institutions. The task of linking learning environments was the same, but the matrices are different. There are, however, some common outcomes, so we can do limited comparisons across institutions.

In College B, design skills were related to lectures as a form of learning for both classes of students. Understanding quantitative skills was tied most strongly to the lecture and, next, to experiences in an internship for both classes. Project management skills were most developed in a project-based learning environment, with internships again making an important contribution. Lifelong learning was most affected by learning situations where students were asked to work on their own. Group project environments were the next most important factor for both classes. Group skills, not surprisingly, were related to project-based work and then experience in working in student clubs outside of regular classwork. Change management skills were not greatly affected by the learning environments. Understanding crossnational issues also was not greatly affected by any learning environment, although

Table 5.2. CONNECTIONS BETWEEN LEARNING ENVIRONMENTS AND LEARNING OUTCOMES

College B

	Design	Quantitative	Project Management	Lifelong Learning	Collaboration	Change Management	Across Countries	Communication
Lecture	88%	80%				44%		
Lab work	56%	•						
Group project work	•	•	84%	44%	80%		48%	80%
Peer teaching		•		•				64%
Learning on your own	•			76%				
Mentoring	•	•		•				•
Internships	•			•	•		52%	48%
Research project	•	•	•	•	•	•		
Studio			•	•				
Student clubs			•		60%		•	72%
Other								
Count	25	25	25	25	25	25	25	25

Note: • = percentages between 20–40, blank = percentages between 0–19.

Table 5.3. CONNECTIONS BETWEEN LEARNING ENVIRONMENTS AND LEARNING OUTCOMES

College C

	Scientific Method	Scientific Knowledge	Problem Solving	Team-work skills	Lifelong Learning	Communication	Design	Context
Lecture	•		•		•			•
Lab work	66%	82%	•	•				
Group project work			57%	86%		68%	43%	
Peer teaching		•	•	•		66%		
Learning on your own		57%	45%		50%			
Mentoring		•	•		•	•		
Internships			•	•		•		
Research project			•				•	•
Studio				•				
Student clubs						41%	•	•
Other								
Count	44	44	44	44	44	44	44	44

Note: • = percentages between 20–40; blank = percentages between 0–19.

there was some influence by internships. The last outcome was communication skills. Group work, peer teaching, and clubs were most important in influencing this learning outcome.

We reported above the strongest links between learning environments and learning outcomes. If we relax the connection to examine those environments where at least 20% or more respondents endorsed a link with a particular outcome, we find the following: Group project work and internships are related to multiple learning outcomes. The lecture and research impact the next number of learning outcomes. Peer teaching, mentoring, and the studio affect the fewest learning outcomes.

If we look at the matrix from the number of learning environments affecting an outcome, it appears that most of the outcomes are affected by at least four or five environments. Design and lifelong learning were affected by the highest number (6) of learning environments. There are a few outcomes, such as change management and cross-national skills, that are not linked even moderately to many of the learning environments. This finding is not surprising. If we did a matrix of courses by learning outcomes for College B, we would see very few, if any, courses that address cross-cultural issues or other topics related to cross-national learning.

In the more traditional College C (see Table 5.3), we observe that the skill of understanding the scientific method is primarily affected by learning in the lab. Scientific knowledge itself is most influenced by the lecture. Problem-solving skills seemed to be affected most by group-project work and the opportunity to learn on one's own. Team skills are most impacted by project-based learning for both sophomores and seniors. Lifelong learning is most influenced when students are given assignments to work on their own. This holds true for the sophomores, but the seniors report no environment as having a major influence on this skill. For communication skills, project-based and peer-based learning are the most impactful environments.

Design skills are most tied to project-based work, but the connection is not as strong as reported above for the other skills. Understanding the context of technical applications is not strongly affected by any learning environment.

If we ask which of the learning environments seem to have at least a moderate effect (20% or greater) on learning outcomes, we find the following: The lecture, project-based learning, and peer teaching and internships influence multiple outcomes. Studio, clubs, and research impact the fewest number of outcomes. These also are the environments used least frequently. Another question is about the impact on learning outcomes by multiple environments. The learning outcome affected by the greatest number of learning environments is problem-solving in College C, for both classes. For sophomores, team skills and communication skills are affected by at least four different environments. For seniors, in addition to problem solving, the learning outcome of scientific knowledge was affected by at least four different learning environments.

There is some complexity in comparing these matrices across institutions, since they have different outcomes; however, there are some themes. First, there are some natural fits between environments and outcomes. Specifically, project-based learning is related to team skills, and learning on your own is related to lifelong learning.

One might argue these are self-evident, but that is not the case. Learning in a project-based environment may be a positive or negative experience. It is unlikely negative experiences would lead to acquisition of team skills. A conflict within the team may create negative attitudes about working on a team and developing skills. From our interviews across all three institutions, work on projects was seen as positive. And as we reported earlier, this kind of environment was more prevalent in the new institutions (Colleges A and B).

We also explored which learning environments had at least a moderate impact on multiple learning outcomes. The lecture environment, project-based learning and internships affected more of the outcomes than the other learning environments. One of these, the lecture, is the most traditional of learning environments. Project-based learning is a distinguishing feature of the new colleges, and internships represent an opportunity to apply classroom learning to real-world situations.

In this analysis of the link between learning environments and changes in learning outcomes, we have not focused as closely on differences between institutions. On one hand, each institution has a different set of outcomes, so the responses are not identical. On the other hand, the question is about how students see the relationship between learning environments and learning outcomes. This type of mapping would not necessarily be affected by differences across institutions. It is not surprising, for example, that students in all three institutions report a connection between project work and obtaining group skills.

At the same time, we do know there are differences between institutions. Colleges A and B have more diverse learning environments and have a more explicit awareness of learning outcomes. This might lead to a more differentiated mapping process. If we look at the total number of entries in the three tables, there are more endorsements of a relationship (20% or greater) in Colleges A and B than in College C.

CRITICAL INCIDENTS

In order to achieve our goals of measuring the OLC and understanding how differences in OLCs affect learning, we explored different measurement techniques. We asked students to describe a critical incident. They were to describe an event they experienced that had some effect on how they think about themselves or the college. This is a fairly unstructured method, but a tested (Flanagan, 1954) measurement approach that elicits important experiences that shape beliefs and attitudes. Students could report up to two incidents. Data were collected at time 1 and time 2.

Time 1 Critical Incident Reports

In the analysis of critical incidents for time 1 at College A, slightly more than half (58%) of the incidents were about positive views of the college. The next highest category (42%) was about a positive aspect of learning. Representative quotes from college incidents included:

> "This is an open, trusting community."
> "It raised my opinion of the kind of work that is done here."
> "Made me feel I belong to this community."
> "We had a town meeting. There were good ideas which contributed to the school."
> "Makes me feel positively about this school."
> "Night before, we were up late helping each other."

For this same group of students, representative learning incidents included:

> "Their dedication to the students is so much."
> "First physics exam, 80% failed first time. What I learned is that this is a different place and learned how to deal with the fact I failed."
> "I needed to set up priorities and stick with them. I needed to do other things than working."
> "Got back quiz. Failed it. Never happened before. I learned to seek help."
> "I learned more in that experience than I had learned in my whole life."
> "I fell in love with the professor and strengthened my beliefs about my major."
> "You really get a sense of what excitement was in college."
> "One teacher comes early and stays past midnight."
> "As a freshman, I was doing professional presentations."

In terms of learning, there are several themes here. There is an acknowledgment of first-time failure. These are talented students who had gotten "A"s in high school. There were initial failures in classes but, in most cases, that led to a realistic appraisal and recognition that failure happens and needs to be dealt with. Another theme is the tremendous dedication of the faculty and their willingness to be available at all times to help the students. There was some acknowledgment of developing specific skills such as presentation, but this was not as dominant as the other two themes. In comparing the new schools, the absolute number of positive incidents in the school and learning category was substantially greater at College A than College B.

In the analysis of the critical incidents students shared for College B at time 1, the highest category (36%) of incidents dealt with positive aspects with learning. These included:

> "I learned how to conduct myself in front of others, how to present."
> "Learning to respect others and gender."
> "I think we learned much more through projects, doing something you have no idea about."
> "Learning different styles of international students."
> "I've learned what I am capable of."

There also were some negative learning-related comments, such as:

"We felt it was a fluffy course."
"Could have got people to cooperate to be better in project management skills."
"The professor had no teaching background."

In terms of the institution itself, there were more positive (21%) than negative (17%) comments. The positive comments include:

"It was a lot of bonding—we're all together as one."
"We had a lot of hours together, but we had fun."
"People really work hard here."
"School really willing to listen to our comments."

Some of the negative comments included:

"I thought (the school's) punishment was a bit harsh."
"It is very conservative—not open."
"Pretty limited electives"

A more detailed analysis of the learning-related comments suggests a number of themes in the positive accounts. Some think of specific skills acquired, such as communication skills. Others focus on the acquisition of beliefs and attitudes, such as enhancement of one's capability and developing respect for others.

The negative learning comments focused on ineffective professors and/or courses. Given that this was a startup institution, having some ineffective courses is not that surprising.

We similarly asked students in College C to describe a critical incident, that is, some concrete event that they experienced, which shaped how they thought about themselves or their college. Fifty-five respondents described 74 incidents. Thirty-one of the 74 (42%) were incidents that affected how they thought about College C. Positive examples included:

"Orientation made me feel this is a great school."
"Very open, explorative kind of place . . . cool being here."

Some of the incidents had a negative tone about the school. There were 10 such incidents. Examples included:

"Grades unfair. School wasn't in the best interests of the students wanting to learn."
"Administration banned fraternities. I didn't like that."

Twenty-eight incidents (38%) focused on learning issues. Examples of positive comments included:

> "It opened a new way of learning. It gave the school more of a human touch."
> "It made me respect how they teach material here; there is always a practical application of what you are learning."
> "It helped me decide that I like it here and that I can do it."
> "It shows they are open to help us embrace other cultures."
> "I've learned a lot about leadership and teamwork."
> "Teachers care to work with us."
> "Opportunity to learn to do research in the Intro class in _____ helped me decide what major to do. Class was intellectual and practical."

Time 2 Critical Incident Reports

We collected critical incidents in our time 2 interviews with College A students. In this case, using the same question, there were the most critical incidents generated of all the interviews at any of the three colleges—107. From this group, 39% were positive incidents about the school. These included comments such as:

> "Everyone wants to help you here."
> "I spoke to the professor and he was very supportive."
> "People here are not risk adverse, they want to change."
> "_____ wants to learn from its mistakes."
> "This place is really a community; people care about you."
> "We can create change around here."

There was a small percentage (12%) of negative comments about the school. These included:

> "We have trouble learning from this professor."
> "It is not what they told us about smaller class sizes."
> "They really haven't made improvements here."
> "There are not a lot of positive things happening."

The other major category of incidents was around learning. At this time period, 38% of the incidents were about positive learning experiences. These included:

> "I'm more effective in teams and communication ... I learned both to fail and to recover."

"I have a lot more confidence in myself."

"I have more of an appreciation of my strengths and my gaps."

"I realized I could learn on my own without some step-by-step guide."

The time 2 learning incidents had some of the same features of the time 1 data. There were clear indicators of personal development in skill areas (e.g., communications) and personal growth (e.g., more confidence). In addition, there was a theme about learning on one's own. Typically, this was tied to some unstructured problem the student had to solve, either in the school or internship context. The underlying idea was the situation was new and the student had to search and find resources to solve the problem.

We collected 58 critical incidents from College B students at time 2. Of these, 26% were positive statements about the school. These included:

"The Dean comes, he sits with the students. I needed some help, and a student I really didn't know helped me . . . I treasure that."

"The school is willing to make changes and listen."

An equal number of incidents (26%) captured the school in a negative light. These included:

"Things are too hyped . . . they're making things up that are not true."

"People are not always willing to help."

"There was a crazy workload, much too much pressure."

"The school had too many A's so they changed the grading system."

The other major category (37%) of incidents focused on personal learning and they were primarily positive. Some representative comments included:

"It meant I am capable of organizing events and getting cooperation from people."

"As a group, we put in tremendous effort . . . we get the highest marks . . . I'll never forget it."

"I've learned about the differences in others."

"I think now I can work in other _____ and feel comfortable."

"I've opened up a lot working on projects."

"I'm very fluent now . . ."

A review of the learning comments shows a major focus on personal development. That is, the students had acquired a better understanding of their own potential or a better understanding of others. The incidents were not about learning strategies, but more about a realization of their own skills or understandings.

We collected 82 critical incidents from the second set of interviews at College C. About 35% were positive statements about the school. These included:

"This is a very open, accepting place."
"Going to that class flipped my view . . ."
"We have a personal touch with the professors."
"It's more a family than an anonymous student ID."

There was a small percentage of negative school-related comments (11%). These included:

"We are not prepared for real life situations."
"Students just think about work."
"I wish people here were more active."

Other incidents were about learning (36%). These primarily were positive and included:

"I'm more independent, but still have a network of people."
"Made me realize I'm more of a leader."
"Showed me how many things I excel at."
"More confident in my ability to guide other people."
"Made me more well-rounded."

A review of the learning incidents shows a common theme. They are all about personal development. This awareness of personal development appears in self-confidence and in skill areas such as leadership. The incidents are not about learning strategies or tactics.

Analysis and Comparison of Critical Incident Reports

What can we learn from these critical incidents from time 1 and time 2? First, incidents about learning were either the first or second most-selected category. On one hand, this is not surprising since the students being interviewed were living in an educational environment. Also, the interview itself primes people to think about learning. On the other hand, college provides a broad range of experiences both inside and outside the classroom. One could expect incidents about sports, social life, and other non-classroom experiences to appear, but incidents about learning seem most salient to the students we interviewed.

Second, there was commonality across the three institutions. Students reported incidents about (1) general personal development—I have more confidence in myself; I know more about what I like and dislike; and (2) specific skill development—I have developed strong communication skills and leadership skills.

Third, persistent differences among the three institutions were harder to determine. In College A, time 1, there was a theme about failing the first time and learning from this experience. Also, there was an emphasis on the availability and openness of the professors. These themes are less pronounced in the other schools. College A in time 1 and time 2 generated more school and learning incidents than the other colleges, which might reflect the stronger OLC in College A. At time 2, there were no noticeable differences in themes across the three institutions. We know from other learning questions (see Tables 5.1–5.4) that there are differences across the institutions. The feature of those questions and the related data are that they are specifically about learning environments, learning environment outcome connections, beliefs about learning, and so on. In contrast, the critical incident question did not focus solely on learning. Although the incidents reported by students were about specific experiences, they were evoked by a more general question. The answers we received captured incidents about personal development or specific skills. We would thus expect more similar answers across institutions on the critical incident questions than on the more learning-specific questions we asked elsewhere in the interviews.

This section on critical incidents is different from the rest of this chapter in that it does not specifically examine aspects of the OLC. The critical incident questions were very open ended and not directly tied to the OLC. At the same time, the questions did evoke beliefs about learning that were consistent with other themes in this chapter and book. For example, students in College A expressed a greater closeness and supportiveness from professors, which appears in other data sources in this book. Further, the absolute number of reported incidents was higher in College A, which might signal the salience of learning at that institution, another concept that appears elsewhere in the data. Also, the form of the presentation— quotes—should provide the reader a different perspective on how students viewed their schools.

PERSONAL MODELS OF LEARNING

Another approach to measuring the OLC and to understanding differences across colleges was to ask students about their personal model of learning. That is, we wanted to know what they had learned about how to learn. The specific open-ended question was:

> You're in your _____ year at [your college]. There is a strong emphasis here on learning and how people learn. We want to explore how you think about effective learning. How would you explain your approach to effective learning to a new student at [your college]?

Several issues underlie students' responses to this question. First, the responses should reflect some of the differences between the learning environments in the new (with stronger contracts) and traditional institutions. If a student is exposed primarily to a lecture discussion format, one might expect his or her personal model of learning to be affected by this environment. Therefore, we should see differences between Colleges A and B and College C. Second, all of the students had to transition from a structured, high school learning environment to a much more challenging, less structured learning environment. Most were very successful in high school, but the challenge of college introduced them to early failures (especially, as we saw above, in College A). This transition should stimulate their thinking regarding their personal models of learning.

We coded the responses to our question in terms of key tactics and strategies. Tactics referred to specific behaviors, such as asking a professor or a teaching assistant for help. Strategies reflected higher-order learning practices, or meta-cognitive strategies (e.g., Garcia & Pintrich, 1994). Self-awareness of one's own learning style is one example of a strategy. Focusing on the basic principles or theory in the learning domain is another. Both of these meta-strategies can facilitate learning across course areas.

Tactics for Learning

Figure 5.3 presents the data for College A. Under tactics, the most common set of responses was to work with others or to ask others for help in learning the materials. In the interviews, students were clear that this was an important change from high school. In high school, they worked primarily alone and did very well. In college, they needed to rely more on others, whether it meant studying together or asking a person for specific help. The next frequently selected category was learning through project teams. A defining characteristic of this institution was to assign people into project groups from the beginning of the freshman year. The students encountered semi-structured problems, such as figuring out how to build an airplane. This was a new form of learning for all of the students, and it is reflected as an important component in how one can learn. The other categories, with around 20% response rates each, included going to class, doing homework and readings and talking to professors. The first two are common for most institutions. Talking to professors was unique to this institution's learning environment. Throughout all of the interviews with students at College A, the idea of faculty availability at all hours of the day was a persistent theme. It is not only that they were available, but they also were motivated to help students, a situation that facilitated learning. This contrasts with a more traditional institution where faculty members meet students in the classroom and have limited office hours.

The tactic-related responses for the other new innovative school—College B— also are found in Figure 5.3. Students' explanations of their personal learning

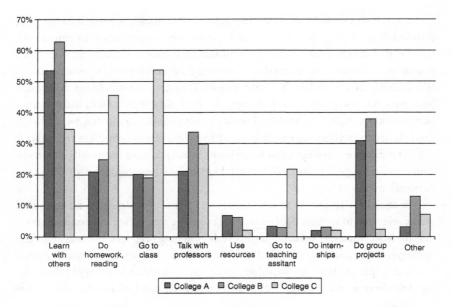

Figure 5.3: Personal Models of Learning—Tactics % of Students

models parallel College A and reflect the role of the OLC. The highest tactical response category was the idea of learning with others and asking others for help in learning. The second most frequent response in this tactical category was to emphasize project-based learning. These also were the two highest responses for College A. In both institutions, there is a culture focusing on learning with others. This appears both informally in asking others for help and more formally by working in project-based teams. The other responses in the tactical area are similar in both colleges. There is a call for going to class and doing the readings, fairly traditional beliefs. The idea of asking the professor also is salient. This response reflects the general norm of talking to others and not learning alone. It also is tied to system mechanisms. In College B, faculty members meet with a group of their students from each course to discuss the strengths and weaknesses of the "learning experience." This, again, reinforces the idea of faculty accessibility and the students' role in contributing to the college.

In the traditional school—College C—the response patterns are quite different. In the tactical category (Figure 5.3), more students talk about going to class and doing homework, both pretty traditional ideas. In Colleges A and B, the responses for working with others (54% and 63%, respectively) were higher than those responses in College C (35%). Also, in Colleges A and B, project-based learning was highly recommended (31% and 38%, respectively) versus the response in College C (2%), where project-based learning barely registered as a tactic. These data reflect different emphases across the institution. As a more traditional institution, College C operates in a high-quality lecture discussion mode. To be successful, it is important to come to class and to do the readings, homework, and labs. College C does not emphasize working with others or using project-based learning, particularly in the first two years. The cultural beliefs and learning experiences are different.

Strategies for Learning

In terms of strategies (see Figure 5.4), students in College A report they should understand their own learning styles and distinguish those that are more or less effective. Another strategy was to select areas for learning that create high levels of motivation, passion, and intrinsic interest. Motivation is at least a necessary condition for learning. Another strategy focused on planning. Students have multiple courses with lots of demands. The challenge is to be explicit about planning time allocation for all these demands. Students in this institution mentioned being proactive in their learning. To do this, one needs to initiate learning experiences in different environments. In addition, these students talked about learning through application of the knowledge they gained.

All of these strategies come from a learning environment utilizing many semi-structured problems that students must figure out how to solve. It is not surprising that proactive behaviors work in this environment and stimulate motivations as

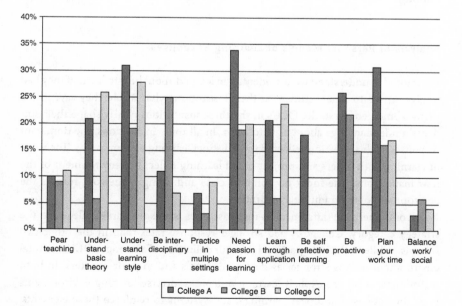

Figure 5.4: Personal Models of Learning—Strategy % of Students

students explore new learning challenges and are successful. The explicit aspect of this learning environment probably evokes more self-reflection on what one learns well and not so well. The fact that project-based learning is a central learning activity in College A accounts in part for the strategic emphasis of applications in learning.

In the learning strategies category (Figure 5.4), there are two dominant responses for College B. First, there is a call for going beyond one's college and doing interdisciplinary work. This is consistent with the learning environment in College B, whose students take more courses outside of their college than students in College A. While they are developing expertise in a core technical area, students are required to take courses in other parts of the university. These areas of the university are characterized by a good but more traditional approach to learning (e.g., an emphasis on lecture and discussion). The second most frequent strategy response for College B was about being proactive. With College B, students are given many semi-structured problems, either individually or in project teams. This type of learning experience evokes proactive learning behaviors.

In the strategic learning category (Figure 5.4), there are no dominant responses for College C. Response categories with some endorsement include: (1) understanding the basic theory and principles of what is being learned (26%), (2) understanding your own style of learning (28%), and (3) learning through applications (24%). This difference between College C and the other institutions is probably related to the lack of differentiation in the students' OLC. There are few dimensions, and "contracts" about learning are less explicit about strategic approach to learning.

Analysis of Personal Models of Learning Responses

We wanted to understand what students had learned about how to learn. If they had to give advice to a new student at their institution, what would they say? Three themes emerged. First, the OLCs in the three institutions clearly shape their students' understandings about how to learn. In all three institutions, the dominant responses to this question reflected their distinct learning environments. The value of learning with others and project-based learning reflect the environment of the new institutions. The focus on going to class and doing homework reflects the environment of the traditional institution.

Second, there are differences in response rates across the three colleges. In the strategy category, College A had stronger response rates than in the other two schools. While both Colleges A and B fit our definition of a stronger OLC, the total environment in A is stronger as discussed in this and in prior chapters. In both institutions, there are explicit learning outcomes, diverse learning environments (e.g., project-based and peer learning), and systems to reinforce these elements. The only difference is that College A's students spend almost all their time within their college environment, while students in College B spend part of their time taking courses outside of the college in a more traditional setting. The higher response rates in College A reflect these differences and the stronger OLC in College A.

A third theme is about what is absent from the personal models of learning. If we went to any good book on learning from a psychological perspective, there would be a discussion about the role of practice and reinforcement/feedback schedules, issues of encoding, memory, forgetting, retrieval, different approaches for learning, different kinds of skills and knowledge, and so on. None of these topics appear with any frequency in the student accounts. In one sense, this is not surprising. There is no direct instructional intervention about these learning topics. Given that all three colleges are primarily technically oriented, the introduction of commonly known learning principles or research on the psychology of learning is not likely to occur with any regularity in class, but this is a potential option.

LEARNING CLIMATE

We have explored some differences between the strong and weak OLCs in these institutions on knowledge of learning outcomes, learning environments, and the relationship between learning environments and learning outcomes. We also have data on some learning climate measures. We surveyed students after the time 2 interview. The goal of this survey was to capture students' overall evaluations of their educational experience in a more structured format.

Table 5.4 provides some overall evaluations of the educational space. College A dominates the other two colleges in overall teaching effectiveness and providing a challenging academic environment. The traditional college exhibits stronger scores on both items than the other new school, College B. This can be explained by two factors. First, College C is a highly ranked college. It has excellent faculty who work hard to create an effective classroom experience. College B, as a new school, suffered some of the risks of being a startup. There were many new faculty teaching a brand-new curriculum, and there were a few cases where courses simply did not work out. These were highly visible courses, and the affected students were very dissatisfied. These "bad courses" were widely discussed among faculty,

Table 5.4. LEARNING CLIMATE IMPACTS—TEACHING

% of Responses–To a very great extent or a great extent			
	College A	College B	College C
Overall Teaching Effectiveness	97	60	81
Challenging High Quality	90	50	84

administrators, and students and probably affected student beliefs about the college's learning climate.

Figure 5.5 captures students' views of the learning climate. Many of these are antecedents of student views on teaching effectiveness and the challenging learning environment. Variation in this table indicates discrimination within and between colleges.

College A has stronger endorsements on most, but not all, of the dimensions. The idea of continuous improvement was a defining characteristic of this college's culture from the beginning. Both new colleges are higher in project-based team learning and opportunities to learn (i.e., lifelong learning) as compared with the traditional school. College A is the lowest in interdisciplinary education, while College B is the highest. College A is a standalone institution that has strong ties with high-quality nearby institutions. However, making these ties work requires much more effort. With College B, as described above, students are required to take courses in other areas of the university that houses the college. College B also has a stronger endorsement for smaller classes. In the traditional school, beginning courses are in large lecture halls, explaining College C's substantially lower score on this measure.

College A has a strong focus on learning activities outside of the classroom. Where College A really stands out is in the quality of its professors and the level of contact with them. This was a persistent theme throughout our visits and data collection in College A. Our assumption is that the rating of teaching excellence and professor contact are closely tied together. The professors at College A are there

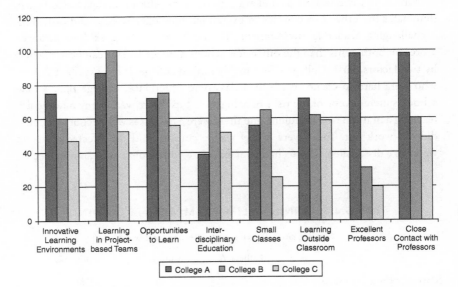

Figure 5.5: Learning Climate—Antecedents to Education Experiences % of Responses—"To a very great extent" or "a great extent"

Theory and Empirical Results

at all hours. They work hard to support students working in project teams, which often run late into the evening. It is probably not that the professors are more qualified or have better credentials than the professors in Colleges B or C. The professors in College A simply are around more, being very supportive to students. This contrasts with a more traditional institution where faculty members meet students in the classroom and have limited office hours.

In terms of learning outside of the classroom, College A has the strongest endorsement followed by B and then C. This also is true for relationships with faculty. In general, College B students also report a strong relationship compared to College C.

DISCUSSION

Our goal was to explore the nature of learning in institutions with stronger versus weaker OLCs. We used the learning contract to organize how to think about the differences between the new and traditional institution.

We expected to find more diverse learning environments in the new institutions with strong OLCs. The mapping of environments to outcomes should be more complex for these institutions. Also, we expected a greater emphasis on active-based learning and a more differentiated view of learning. The overall assessment of the learning climate also should be stronger in colleges with strong OLCs.

In terms of learning environments, Colleges A and B used more diverse environments, with a stronger emphasis on project-based learning. There were both commonalities and differences across institutions in mapping learning environments to learning outcomes. Group project work was more strongly tied to team skills, and learning on one's own seemed to facilitate the outcome of lifelong learning. Since the exact set of learning outcomes differs for each college, it is harder to identify other common themes. However, in College A there were more differentiated mappings. In the critical incident question, learning was the first or second most mentioned category. Learning incidents mainly focused on personal development or specific skill development. In College A, there was some differentiation in the frequency of incidents dealing with failure and developing a realistic appraisal of failure. Also, the theme of closeness to faculty was more pronounced. In terms of personal models of learning, there were stronger themes about working with others and working in team-based projects compared with the traditional college. The questions about learning climate and teaching indicate strong endorsements for College A.

At one level in this and the prior chapter, we indicated that the learning environments in Colleges A and B had an impact on students' expectations and learning. We also discussed why these explicit organizational learning contracts are important. With explicit learning outcomes, students know how they should focus their attention. If team learning is an outcome, then students are more likely to practice skills that drive this outcome and to be open to feedback on their performance with respect to team learning. Students also experience a more diverse set of learning environments that are linked to different outcomes, and these environments require more active forms of learning. This is in contrast to an OLC that is more diffuse, general, and open-ended. In the latter environment, students will focus on what they have to do in each of their courses, but they will have less opportunity to achieve integrated learning outcomes that cut across any single course.

At a different level, the experiences in strong OLC Colleges A and B influenced students' views about learning. This is probably best illustrated in the question about personal learning models. We asked what students had learned about learning. This obviously is an important question within a college, but probably is even more important when students move to the work environment. In response to our question, there were similarities in Colleges A and B, as contrasted with College C, regarding the concepts of working with others to learn and having close contact with professors as a means of learning. Students in College A had a more differentiated view of learning strategies (i.e., understanding one's learning style) than students in Colleges B or C.

Some of the other striking contrasts came from our post-interview survey of students. In terms of overall teaching effectiveness ratings, College A is almost off the charts. In terms of learning antecedents, such as excellent rating for professors, College A is stronger than the other colleges. In terms of other antecedents, such as innovative learning environments or learning in project teams, Colleges A and B have higher response rates than College C. When we asked students about their personal feelings about the college, College A engendered the strongest positive feelings, and in a number of learning climate dimensions, Colleges A and B are stronger than College C.

Although we have tried to provide a more differentiated picture of three institutions and their varied roles in impacting student learning processes, our general findings are consistent with the most recent literature on learning in colleges. The impacts of faculty availability, active-based learning, working with others, and project work in these studies parallel themes in this chapter. However, our focus on the OLC provides a different perspective. We argue that in institutions that have explicit contracts about these learning activities, the impact will be stronger. College A is one illustration.

In this chapter, we have tried to provide a representative picture of the three colleges; however, there are some gaps in our conceptualization and measurement of learning. In terms of outcomes, such as group work, students reported they got a lot of practice, which is desirable. But if we asked students about the dynamics of group learning, such as the key activities that can make groups more effective (e.g., strategic planning, conflict resolution), most of them likely would not have had a clear response. Also, lifelong learning is a common outcome across all three colleges. But what does it mean? I think we would find few students with clear understandings about this outcome. Now, it is clear that students in the new institutions faced many unstructured problems. These types of problems are good practice, requiring students to learn a lot on their own. However, it appeared that there was little feedback about how people were learning on their own or how they should think about what lifelong learning means. The conclusion is that the new college had explicit learning contracts, diverse learning environments, and many practice experiences in the two learning outcomes we discussed. This is what we call first-generation learning. The next challenge is how to take an outcome, such as lifelong learning, and build a set of learning experiences that will provide a better conceptual map about what lifelong learning means, as well as opportunities to practice it with feedback given to students along the way. These are necessary conditions to learning development.

As in any study, there are limitations. We only reported results for a small number of colleges. The problem with developing a larger sample is there are not a lot of innovative startups. There are new universities, but for the most part, they are modeled after traditional universities with only incremental improvements. Second, we are operating with relatively small samples within each college. Effective data collection in this domain really requires interviewing, a very labor-intensive activity. We chose to do a more intensive study at two time periods and operate with a smaller sample. A third issue is that we haven't captured all aspects of the learning experience. For example, in College A there is a persistent theme that faculty are around all hours of the day to help the students. That is an important predictor. We didn't independently measure this, although there are a variety of other measures indicating faculty availability and closeness in College A. Finally, it remains to be seen whether the character of Colleges A and B will remain the same or revert to more traditional forms over time. More time needs to pass before we can make that assessment.

CHAPTER 6

Effectiveness

In this chapter, we explore some of the effectiveness indicators of the institutions we studied. One major goal of this study was to examine the effects of different OLCs on multiple indicators of effectiveness. We will review effects on the students in the institutions as well as the institutions themselves. Some major questions include: Are these colleges able to maintain or improve on the quality of students or faculty admitted to the institution? How are the colleges evaluated on the quality of their educational processes? What happens after students graduate? How are they placed in work organizations or graduate schools? How do differences in OLCs affect the answers to these questions and other questions? Where do differences in OLCs have a significant effect, and where do they not have an effect?

In order to fully answer the above questions, we need to be able to explain why certain effects occur and recognize alternative explanations for those effects. Given this focus, we needed to develop conceptual dimensions of effectiveness, figure out how to operationalize these dimensions and explain the differences in effectiveness indicators across the three colleges. We turned to the effectiveness literature to inform our approach. A host of books and articles address the effectiveness of organizations (cf. Goodman & Pennings, 1977; Goodman, 1979; Lawler & Worley, 2006). Some focus on theoretical issues (cf. Goodman & Pennings, 1977; Birnbaum, 1989). One of the fundamental issues in assessing organizational effectiveness is the underlying model of organization. Some representative models include the goal and system models (Goodman & Pennings, 1977). Which model one adopts affects the approaches to understanding organizational effectiveness. Other issues include the role of constituencies in defining the meaning of effectiveness (Zammuto, 1982) as well as the role of time (Ancona, Goodman, Lawrence, & Tushman, 2001). Different constituencies may select or have different priorities for different types of effectiveness indicators. Time is especially important in our context because we want to examine the effectiveness of the new institutions we studied over time. For example, does the quality of students get better or worse or remain the same?

Other approaches to organizational effectiveness have focused on the assessment issue (cf. Goodman, 1979; Cameron, 1981), that is, methodological issues in effectiveness research. Here the attention has been on research design, the use of multiple methods, and questions of the reliability and validity of measures.

Other approaches to effectiveness begin with major institutional changes affecting the viability of universities and colleges. Work in this area has examined (1) changes in financial pressure and their impact on the economic viability of tertiary institutions (Rhodes, 2004); (2) the increasing globalization of higher education, which can affect the flow of high-quality students and has important cost and quality implications; (3) changes in student demands in terms of students with more diverse backgrounds, and the implication for tertiary institutions to adapt to these changes (Zemsky & Duderstadt, 2004); and (4) the information revolution, which leads to different forms of competition (e.g., the University of Phoenix), which in turn affects the functioning of traditional face-to-face universities (cf. Duderstadt, 2000; Goodman, 2001). There obviously are other external forces impacting the effectiveness of tertiary institutions. A key issue is the ability of existing organizations to sense these changes and adapt to them.

Our interest here is to acknowledge the wide range of effectiveness literature, rather than review it in detail. Some themes emerge from this literature. First, there are multiple dimensions of effectiveness (e.g., financial growth, student satisfaction). Different theoretical positions use different dimensions, but the idea of assessing institutions based on multiple indicators is important. Second, the role of constituencies is important in mapping out relevant dimensions for a particular kind of organization. In institutions of higher education like the colleges we studied, students, faculty, and administrators are obvious constituencies that may key on similar or different effectiveness dimensions. Other constituencies such as alumni, the community in which the institution is located, accrediting agencies, and so on also may play a role in defining effectiveness indicators. Finally, organizations are dynamic entities, so time plays a role in assessing effectiveness. New institutions enter very competitive environments. Simply being sustainable over time is one measure of effectiveness. Although there are other themes in the literature, our focus will be on the OLC framework and the related data we collected in our study.

An important part of assessing effectiveness is having an organizing model (Goodman & Pennings, 1977). This is preferable to merely analyzing variables and data that happen to be available. We use a simple model of inputs, processes, and outcomes. "Inputs" are the quality of resources attracted to the institution of higher education. Examples of these inputs include student quality, faculty quality, and the institution's ability to attract financial resources. One major challenge for new institutions is initially attracting high-quality students and faculty. A bigger challenge is maintaining or increasing the quality of these inputs over time. "Processes" refer to the transformation processes that occur within the institution. Our focus has been primarily on the educational learning activities that take place in the colleges we studied. Research is another process element, but it has not been central to our work. "Outcomes" include a range of outputs of the institution. Examples include graduation rates, student satisfaction with their four years, job or graduate school placement, and the transfer of skills acquired in college to the world of work.

While our approach reflects multiple dimensions of effectiveness—inputs, processes, and outcomes—an important qualification is that we are not testing causal links between these dimensions. Rather, we treat inputs, processes, and outcomes as multiple dimensions that can each be used to measure effectiveness. Basically, we are asking: What is the quality of the students or faculty who came to this institution and does it improve over time? What is the quality of the teaching-learning process and does it improve or decline over time? What do we know about the quality of outputs (e.g., student job placement) for this institution and do they change over time? This input–process–outcome model simply is a way to organize one's thinking in order to assess multiple dimensions of effectiveness.

While our study has primarily focused on the student as a major constituency, we do present organizational-level data, including data that are independent from subjective interviews or surveys. In addition, when possible, by looking at changes in different effectiveness indicators, we do incorporate time as a factor. As explained above, we collected data from two different classes and completed two time waves of data collection within each class. Where possible, such as with information on quality of students and faculty (both input effectiveness measures), we present data over multiple time periods.

INPUTS

Inputs represent the quality of resources the institution is able to attract. Two of its most important resources are students and faculty. The question is to what extent does the quality of students remain the same, increase, or decline over time? Both the absolute values of quality as well as changes in quality over time address one part of the effectiveness question.

Student Inputs

As outlined in chapter 3, we examined differences in student quality with scores from the Scholastic Achievement Test (SAT). We had full data from Colleges A and C beginning with classes entering in 2005 through 2008. This period reflects the time when students in our interview/survey study were on campus and beyond. Since we have limited data on College B, which does not require all students to take the SAT, we will treat those data separately.

Table 6.1 shows SAT scores for Colleges A and C over the four-year time period. The basic question is whether student quality remained the same, increased, or decreased over time as a measure of input effectiveness. Since the composition of the test changed between 2005 and 2006, focusing on the percentiles may be most informative. The basic finding for College A is that the input scores remained the same. However, the critical finding is that College A was able to attract the highest quality students when it first began admitting students and continued to attract students at the 99th percentile for the entire four-year period. College C also was able to attract very high quality students and to maintain this quality over time. While there are *statistically* significant differences between Colleges A and C, we do not believe their differences are *practically* significant. We doubt there are substantial differences in ability of the students in these two institutions at a point of time or over time. Students in the 94th, 96th, and 99th percentiles are all high-ability individuals.

Based on these data, our overall finding is that Colleges A and C were both able to attract high-quality students and maintain the high quality over time. In the case of College C, that is not surprising. This is a well-established, highly ranked institution that attracts high-quality students to apply. In the case of College A, the findings are less obvious. If College A had start-up problems, these issues clearly would have affected their intake of new students. However, the data show this school was able to attract top students, and it maintained that quality of student input over time. Thus, both Colleges A and C appear to be effective on the measure of student inputs.

For College B we have limited data because SAT scores are not required. However, the SAT scores remain basically the same for College B over time (2003–2008). The actual scores over time are slightly lower than for Colleges A and C.

A second input effectiveness measure is retention rates. That is, how many students graduated compared to those that entered the college as freshmen? Overall the retention rates were high and similar across all three colleges (92%, 98%, and 89% for Colleges A, B, and C, respectively). Again, the meaning of these rates is similar to the SAT analyses. College C is a stable high-quality institution. One would expect high retention rates. But Colleges A and B are start ups. This is a more

Table 6.1. SAT TOTAL SCORES FOR CLASSES ENTERING 2005 THROUGH 2008, BY COLLEGE

College	SAT total score (%tile)	2005*	2006	2007	2008
A	Mean	1493 (99)	2203 (99)	2205 (99)	2217 (99)
	Median	1490 (99)	2210 (99)	2230 (99)	2210 (99)
C	Mean	1412 (94)	2033 (94)	2069 (96)	2095 (96)
	Median	1420 (95)	2080 (96)	2095 (96)	2110 (97)

Notes. N = 77 to 86 for College A. N= 190 to 225 for College C. *Writing section was added to the SAT after 2005.

risky, untested environment. Any mistakes would mean students might exit the institution. We do not find that phenomena. However, we know Colleges A and B were able to attract high quality students over time. Students in general had positive evaluations of their college (see Table 6.5), particularly College A. High graduation rates are not surprising.

Faculty Inputs

We assessed differences in faculty inputs by comparing the relative quality of the schools where each college's faculty had completed their doctoral training. School rankings are one approximate indicator of quality. We used two rankings recently done by *U.S. News and World Report* (2008). These include 1) American universities (top 130) and 2) international universities (top 200). We identified all schools from which faculty graduated for each of the three colleges and coded them by ranking in each category. Faculty who graduated from unranked schools were excluded from the analysis. Almost all faculty in Colleges A, B, and C were in ranked colleges. Table 6.2 displays the results of these rankings by college. This table shows the number of faculty who graduated from institutions that were ranked on the two *U.S. News and World Report* lists; the percentage of total faculty they represent; the highest and lowest ranking schools of these faculty; and the median and mean rankings of the universities from which ranked faculty graduated.

Table 6.2. U.S. NEWS RANKINGS OF FACULTY DOCTORAL INSTITUTIONS BY COLLEGE

College	U.S. News Ranking Source	Number of faculty ranked	% of total faculty ranked	Highest ranking school	Lowest ranking school	Median rank	Mean rank	Std. Dev.
A	Universities- U.S. only	34	97%	1	102	21	18.2	24.5
	Universities- International	34	97%	1	165	21	28.5	37.0
B	Universities- U.S. only	17	53%	1	102	26	34.4	24.3
	Universities- International	26	81%	1	165	39	52.4	45.4
C	Universities- U.S. only	92	90%	1	83	6	19.4	15.7
	Universities- International	95	93%	1	174	10	31.8	31.6

Notes. Faculty who graduated from unranked institutions excluded from analysis. Total faculty by college A, B, and C N=35, 32, 102.

The results show that the percentage of faculty coming from the two ranking systems is pretty comparable for Colleges A and C. For example, about 97% of the faculty from College A and 98% from College C attended universities included in the top 200 international institutions. The percentages for College B for both ranking systems are lower. Each college had faculty graduating from the highest-ranked school in each category. For example, the median rankings for Colleges A, B, and C faculty institutions were 21, 26 and 6 respectively for U.S. universities. The mean rankings were about 18, 34, and 19 in the same category. The median ranking indicator is probably more relevant since it is less sensitive to rankings at either end of the continuum (i.e., very high or very low rankings). The rankings for the newer schools, A and B, are comparable and reasonable, given they are start-up institutions. College C, which has an established reputation, is higher in the median rankings.

We also looked at faculty doctoral university rankings over time. One needs to be cautious in reviewing these data because the number of faculty hired over time (particularly after the first two years) is relatively small, particularly for Colleges A and B. However, keeping this qualification in mind, the quality of institutions granting the new faculty hires a doctoral degree remains pretty much the same over time for all three institutions.

We recognize these rankings are an imperfect indicator of the quality of faculty inputs. For example, they only provide an indicator of institutional quality at one point in time—when they were ranked in 2008. They do not account for the quality of institutions when faculty members completed their degrees. They also do not account for specific areas of specialization that may be overlooked by these general measures.

Subjective Measures

Another way to look at the quality of students and faculty is through our survey of students at time 2 in our longitudinal study. For College A, 95% report they are satisfied or very satisfied with student quality, 69% report the same responses for College B, and 77% for College C. College A shows substantially higher satisfaction than College C, and College C has slightly higher responses than B. Comparable data are available for quality of faculty. For College A, 98% report they are satisfied or very satisfied with faculty quality, 55% for College B, and 78% for College C. These results for College B are not surprising. There were a few courses in the first two years that were not successful.

Discussion

What conclusions can we draw from these data? First, for students at Colleges A and C, where we have more comprehensive data, both draw high-quality students (in the middle and upper 90th percentile range). Differences between the colleges in this and other chapters probably are not explained by student quality. Also, they both attract high-quality students over time, another measure of effectiveness that is particularly relevant for College A, as a new institution. Second, for quality of faculty, College C has a slight edge in the median rankings, but the mean ranks are relatively the same for Colleges A and C. The differences between the median and mean data probably represent the sensitivity of mean rankings to extremes in the ranks. Again, the strength of College C is not surprising because it already has a strong reputation. For College B, where we have less data for students, the quality of students seems to be the same over time. This observation holds true for faculty over time. In both cases, College B scores are below College A and C.

The strength of College A in the subjective measures is not unexpected. Students really like the institution, and faculty spend a lot of time with students—both factors that should lead to high very positive subjective ratings.

PROCESSES

Another way to assess effectiveness is by reviewing critical processes that occurred as students moved through their four-year college experience. Some critical processes concern whether the expectations in the OLC were met, the teaching-learning process, and the role of decision making in each institution.

Expectations

As chapter 4 indicated, the expectations were different between the new and traditional institutions. The data also indicated that the student expectations were met or exceeded in all three colleges.

Teaching-learning Environment

Chapter 5 provided a fairly detailed picture of the teaching-learning environments in the three colleges. This is the central process variable in undergraduate higher education. College A had the strongest ratings in overall teaching effectiveness (97%). Also, Colleges A and B reported more active, project-based learning environment (87% and 100% respectively) as compared to College C.

Table 6.3 provides some additional survey information on the teaching-learning environment. These results are consistent with other findings that have been presented. Both Colleges A and C had strong positive ratings on having a "challenging, high-quality education." College B's lower ratings may be explained by the fact that its learning experiences occur both within the college and other parts of the

Table 6.3. OTHER LEARNING/TEACHING INDICATORS

| | % of Responses–Strongly Agreeing or Agreeing | | |
Indicator	College A	College B	College C
Challenging, High-Quality Education	87	50	83
Innovative Learning Organization	77	59	47
Learning on Your Own	70	75	56
Flexibility in Selecting Courses	27	50	49
Small Classes	62	65	27
Learning outside Classroom	75	62	58
Close Contact with Professors	97	59	49

university. Also, as we mentioned before, start-up institutions are likely to have problems, such as some courses within College B were not successful. Across many of the other dimensions (e.g., "innovative learning, learn on your own, small classes"), Colleges A and B had a higher number of students endorsing these dimensions than did College C. College A had the lowest endorsements for "flexibility in scheduling." That is because there was a limited set of courses that everyone took, and not a lot of electives. On "close contact with professors," College A had 97% of the student endorsements. This strong response probably affects other views these students have about learning.

Decision Making

One part of the "contract" that was not picked up in chapter 5 concerned students' roles with respect to college decision making. Students in the new colleges were expected to be involved in decision making across a variety of areas, in contrast to the traditional institution. This was part of the OLC for Colleges A and B.

We asked students a series of questions about their role in their college. They provided information about their experiences over time, when they first came to the college and at the time they were surveyed ("now"). They were provided a five-point scale measuring the extent to which something was true (1 = "to a very great extent" to 5 = "not at all"). Typically, we group responses 1 and 2 ("to a very great extent" and "to a great extent") together.

The first question dealt with student involvement in the design and redesign of the college. A greater percent (76%) of College A said they were involved in the design of the college when they first came. College B also was higher than College C. When respondents rated their involvement "now," there was a drop in involvement in Colleges A and B, but both remained higher than College C. Part of the contract in the new institutions was to involve students in decision making. Such was not the case for College C. The decline in the percentages for the new schools was not surprising, given that the organizational form of the new institution was more stabilized at the time of the survey. These results reflect the natural development of the colleges. In year 1, there were a variety of activities still to be designed. Over time, as the organizations' activities and procedure became more stabilized, the opportunities for designing the colleges were reduced.

We also asked about student involvement in course/curriculum design. College A showed higher student involvement than the other two colleges, both when the respondents first came (69%) and "now" (61%). College B respondents report greater involvement when they first came compared to College C. The level of involvement for Colleges B and C are the same at time "now." These differences probably reflect the stronger focus in College A on continuous improvement and the involvement of its students. One should note that redesigning the curriculum is a continuous process, while redesigning the college itself has limiting conditions, particularly over time.

Another question concerned student involvement in contributing to the community outside of the institution. Both new institutions reported higher involvement in the community, with College B showing the strongest involvement.

Discussion

We highlight these questions because they were part of the explicit contract in Colleges A and B, but not in College C. Many of the results support the differences between the new and traditional institutions. We also focused on these questions because we have data on how things were when they "first came" and "now." It is one thing to contract with students when they first come to campus and then deliver on that early promise. It is another thing to maintain that promise over time. The institutionalization or sustainability of the contract is a measure of effectiveness. In terms of involvement of students in the design of the college, that figure declined over time in both new institutions, but it remained higher than College C. In terms of involvement of students in curriculum design, College A was dominant and maintained the level of student involvement. In College B, there was a slight increase in involvement over time, but there were no real differences between College B and College C in the "now" category. In terms of involvement in the outside community, Colleges A and B increased student involvement over time. There was some percentage increase in College C, but the absolute values were lower compared to the new institutions.

OUTCOMES

Outcomes represent another way to assess effectiveness. The basic concept is to focus on the student outside of the four-year college experience. In order to evaluate students' outcomes across the colleges, we asked them about an internship or paid job that was important to them, as well as how their personal competencies had changed over time. We also compared the placement of students after college. Finally, another outcome that can be measured is how constituencies (in this case, students) evaluate their total experience with the institution.

Impacts on Work Experience

We asked all the students whether they had any work experience during their time at college. If yes, we asked for a description of the job. If there were multiple jobs, we asked for information about the most important. Students' responses were coded into formal internships or non-internship jobs. Formal internships are specific jobs where the hiring organization wants work done, but they also are building relationships with the student and college for future employment needs. Non-internship jobs were work for pay and could include working in a research laboratory, teaching in a school, or working in a family business. The next set of questions and probes focused on what effect, if any, their educational experiences at College X had on work effectiveness in their summer job. The students responded by describing their job experiences and how their educational experiences at the college (inside or outside of the classroom) impacted their work effectiveness. The rationale for posing questions in this format was to identify what was salient to the student and to avoid the "priming" that a more structured format would have elicited.

Student responses to this question—what effect, if any, their educational experience had on work effectiveness in their summer job—are included below. We also note the learning outcomes to which these answers related (in parentheses).

College A:

- I was assigned a lot of things that I didn't know anything about and I researched it and I figured out. I also had to do presentations and I had a lot of College A presentations that really helped me. (Lifelong Learning, Communication)
- Even though I didn't know anything, I made headway. I have a lot more confidence in myself. My image here and work here contributed to this. Here you're really smart, and there are a lot of amazing people. You know you're special, that helps you in jobs like this. (Lifelong Learning, Confidence)
- Being able to investigate things on my own—Being able to learn by myself— Being able to ask for help when I didn't know how to do something or did not know how something worked. (Lifelong Learning)
- Believe it or not, it was the teamwork stuff. That was the most challenging. Part of the job involved change that was difficult like communication. (Teamwork)

College B:

- In the soft skills side, I learned a lot. I learned how to deal with the bosses and team members. There was a lot of political stuff going on, and I learned how to work both with the staff and the boss. And this came from my experiences in improving communication here. (Teamwork, Communications)
- Well, initially I wouldn't have said a lot. But some stuff in the management of people was important when I was doing that job. That's something we are trying to learn here is how to deal with people and I would say that was also relevant when I had this job. (Teamwork)
- Project management skills made a difference and so did my communication skills. (Project Management, Communication)
- Some of my technical skills have increased here at College B, and I've also learned to do things on my own. In terms of communication, that helped working with other people. I had learned a lot at College B about document requirements and that helped. (Technical Skills (e.g., design), Lifelong Learning, Communications)

College C:

- I did learn how to present things, and that helped. I had to present in this job, that's something we totally do at College C. (Communications)
- I had internships my freshman and sophomore year. The sophomore year was more significant. I worked in a clinic in _____. It was a really good experience. I didn't really apply engineering, but I learned about teamwork and thinking analytically. I had to figure out a computer problem at the clinic that they were having with transferring results from their patients to a laboratory system that was outside the clinic. (Teamwork, Problem Solving)
- Teamwork and communication, a lot of things I did I had to rely on people who didn't understand the system I was working with. At College C, I had to communicate with people at different levels. I had to communicate with people with different backgrounds. Also problem solving, being able to break down a problem, I set up spreadsheets. I think that helped a lot. (Teamwork, Communication, Problem Solving)
- Some classes give you problems where the parameters aren't clearly defined. I had to figure out what the constraints were in my summer job, so those problem-solving skills really helped me as an intern. (Problem Solving)

We also coded students' responses to the question that asked how their experiences in college impacted their experiences at work. Table 6.4 examines how competencies or skill development during college impacted work effectiveness for students in internship and non-internship jobs. Each college had a different set of competencies. However, the three colleges emphasized some common competencies.

Table 6.4. INTERNSHIP EXPERIENCE

College A

Impacts of College Competencies % of Students Reporting

	Total	Percent
Quantitative	2	7%
Qualitative	1	4%
Diagnosis	4	14%
Teamwork	11	39%
Lifelong Learning	10	36%
Communication	4	14%
Context	1	4%
Design	1	4%
Opportunity	2	7%
Total number with internship	28	

College B

Impacts of College Competencies % of Students Reporting

	Total	Percent
Design	3	17%
Quantitative	1	6%
Project Mgmt. Skills	6	33%
Lifelong learning	3	17%
Teamwork	2	11%
Change Mgmt.	0	0%
Cross Cultural	0	0%
Communication	7	39%
Total number with internship	18	

College C

Impacts of College Competencies % of Students Reporting

	Total	Percent
Scientific Method	0	0%
Scientific Knowledge	0	0%
Problem Solving	7	30%
Teamwork	9	39%
Lifelong Learning	1	4%
Communication	4	17%
Design	0	0%
Context	1	4%
Total number with internship	23	

In College A, Teamwork and Lifelong Learning seemed to be most impactful on work experiences with Communication and Diagnosis next in importance. In College B, most of the impact came from Design, Project Management Skills, and Lifelong Learning. In College C, Problem Solving and Teamwork were selected as most impactful on work experiences, with Communication as the next level skill in importance.

In comparing the three institutions, the level of competencies affecting work was slightly higher in College A. Lifelong Learning was higher in impact for both new institutions A and B. Teamwork consistently received endorsements across all three institutions, with a stronger endorsement in Colleges A and C. This was a little surprising, because the role of teamwork throughout our analyses had been stronger in Colleges A and B. Communication Skills appeared as a factor in all three colleges, with a slightly more impactful role in College C.

We also looked at the same question only for formal internships. The results are basically the same as reported in Table 6.4. Teamwork and Lifelong Learning were more impactful in College A, Project Management in College B, and Problem Solving and Teamwork in College C. In this analysis of only formal internships, the magnitudes or percentages of the dominant skills were pretty much the same across colleges. Since the number of responses and the absolute percentages are lower in this category, the above information on internship and non-internship jobs is more informative.

One conclusion from these data is that the college experience impacts work effectiveness beyond the classroom. Remember, how we formatted the question placed the burden on the respondents. They had to think first about an effective work experience and then think back to link their work experience to one or more experiences in their college. In College A, where 39% of the students said that team work positively affected their work effectiveness, that is a good endorsement because we did not prime them with a list of competencies from which to choose. It also is clear that in this format, students will not tie all the institution's competencies to their response. We expected that only some competencies would be elicited. Those that were mentioned were consistent with the learning environment in the college. There is a major emphasis in College A on working in teams and solving semi-structured problems (Lifelong Learning). In College B there is a strong focus on project management. What may be surprising is that teamwork was not more dominant there. In College C, problem solving is a central skill, which was shaped by multiple learning environments.

The basic conclusion is that there is some transfer of learning from the college experience to the work experience. While we saw this for all the colleges, the effects were strongest in College A. This is partially reflected by the fact that more students reported a connection between school and work. The actual percentages also are higher. But the competencies selected in College A and also for Colleges B and C are consistent with other data we selected on these institutions.

Impact on Competencies

Another measure of effectiveness is changes in student competencies. During our interview at time 2, we asked students to select six of the college's learning outcomes or competencies and then rate themselves on each competency over time. They were asked to select and rate themselves on the three competencies that were most important to them and the three that were least important. We used that format to generate competencies in a systematic way across respondents. Also, we wanted to reduce the number of competencies to make the rating task easier. We gave them a six-point scale where 1 was low and 6 high and specifically asked them, "Thinking about when you first came here and now, please rate yourself on the following competencies."

Table 6.5 shows the total change score and the subtotals by class. We calculated a total score by subtracting the "first came" rating from the "now rating" and then summing across all six competencies for each respondent. The figures in the table represent the mean change across all the respondents and for the respondents sorted by class.

We can make a number of observations about this table. First, College B shows the most change in all the competencies or outcomes. Second, there is a 2007 vs. 2009 effect where the class that has been in the college longer (the class of 2007), changes more. Third, there is a natural bias in self-ratings to inflate the estimates. However, the change values in the table are relatively conservative—somewhere between 1- and 2-point changes.

Table 6.6 is based upon the same question, this time sorting the changes by competencies. Since each college has a different list of competencies, we examine them separately. In College A, the highest changes are in Qualitative Reasoning, Teamwork, and Design. In earlier chapters, we presented data on team projects as a major form of learning. This is explicit in the OLC. Recall that design tasks begin very early in the curriculum at College A. The emergence of qualitative reasoning may be explained by the following: Most students of College A started with strong quantitative skills, and were less experienced in qualitative reasoning. While this

Table 6.5. AVERAGE CHANGE IN COMPETENCIES BY TOTAL AND CLASS

	College A	College B	College C
Total	1.44 (1.13)	2.28 (1.23)	1.37 (1.04)
2009	1.28 (1.05)	2.12 (1.21)	1.18 (0.91)
2007	1.62 (1.20)	2.61 (1.23)	1.56 (1.13)

Note. Standard deviation in ().

Table 6.6. CHANGES IN COMPETENCIES OVER TIME,
AS SELF-REPORTED BY STUDENTS

	College A	
	"At Entry"	"Now"
Quantitative	1.36 (mean)	1.25 (std dev)
Qualitative	1.86	1.30
Diagnosis	1.74	1.19
Teamwork	1.94	1.15
Lifelong Learning	1.54	1.08
Communications	1.34	1.06
Context	1.30	1.10
Design	1.80	1.01
Opportunity	1.18	.93
	College B	
Design	2.42	1.23
Quantitative	3.30	1.22
Project Management	2.20	1.15
Learn to Learn	1.66	.99
Teamwork	2.04	1.19
Change Management	2.25	1.12
Across Countries	2.13	1.21
	College C	
Scientific Methods	0.76	0.89
Scientific Knowledge	1.52	1.03
Problem Solving	1.56	0.92
Teamwork	1.48	0.93
Lifelong Learning	1.19	1.21
Communication	1.36	0.99
Design	1.57	1.17
Context	1.02	1.02

observation is tentative, there is more room for students to move in the qualitative reasoning area than in quantitative skills.

In College B, as we have mentioned above, there is more change across most of the competencies. The higher score in quantitative skills is probably related to the mix of courses students are required to take inside and outside the college. The changes in Design and Team Work are consistent with the educational emphases in this college. What is surprising is there is movement in the Change and Across Country competencies. This is surprising because there are no direct courses on this topic. However, learning can occur outside of the classroom. There are students from other countries. They participate together in a lot of project work. One consequence is learning about change and global differences in the process of completing project work. Another issue in reviewing College B's different scores is that they are higher across competencies, compared to the other two colleges. There could be an upward rating bias. But it is not clear why this should happen in this college compared to the others.

College C exhibits the lowest competency change scores. The most change ($x = 1.56$) occurs in Problem Solving, which has been a central competency at this institution. It is difficult to know why the competency change scores are lower than in the other schools. We do know that students in College C are less familiar with the competencies and in general their OLC is weaker than the other colleges.

Placement

Overall, all three colleges seem to place students with employers or graduate schools. The overall placement percentages are 98%, 61%, and 90% for Colleges A, B, and C, respectively. The lower rates in College B represent lower reporting rates about placement. That is, the difference between the number of graduates in a year and those reporting placements. Also, all schools seem to have consistent placement over time. In one sense, that is more impressive for the new colleges which have no established reputation.

Another way to assess outcomes is to examine the specific types of placement. Figure 6.1 displays differences between Colleges A, B, and C for different categories of placements. A couple of differences are worth noting. First, 33% of College A's graduates went to graduate school and less than 5% from College B, compared to 48% of College C's graduates. The reason for this might be explained by differences between the institutions. College C has many graduate-level programs, as does the university of which it is a part. The visibility of these programs might have influenced the propensity of College C's students to go into graduate school. Graduate programs were not found within Colleges A or B. Second, College A's graduates were more likely to work for smaller or non-profit organizations (48%). In contrast, Colleges B and C's graduates were more likely to work for large firms.

Another way to look at placement is by Fortune Global 2000, which ranks the largest and most profitable employers (see Table 6.7). Noting the differences in percentage of students working for large employers, College C seems to place students with higher-ranked employers than Colleges A or B. This college has a long-standing high reputation. The entrepreneurial focus of College A (e.g., entrepreneurial skills or "opportunity recognition" was part of College A's learning contract) may have motivated students to seek employment with smaller, more entrepreneurial organizations. On the other hand, College B has a strong work focus and there are many large organizations in its geographic area. College C, because of its 100 year history, should have stronger relationships with established employers. There are differences in job placement noted above, which seem consistent with the structure of the colleges, their reputation, and environment.

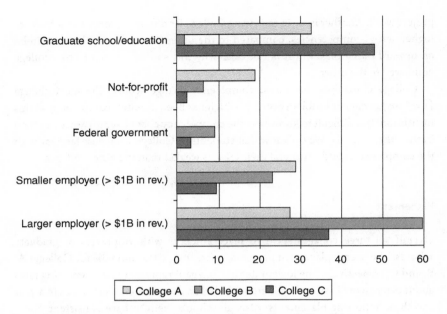

Figure 6.1: Percentage of post-graduation placements for Colleges A, B, and C
Notes: N=109 for College A (Classes '06–'07). N=241 for College B (Classes '07–'09). N=439 for College C (Classes '06–'07). Forbes Global 2000 ranked companies included in larger employer (> $1B in revenue) category.

Students also pursued graduate studies after completing their degrees. Table 6.8 compares the quality rankings of graduate schools that Colleges A and C graduates attended (*U.S. News and World Report*, 2010). College B had too few students going to graduate school to be included in the analysis. The results show Colleges A and C placed alumni into graduate schools of comparable quality. For example, 96% of the graduate schools that College A and College C alumni attended were ranked in the top 120 of U.S. universities. College A alumni entered graduate schools

Table 6.7. FORTUNE GLOBAL 2000 PLACEMENTS BY COLLEGE
(CLASSES OF 2006 & 2007)

College A–2006–07 (2 years), College B–2006–07 (2 years), College C–2006–07 (2 years)

College	Number of students	% of for profit employers ranked	Highest ranking employer	Lowest ranking employer	Median rank	Mean rank	Std. Dev.
A	18	28	2	904	288	293	261
B	110	55	1	1879	215	375	479
C	167	58	1	1870	186	461	554

Table 6.8. RANKINGS OF GRADUATE SCHOOL PLACEMENTS BY COLLEGE (CLASSES OF 2006 & 2007)

US Rankings based on U.S. News and World Report 2010

College	U.S. News Ranking Source	Number of students	% of schools ranked	Highest ranking school	Lowest ranking school	Median rank	Mean rank	Std. Dev.
A	Universities-US only	42	83	1	106	24	30	26
	Universities-International	43	87	1	262	100	91	81
C	Universities-US only	281	87	4	115	27	40	31
	Universities-International	298	84	5	397	42	92	102

Note. Due to a very small sample size, College B data has not been included in this table.

in U.S. universities with an average ranking of 30, compared to 40 for College C alums. Many College A alumni who attended graduate school attended comparable universities (54%) to College C alumni.

Overall, students from all three colleges are placed either in a job or graduate school. College C places students in high-quality established companies. That is not surprising since it is a high-quality institution that has been building relationships with employers for more than 100 years. The challenge for Colleges A and B is different because they do not have an established track record of producing high-quality graduates. A higher percentage of College A's placements go to smaller employers. This is consistent with an explicit entrepreneurial focus at the college. More of College B's students go to larger established employers, which is also consistent with their focus of solving technical problems in large systems. Students from Colleges A and C who go to graduate school are accepted in similar institutions.

Impact on Attitudes

An additional outcome-related indicator of organizational effectiveness is how students evaluate their experiences. In our context, the students are like "customers" (Schneider & Bowen, 1995). They pay for and receive a service. Their attitudes and attachment to the institution are important indicators in their own right; if that attachment continues over time, there are benefits to the institution in recruiting new students, receiving donations, and so on.

Earlier in this chapter we explored some outcomes such as experience in internships and job placements. In our wave 2 survey, we asked students to what extent their college prepared them for these opportunities. In terms of opportunities for internships, students at the three colleges reported similar support. Responses (including to a "great" or "very great" extent) were 68%, 84%, and 74% for Colleges A, B, and C, respectively. For opportunities for job or graduate school placement, respondents in College A reported 60% and Colleges B and C reported 75% and 91%, respectively. The higher response rate in College C is consistent with its long run and high reputational standing. That leads to many ties with companies and other universities. The lower percentages from College A may reflect this is a stand-alone institution just starting its own placement activities. The other new institution, College B, had an established placement service at the university level.

In the chapter on learning, students' ratings of the overall effectiveness of teaching were much stronger in College A than in the other colleges. Many of the antecedents of teaching effectiveness, such as learning in teams, opportunities to learn, and small classes were stronger in Colleges A and B vs. College C. (See Table 6.3.)

Table 6.9 presents some global attitudes directed to each college. The students we surveyed were presented with three statements: (Affective Commitment Scale [Allen & Meyer, 1990])

I have a strong sense of belonging to College _____.
College _____ has personal meaning for me.
I enjoy discussing the College _____ with others.

As with most other questions, responses were captured on a five-point scale, and we summed the two top categories—"to a very great extent" and "to a great extent." The results in Table 6.9 show a very strong attitude endorsement from the students of College A. This is much stronger than the other two colleges. College B is slightly stronger than College C on the first two items. In terms of "I enjoy discussing [the College] with others," both College A and College B have strong scores.

The three items capture global identify or attachment to the institution. They are not tied to specific persons or activities, such as professors or project-based learning.

Table 6.9. LEARNING CLIMATE IMPACTS–PERSONAL AFFILIATION

Percent of Positive Responses–To a very great extent or To a great extent			
	College A	College B	College C
Strong Sense of Belonging	97	78	72
College has Personal Meaning	96	75	60
Enjoy Discussing College X	96	90	79

They are good summary judgments of each institution. The strength of College A is worth noting.

DISCUSSION

Which college was more effective? There is probably no clear answer to that question. Effectiveness is a multidimensional concept. There is no simple way to add the multiple dimensions together. Even in the for-profit sector, a company would evaluate their performance on dimensions such as profitability, market share, and employee and customer satisfaction. Typically, they do not try to add these different dimensions together, but rather evaluate their progress on each of the dimensions.

We know particularly where we have the best data that Colleges A and C attract very high-quality students. This is not so surprising for College C, which has a long-standing reputation as a highly ranked institution. On the other hand, College A is a start-up, with no track record or accreditation. It was impressive that this newer, less-established college consistently attracted the highest-quality students over time. The faculty quality data over time are more difficult to assess because the numbers of entering faculty are low, particularly past year one, and there is natural variability in the data. Looking at the big picture, the three colleges have relatively comparable faculty and are selecting some faculty from the best universities. In terms of organizational processes, we have a variety of data from chapters 4 through 6. Across all of these colleges, expectations have been met or exceeded. It is important to note that there were more expectations in College A, and to some extent College B, than in College C. The more expectations created, the harder it is to meet them. In terms of learning, a central process, College A had the highest rating in teaching effectiveness, and Colleges A and B had higher responses on working in an active team-based learning environment. Another outcome dimension examined the students' role in the design process of the college, on curriculum, and relationships with the community. In general, students in Colleges A and B were more involved in these elements than in College C.

In terms of outcomes, we had a variety of measures. Students were placed post-graduation, but in different kinds of settings. More students went on to graduate school from College C than College A. More College A students selected jobs in smaller firms. To some extent, these differences reflected institutional differences. In terms of internship experiences, College A reported a higher level of transfer of learning from college to work. In terms of self-rated changes in competencies, College B had higher change scores. In the other colleges, the greatest change scores occurred in dimensions where there was a lack of skills or where the competency had a greater emphasis placed on it. A final question asked students about their overall identity and satisfaction with their college. On these questions, College A has the strongest endorsement.

Although there is not one single composite effectiveness indicator, across most of the subjective indicators in chapters 4 through 6, particularly as summarized in Table 6.9, College A has both the strongest OLC and the most positive ratings across a variety of questions. Second, the new institutions were in a risky position. They were start-ups with no record and no reputation. Also, as start-ups, there were lots of opportunities for mistakes that would have been costly both in terms of recruiting students and faculty in subsequent years and in placements post-graduation. These risks were not borne out, although College B had a few problematic courses. Both institutions had stronger and more differentiated OLCs. Yet in the final analysis, their higher expectations were met or exceeded.

In conclusion, we want to note some limitations of this chapter. First, most of the data come from students and institutional records. Although we did conduct interviews with faculty and administrators, these were more for context than for formal data analysis. Ours was a fairly expensive study to conduct because of the selection of interviews as the mode of data collection. This, to some extent, limited our expansion of the formal sample. Second, there are some missing data, particularly in College B, on the input indicators. However, most of the data we presented cover all three colleges. Third, we chose not to do a multivariate study that would assess individual characteristics, teaching features, and organizational dimensions. While such a study would have helped us understand the contribution of these different levels of analysis, our design was driven by our research questions. We wanted to assess OLCs and their consequences for the different colleges. This led to a smaller-sample, more intensive interview study. This design is not compatible with the large-scale multivariate studies that are more typically found in the literature.

One contribution of this chapter is that it links the OLC concept to a variety of effectiveness indicators. In the college with the strongest OLC (College A), you see a variety of linkages between an explicit and differentiated OLC and indicators such as the quality of the educational experience and the identification with the institution. Since the OLC is a new concept, these data provide a new perspective on factors related to organizational effectiveness of institutions of higher education. Another feature of this chapter is its use of both qualitative interviews and coding schemes, which provide opportunities for quantitative analysis. In the current literature there tend to be purely qualitative accounts or purely quantitative accounts, primarily using key survey data. The use of the interview is very important in this study because we want to elicit OLCs from the students and not prime them about possible OLC dimensions. Also, the data we used came from multiple sources (e.g., recorded data, interviews, and surveys).

Another contribution is that we provided data on both convergent and discriminant validity that was pretty consistent over time. College A was the strongest in educational processes, with College B next and then College C. College C was strongest in an area such as placement. This is expected, given its strong reputation and longevity. In some cases where the scores were relatively the same (i.e., SAT-input measures), the meaning was different. Both Colleges A and C had strong

SAT scores, but College A was a brand-new institution with no reputation. College C is a long-standing institution with an excellent reputation.

This chapter also captured some information on transfer of learning. This is important because what gets learned in one setting may not transfer to another "similar" setting. The data suggest that there is transfer in some competencies from college to the workplace.

PART TWO

Practice

CHAPTER 7

Some Challenges of Creating an Entirely New Academic Institution

RICHARD K. MILLER

President and First Employee
Franklin W. Olin College of Engineering

This chapter presents a timeline for the formation of Olin College and an outline of several of the major challenges encountered in establishing the institution, which may be instructive for other start-up institutions. This institution was chartered in 1997 by the F.W. Olin Foundation of New York, NY, and presents a very special case of starting an entirely new institution by a private foundation.

GENERAL TIMELINE[1]

The F.W. Olin Foundation was well known in higher education for its philanthropy in the form of generous grants for new facilities at private colleges and universities.

---

1. A more detailed account of the founding of Olin College is contained in the recent book by Gloria Polizotti Greis, *From the Ground Up: The Founding and Early History of the Franklin W. Olin College of Engineering, A Bold Experiment in Engineering Education*, Needham, MA 2009.

Over approximately the last 50 years, the Foundation provided funding for a total of 78 buildings on 58 different campuses across the United States.

1993–1997

In 1993, the Foundation began to consider ending its long-established building grants program. For the next four years, it explored a number of alternatives. These included (1) making a single large gift of all the remaining funds in the Foundation to a deserving college or university, (2) establishing a new college of engineering as part of an existing private university that did not already have such a program, and (3) establishing an entirely new and independent academic institution devoted to engineering education. During this period the Foundation also explored various locations throughout the United States as potential sites for a new institution, should that be the chosen route.

1997

In 1997, the Foundation announced its intent to establish an entirely new independent college devoted to innovation and change in the education of undergraduate engineering students. It submitted a proposal for a charter from the Massachusetts Board of Higher Education (MBHE) for the establishment of the Franklin W. Olin College of Engineering, to be located in Needham, MA. The college would be adjacent to Babson College, a well-known independent college devoted to business education, and about two miles from Wellesley College. The charter was approved in November 1997.

In order to obtain the MBHE charter, it was necessary to hire an academic consultant (Dr. James Eifert of the Rose-Hulman Institute of Technology) to draft a detailed proposal laying out a preliminary vision for the scope of the institution and its academic program. The College was envisioned to be a residential undergraduate engineering school that would eventually grow to a total enrollment of about 650 students with a student/faculty ratio of 10:1. The MBHE proposal required a great deal of creativity and some discussion with the Foundation, as it needed to describe in some detail a complete college (including faculty, students, facilities, finances, governance, curriculum, etc.) that did not exist at the time. The MBHE proposal also contained a clear vision for the overall goals of the academic program and several of its operating principles.

Before the charter was received in 1997, the Foundation also initiated efforts with a team of planners and architects to develop a master plan for the campus and design its major buildings. Since it takes several years to purchase land and design and construct facilities of this nature, this task would take longer to complete than most other tasks associated with the creation of an institution, and therefore it had to be one of the first tasks undertaken.

1998

In 1998, the Foundation conducted a national search for the first operating president of Olin College. The search resulted in hiring the author of this chapter as the first employee of the College, effective February 1, 1999.[2]

1999

The efforts to establish Olin College accelerated considerably in 1999, with the arrival of the first president; the recruitment of a provost, three vice presidents, and a few key administrative staff; initiation of negotiations with Babson College for the purchase of the land for the site of the campus; and continued work on the detailed architectural plans. During most of 1999, all of the College staff were housed temporarily in a few offices on the campus of Babson College. Site-work construction on the new campus began in August 1999.

2000

On May 1, 2000, ceremonial groundbreaking took place for the construction of the first phase of the campus facilities, including four buildings: a large academic/classroom building, an administrative/faculty office building, a student center/dining hall/heating and cooling plant building, and a residence hall. On September 1, 2000, the senior administrative team was complete and the first eight "founding" faculty members were hired. The first strategic plan (*Invention 2000*) was developed as a "blue print" for how to create an entire institution from scratch. The plan required a pattern of Discovery, Invention, Development, and Test for all aspects of the College, from curriculum to administration to governance.

2001

From the fall of 2000 to the fall of 2001, the founding faculty and administrators visited many universities and corporations to explore existing best practices and future aspirations, and developed a set of "bold goals" for the new learning experience. In the fall of 2001, an additional eight faculty were added to the original eight to create a group of 16, and a unique group of 30 students arrived at Olin. These 30 students—15 men and 15 women—were called "Partners" and they

---

2. Dr. Miller had been Dean of Engineering at the University of Iowa and held other leadership positions in engineering education.

did not take formal classes or make progress toward their BS degrees. They were all recent high school graduates, and their role for the next year was to become partners in invention with the founding faculty members and test various learning models before the launch of classes in 2002. These students would return in the fall of 2002 to join others in becoming first-year students in the four-year BS program.

2002

The first four buildings of the new campus opened and the first courses were taught at Olin College beginning in the fall of 2002. The college welcomed its freshman class of 75 students, including 29 of the original 30 Olin Partners, who returned from the year before. Only first-year courses were offered in the 2002–2003 academic year. The college also recruited an additional four faculty members, bringing the total to 20 in the fall of 2002. Each year, for the next three years, the highest level courses offered progressed by one year, until in the fall of 2005 the first senior courses were offered. Each year, new first-year students were welcomed to campus, until a full complement of students, from freshmen to seniors, was attending the college. In December 2002, the Olin Foundation completed work on an Endowment Grant Agreement that finalized the terms of the transfer of the endowment funds from the Foundation to the College over several years, and established the Founding Precepts of the College.

2004

In 2004, The New England Association of Schools and Colleges provided Olin College with "Candidacy" status, the first step toward regional accreditation. In addition, the college arranged to bring several experienced accreditation evaluators from the Accreditation Board for Engineering and Technology (now called simply "ABET") to visit the campus and offer advice and suggestions to help guide the efforts to obtain accreditation of the three BS degree programs in engineering offered by the college: Engineering, Electrical and Computer Engineering, and Mechanical Engineering.

2006

In May 2006, Olin College held its first Commencement exercises, awarding about 66 BS degrees to the first class of students. In December 2006, the New England Association of Schools and Colleges granted Olin College institutional accreditation.

2007

In July 2007, ABET granted accreditation to all three engineering degree programs.

CRITICAL DECISIONS AND CHALLENGES

Locating the Campus

When building an entirely new institution, the first decision—before even designing the campus—is where to locate. In most cases, this decision may be prescribed by an initial donation of land on a specific site or prescription of a site by a government agency. However, in the case of Olin College, the founder brought sufficient liquid assets (rather than real assets) to the table, enabling the option of considering a location anywhere within the United States.

In retrospect, Olin College was enormously fortunate to have the opportunity to locate in the Boston area, near Babson College. If we had been restricted to a site in a rural community far from a major industrial center or airport, I do not believe we would have succeeded in attracting the quality students and faculty that now characterize the institution. In some sense, Boston is the "Silicon Valley" of higher education. There are literally dozens of colleges and universities within a few miles of the city center, and more than 250,000 college students live in the greater Boston area. It has long been established as a desirable location for students to spend their college years, and the resources nearby for academic enrichment, arts, and entertainment are extraordinary. The community is rich with academic talent, and it is a desirable location for world-class faculty members to spend their careers or to spend a sabbatical leave. Boston is the only place in my career where we have benefited from the "two body problem" in faculty recruiting as often as not.

Furthermore, Babson College welcomed Olin College as both neighbor and partner. Olin College's founders planned to develop a partnership with Babson. As a result, Olin's campus master plan did not include an athletic facility, a performing arts center, a health center, or a chapel or religious center. Instead, from the start we planned to contract with Babson for access to these services for all members of the Olin College community.

It is impossible to over emphasize the value to the founding team at Olin to have the opportunity to learn from such an entrepreneurial and innovative institution. We learned a great deal about innovative undergraduate education by simply observing the remarkable hands-on pedagogical approach to business education that exists at Babson. Their faculty and staff were very generous with support in our critical first two years. It would have been enormously more difficult to attempt to start everything from a blank sheet, from the first day. Instead, they provided a few empty offices for the founding team, and we were able to rely on their human resources department to process the paychecks for our initial employees. In addition, they provided access to benefits programs, athletic facilities, a health center, and food service from the first day.

Campus Design, Construction, and Learning Model

After the site was chosen, the next step in creating an entirely new institution from an open field is the design and construction of the campus facilities. Since the time required to complete this task is several years, and because it is generally impractical to recruit faculty and students before basic facilities are available to them, the design process must begin before any faculty or staff have been hired. This presents a number of special challenges.

First, note that it is extremely rare to have the opportunity to design a complete campus at one time. Most campuses have been built over many decades, with one or two buildings added at a time. As a result, the age and architecture of the various buildings on campus are often quite diverse. One of the major design constraints for new buildings on a mature campus is the location, contents, and appearance of the existing adjacent buildings. This often limits the range of possibilities in important ways.

Obviously, starting from an open field and designing the entire campus at one time provides a great advantage in that the overall location and layout of each building on the campus may be planned at once, and the content and architectural style of all the buildings may be designed to complement each other as a coherent system. On first glance this would seem like an ideal situation that will almost ensure an outcome that meets all programmatic needs and pleases everyone on campus. However, in reality, it presents some inherent problems that almost guarantee disappointments.

One example of the critical challenge posed by designing an entire campus from the ground up is the first step in the architectural design process, which involves "programming" the building by the architect. During this early phase of design work—where all the advantages of starting from a clean slate should manifest themselves—the architect generally takes the time to interview each member of the faculty and staff to ask them basic questions. For an existing campus that is adding one or more new buildings, these questions normally include such things as: How many linear feet of shelf space do you need? Who are the three or four people you interact with most frequently during a typical work day? What laboratories do you need, and what equipment is required (fume hoods that require special air-handling facilities in the walls, wet chemistry labs that require hazardous chemical disposal plumbing, heavy machining or testing equipment that require vibration isolation and special foundation reinforcement, etc.)? However, when starting an entirely new institution, no faculty or staff are yet associated with the institution. In the case of Olin College, the organization chart was not yet developed, and it wasn't certain how many employees the college would even need.

As a result, the architects were forced to substitute the general advice and suggestions of the academic consultant (James Eifert) for the results of these detailed interviews. This required substantial degree of estimation and extrapolation from existing conditions on campuses well-known to Dr. Eifert. The architects then did their best to develop an attractive campus that met the expectations for this envisioned "program" as well as the cost restrictions and expectations for appearance.

The campus designs were well along in the spring of 1999 when I arrived, and by the fall of 2000 when the first faculty arrived, the detailed architectural plans were essentially complete. Construction of the campus began in the fall of 1999, but the efforts to develop the curriculum were just beginning. The Olin Partners arrived in the fall of 2001 when campus construction was well along—long after it would have been feasible to make any significant changes in the construction plans. This is unfortunate, because the innovative curriculum developed by the founding faculty could not have been anticipated in 1998–2000 when the basic architectural plans were developed and, as a result, the Olin campus facilities are very attractive and modern in appearance but do not fit perfectly with the academic program needs. For example, the curriculum that was developed featured a strong emphasis on project-based learning in design studios. However, there are no spaces on campus that were specifically designed to perform as design studios, and the numbers of shop and project design spaces in general were inadequate. Many of the needed shop and project spaces were intended to be included in a "Building B" that was not included in the phase 1 construction plan (and has yet to be constructed).

This general conflict was first anticipated in 1999, but the only accommodation available (absent a finalized curriculum or any faculty on board) was to provide as much flexibility in building design as possible in order to facilitate reconfiguration and modification of the spaces after the faculty and students were in place. We asked the architects to place the structural walls along the outer perimeter of the buildings as often as possible to allow for later reconfiguration of the interior spaces if needed, and to provide utility chases in ceilings and walls to accommodate the later addition of fume hood exhaust fans in case they were needed to convert classrooms into wet laboratories.

Designing for flexibility in the use of the facilities is bound to add a little to the cost of the buildings as some "just in case" capability is added to the design of the buildings. I strongly suspect that architectural designers for any new campus will face a similar problem, and perhaps they can learn from our experience in this area. The construction plans should anticipate early reconfiguration of the spaces as faculty members are added, and the design budget should include a larger than normal contingency for just-in-case features to allow alternative uses of spaces that are not currently called for in the architectural program.

A more aggressive way to provide flexibility in the design is to delay the construction of some of the buildings to enable revision of the plans as more details in the academic program emerge. One way to do this—while retaining some of the price advantages of simultaneous construction—is to build only the outer shell of some buildings. The detailed design of the interior spaces can then be deferred for a year or two, when more faculty are on board and the academic program is better defined.

While making campus design and construction decisions, we noticed that three factors always seem to be involved. One of the factors is cost. Because budget constraints are always important, the idea of making choices about materials, schedules, vendors, and so forth that minimize costs should be ever present in the decision-making process. Another factor is speed. Staying on schedule as unexpected problems arise during construction (delays in obtaining legal permits, weather-related delays, labor conflicts, etc.) is a major concern when the facilities must be available on the first day of classes. The third factor is quality. Making the most of a rare opportunity to build an entire campus from the ground up requires a great deal of thought and attention to detail. The quality of the result will depend on taking the time to explore alternatives and choose design configurations, materials, and vendors that will maximize the quality of the facilities and the resulting learning environment.

Each decision made during such a project may be considered the result of a deliberate balance between these three competing factors. Each decision can be visualized as a point somewhere inside a triangle with its corners labeled as Cost, Speed, and Quality (see Figure 7.1). Over time, the location and sequence of these decision points creates a trajectory that provides an indication of the degree to which one of the three factors dominates the others in the design and construction process. If cost dominates, then the quality of the facility is bound to suffer to some degree and the schedule is bound to fall somewhat behind. If speed dominates, then both cost and quality are certain to be compromised to some degree. If quality dominates, then it is going to cost more and it is more likely to fall behind schedule.

A final challenge we faced had to do with assigning offices and laboratories to the faculty and staff as we moved into the new campus facilities after they were completed. Most of the facilities required to accommodate a full-sized campus

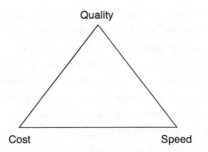

Figure 7.1: Criteria for Architectural Design

community had been built in phase one of the construction, yet we had only a small number of people at that time (fall 2002), resulting in an abundance of office and classroom space. The campus facilities were seriously over built relative to our immediate needs. (We had the opposite problem of most colleges and universities, which typically face a severe shortage of space even after the addition of a new building.) Obviously, this problem would fade away in the next few years as we systematically ramped up the enrollment and the size of the faculty and staff, but on move-in day we had some unusual issues to contend with.

It is expensive to place a new building into service, and it is also expensive to maintain it once it is open. As we had a lot more classroom space than we needed for the first year, we simply blocked the entrances to entire floors of the classroom building and minimized the heating and air conditioning to cut costs. These blocked floors were later opened as they were needed during the growth in enrollment.

In assigning offices and laboratories, it is tempting to allow the faculty and staff to take control of some of the empty spaces and spread out since so many rooms remained empty for the year. However, we found that this has significant negative consequences on the culture. Once a room is "claimed" by someone, it is difficult for them to return it to the College for reassignment. Each year as more people arrived and more rooms were opened or reclaimed, the population density increased. The problem is that this process feels to the faculty and staff like a steady and predictable reduction in the perceived quality of their lives year after year. They lose the ability to store their bicycle in the empty room next door; they have to vacate the empty laboratory next to the classroom they use all year. *Managing expectations* during the process of moving in to the new spacious facilities may seem trivial—but it can have long-lasting effects on the campus culture.

Designing the Initial Curriculum

One of the most important opportunities presented by starting an entirely new institution is the ability to create a new learning culture. This is not only a great opportunity but also a great responsibility. It is very rare—perhaps less than a once-in-a-lifetime opportunity for most educators—to rethink the educational process and deliberately design all of the aspects of the learning environment in a holistic and coherent way. Of course, Olin College was specifically created for this particular purpose. It was designed as a new, independent institution for the purpose of creating a new paradigm for engineering education.

Given that the process of curriculum revision in almost any existing university involves excessive levels of consensus among the faculty—often at many levels—it can be very difficult to make significant, sweeping changes. This decentralized process of decision-making among faculty, coupled with the widespread tradition that empowers only the faculty on the local campus to have any significant voice in the matter, creates enormous barriers to consideration of "big ideas" or alternate approaches to education. It also works against a coherent vision of the educational experience.

As part of the process of being selected as the first president of Olin College, I had created a personal vision for a new engineering curriculum before being appointed. This vision was expressed in a white paper that was shared with the presidential selection committee, but very few others. As the first few faculty members arrived, it was tempting to distribute this vision for the curriculum and instruct them to lay out the courses needed to deliver it. However, I did not do this, and I am now convinced that doing so would have been a serious mistake. The primary reason for this is that an effective learning environment requires much more than a thoughtful and coherent curriculum. It also requires the passionate commitment of the faculty and students to the learning model. In retrospect, I believe that the latter may well be the most important ingredient in achieving exceptional student achievement.

Dr. Charles Vest, President of the National Academy of Engineering and former President of MIT, recently observed that "making universities and engineering schools exciting, creative, adventurous, rigorous, demanding, and empowering milieus is more important than specifying curricular details." I believe that engaging the faculty and students in the process of inventing the curriculum is essential to achieving this outcome.

Because of this, instead of handing out the vision and asking faculty to implement it, we decided to ask the founding faculty members (8 the first year, 16 the second) to take the first two years to rethink the way engineering students are taught and to propose a new model that would provide a fresh approach. It is important to note that these faculty members were very well qualified by all conventional measures. Although they came from traditional institutions, they were clearly self-selected risk takers who were passionate about the opportunity to create an entirely new learning model for engineering.

This process of inventing the learning model included four distinct phases: discovery, invention, development, and testing[3]. During the discovery phase, we visited or hosted visits from about 35 different colleges and universities and about 20 corporations around the world. We set out to identify best practices and to learn what leaders felt the future would hold for the field of engineering. During the invention phase, our faculty began to develop specific "bold goals"[4] for the

---

3. An outline of the process used in developing all aspects of the College, including the curriculum, is contained in the document "Invention 2000." This document was developed by the founding team of senior administrators before any faculty members arrived, with R.K. Miller as the principal author. It clearly lays out the need for the four-phase approach of discovery, invention, development, and testing. This document is available on the Olin College web site, under the tab About Olin. - http://www.olin.edu/about_olin/invention2kf.asp.

4. Somerville, M., et al. (2005). The Olin curriculum: Thinking toward the future. *IEEE Transactions on Education, 48,* 198–205.

curriculum and then identified new approaches to meeting these goals, using both traditional course structures and new studio-based design approaches. Due to our proximity and good relations with neighboring Babson and Wellesley Colleges, our plans included the academic programs in place at these institutions as well. The invention phase culminated in a report from a special curriculum decision-making board made up of faculty.

A hallmark of the new learning model developed by the faculty is the "Olin Triangle." This symbol (see Figure 7.2) illustrates graphically the intended balance between "superb engineering" (intended to emphasize rigorous preparation in the engineering sciences and design), "entrepreneurship" (which we interpreted as entrepreneurial thinking), and "arts, humanities, and social sciences" (which we intended to mean a broad and rigorous interest in the human dimension of all engineering activity). These three fundamental aspects of the learning model are held together by a strong central focus on design, creativity, and innovation.

The development and testing phases of the process involved the need to implement and test the new approaches before attempting to deliver the material to enrolled students. For this phase, we recruited a group of 30 recent high school graduates—15 young men and 15 young women—to work with the faculty as "partners in invention" in testing different learning models. These 30 students were known as the Olin Partners, and they received a unique academic experience. They were selected through a rigorous and unusual process that required—in addition to exceptional academic preparation, grades, and test scores—team design exercises as well as in-depth interviews. We received more than 600 applications for the 30 positions. Many of the students who applied had been accepted at several of the most prestigious institutions in the United States, yet chose to attend Olin College because of the unique opportunity to become partners in inventing the

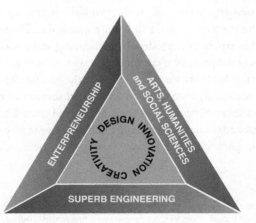

Figure 7.2: Values in Curriculum Design

academic program. They arrived in the fall of 2001 and spent the 2001–2002 academic year (known to us as the Partner Year) helping test various aspects of the plans for the new academic program. After the Partner Year they returned to enroll as first-year students in the regular four-year degree programs. For the Partners, the Olin experience was unique and involved a total of five years on campus.

During the Partner Year, the students participated in a number of experiments designed to test the hypotheses behind the traditional approach to engineering education. For example, early in the year we assigned a small group of students to work together for a few weeks to attempt to build a prototype of a pulse oximeter.[5] The students were given very little background on the device but were directed to the library for reference material. For example, the patent literature contains information on the purpose of the device and a schematic of its design. Several faculty members were available to answer questions and provide coaching and suggestions. We expected this project to fail because the students had no background in college physics, mathematics, electronics, or other areas that seemed necessary to the task, and we were planning to conduct a post-mortem to learn what the critical missing factors were. However, to our surprise, the students were successful in building and demonstrating a prototype for all of us to see. We learned from this that not only are students capable of undertaking significant technical challenges without the benefit of standard course work, but in addition, the students seemed to be personally affected by the experience. They developed a strong "can do" attitude and an eagerness to learn more about engineering. Many other experiments of this type were conducted, and the students frequently exceeded our expectations, demonstrating their ability to learn on their own in an iterative "do-and-then-learn-and-then-do-and-then-learn" cycle. We came to believe that this cycle is the dominant mode of learning in the practice of engineering, and it presents many advantages, including increased motivation to succeed, retention of knowledge, and integration of knowledge across disciplines.

These experiences gave us confidence that integrating real design-build challenges into the new engineering curriculum would not only succeed but also further motivate the students to want to learn engineering. Obviously, it also gave them considerable experience in independent learning and working in teams.

By approaching the process of curriculum design the way we did, by delegating authority to the faculty, there was some risk that the first faculty would settle on a curriculum not adequately innovative or was unworkable in some way. That would have required an intervention late in the process and most likely, some conflict between the senior administration and the faculty. However, since the faculty came to the college in part to design a new innovative curriculum and were deeply

5. A pulse oximeter is a medical instrument that measures the patient's pulse rate and the oxygen content of the blood. It works by clipping onto a finger and sending a light beam through the skin. It does not pierce the skin.

involved in inventing the particular version of the curriculum that we now use, they are passionate about it and they believe in its effectiveness. Curriculum design came from a faculty team, individual contributors, and faculty-student interactions. I believe this level of passion and buy-in from the faculty is very important to the positive learning outcomes that we have obtained.

Unless the faculty members believe in the curriculum and are passionate about it, they are unlikely to deliver it with enthusiasm and dedication. If faculty are not excited about the content and able to share their personal passion for engineering, it is unlikely that the students will become motivated to persist through difficult subjects.

Olin faculty members are expected to become inspirational teachers of undergraduates. This is a carefully crafted expectation. It comes from selecting people passionate about teaching, providing models of other inspirational teachers, and formally and internally reminding faculty of the uniqueness of the Olin model. To inspire students, it is necessary to transmit to them the knowledge to succeed in the exams and projects, but in addition, a passion to learn more about the subject. Our ultimate goal is to move beyond the mere transmission of knowledge to include attitudes, behaviors, and motivations. So, it is necessary to create a process for the development of the learning model and curriculum that results in a high level of enthusiasm and buy-in from every member of the faculty.

Since the design of the learning environment—including the curriculum—is perhaps the single most important aspect of creating a new academic institution, it is critically important to give this process the highest priority in creation of any new institution. In the past few years, Olin College has been visited by several teams of visitors from abroad who are involved in the process of developing a new university. In talking with them, it appears that they have sometimes adopted a commitment to complete the campus and launch the academic program very quickly to meet a rushed schedule. In my judgment, such a decision may cause substantial disappointment later in the reduction of the quality of the learning environment. Thinking back to the triangle presented in Figure 7.1, above, by placing too much emphasis on speed rather than quality, it is likely that the team of faculty charged with developing the curriculum will be forced to take courses and programs already in existence elsewhere from "off the shelf" and attempt to deploy them with minimal modification in the new environment solely to meet the rushed schedule for completion. Not only is this unlikely to duplicate the successful learning outcomes from the source campuses, but it also minimizes the opportunity to allow the founding faculty at the new institution to establish ownership of and passion for the learning model. Attempting to directly reproduce existing curricula, instead of developing a new learning environment from the ground up, might minimize the time required to launch the academic program, but it simultaneously forfeits all the opportunity for innovation and improvement that is inherent in starting a new institution.

In concluding this description of the invention of the Olin College learning model, it is important to add a few comments about the particular outcome we achieved. However, many visitors to our campus notice that nearly all members of our campus community are able to describe the purpose of the college and its learning objectives in the same way. This is an unusual feature of the academic community that has developed at Olin College. The level of common understanding of and commitment to the learning environment we have created is a hallmark of our program. It does not depend on a single pedagogical approach, but is diversified to recognize the many different ways in which people learn about the world.

Recruiting the Founding Faculty—Without Tenure

Another of the principal challenges of establishing Olin College was attracting the founding faculty. This challenge was made more difficult by the founding precept that Olin will not offer the opportunity for faculty members to obtain a tenured appointment. In addition, Olin is an undergraduate institution that does not (at this time) have any plans to offer graduate degrees, so there are no opportunities to work with graduate students. Furthermore, when the first faculty members were recruited, the campus facilities were under construction and there were no permanent offices or laboratories available. (Make-shift faculty offices were provided in a large residential house on the perimeter of the campus property for the first year and in temporary modular building units on the parking lot of a nearby athletic field in the second year.) At that time it was also very uncertain how successful Olin would be in attracting students of high ability.

The primary responsibility for attracting the founding faculty was that of Dr. David V. Kerns, Jr., the first Provost of Olin College. He worked closely with Dr. Sherra E. Kerns, the Vice President for Research and Innovation (who also happens to be David's wife) and me as the only three employees at the time who were also faculty members.

We decided that faculty members from a range of disciplines would be required. Since we planned to build the academic program one year at a time, starting with the freshman program in year one and then adding the sophomore program to the newly-created freshman program in year two, etc., this meant that the founding faculty *must* include those most responsible for the first year of the engineering curriculum. So, we included advertisements for a mathematician, a physicist, a chemist, and a biologist.

However, since the college offers only engineering degrees—and we envisioned an integrated and interdisciplinary approach to curriculum design—we also included advertisements for two electrical engineers, two mechanical engineers, and a computer scientist. This resulted in an interdisciplinary team of natural scientists, engineers, and mathematicians. The arts, humanities, and social sciences (AHS) were not explicitly represented. However, two of the original faculty members, one of whom was an electrical engineer and the other a biologist, each had nationally visible careers in the arts—music and visual arts. We originally intended to utilize existing course offerings in these areas from neighboring Babson College to avoid duplication of faculty resources.

To recruit faculty, we placed advertisements in the major national journals. In addition, we made numerous presentations at national conferences attended by engineering faculty members and administrators. Since the Olin Foundation had made special efforts to nationally publicize[6] their plans to create Olin College as early as 1997, many faculty members around the nation had some level of awareness of the project. This resulted in more than 1,500 applications for the (relatively few) available faculty positions. The quality of the applications was very high by any standard. Included in this first wave of new faculty members were two faculty members on the tenure-track at MIT, one of whom had taught there for 10 years. Another was a senior faculty member from Vanderbilt, who had more than 30 years of experience. Another came to Olin from NASA Goddard Space Flight Center where he retired as Director of Space Sciences. Yet another had a unique background as both a concert pianist and an electrical engineer. (She now holds a faculty appointment in both electrical engineering and music.)

It is impossible to overestimate the importance to the success of Olin College of attracting a group of founding faculty members of outstanding quality and diversity. Nearly half of the founding faculty members were women, which is quite unusual in engineering schools. Everything that followed was dependent on the knowledge, passion, vision, and resourcefulness of this group. They set the tone and the expectations for others to follow. We were exceptionally fortunate to secure a team of this quality for the unique challenge of inventing the learning model and curriculum.

It is interesting to speculate on what factors were most important in our successful attraction of so many highly qualified applicants. Many factors were likely involved. The unique mission of Olin College and its plan to develop a completely new paradigm for engineering education surely played an important—possibly the central—role in the attractiveness of Olin to the applicants. After all, the opportunity to start with a blank slate and invent an entire curriculum is extremely rare in higher education, and I believe a powerful magnet for creative and experienced faculty members.

In addition, the Olin Foundation had a long reputation for investing in high-quality facilities at more than 50 private universities and colleges throughout the nation, so its name recognition was high. This was enhanced by the well-placed national news releases about the project. In addition, the location of Olin College in Needham, MA, near Babson College and Wellesley College—only about 15 miles west of Cambridge in a very pleasant suburb of Boston—is a very significant advantage. Boston is the hub of the extraordinary academic resources of New England,

6. Honan, William H. (1997, June 6). $200 million, largest gift ever, endows new engineering college *New York Times*.

with many world class universities a short distance away. In addition, the high concentration of young professionals and academics in the Boston area provides a comfortable environment for young faculty members and for two-career faculty families to make their home. Finally, the strong national reputation of Dr. Kerns and our collective network of respected colleagues in other engineering schools around the nation also helped to steer good candidates to Olin.

The absence of tenure at Olin was surely an important deterrent to some potential applicants, but obviously not for the 1,500 who chose to apply. Because this feature was well-publicized, we felt confident that the applicant pool self-selected for their tolerance for this innovation in employment relations.

Some may speculate that Olin College provided extraordinary compensation to its founding faculty that could account for its success in attracting such quality applicants. However, this is definitely not the case. Olin's faculty salaries are competitive with a group of distinguished engineering and liberal arts schools around the nation, but they are not significantly higher. We did not offer candidates a compensation level exceeding that at other schools by more than a few percent.

The process of screening, interviewing, referencing, and selecting the faculty members was an enormous task in the first year. With 1,500 resumes to read and only three senior faculty members employed by the college, the sheer numbers were a challenge. We reached out to trusted senior faculty colleagues at other institutions and sent them boxes of resumes for them to review, and we also asked them to recommend a short list of top candidates in their field for our consideration. This parallel processing accelerated things considerably. We also asked the outside faculty to help with the referencing of finalists by making phone calls to references and providing us with summaries. When it came time for the faculty interviews, we asked all Olin employees to attend the seminars and to ask questions, even though many of the people in attendance were administrative or clerical staff. We explained to the candidates that they would need to be able to explain their research with such clarity that even our clerical staff could understand the main ideas. This worked better than we expected, and was quite revealing.

The requirements for faculty appointment at Olin start with the need to provide evidence or promise of becoming an inspirational teacher of undergraduate engineering students. In addition, since faculty members can only teach what they know and engineering is a fast-evolving field, they are also required to develop a life-long commitment to intellectual vitality and professional growth. Measures of both of these dimensions to their career are based on both external and internal assessments, with the expectation that our faculty will earn a degree of national visibility in their principal achievements.

The founding faculty members were expected to not only demonstrate all the requirements for faculty appointment to Olin but also a high degree of creativity, flexibility, vision, teamwork, and passion for establishing a new paradigm for engineering education. Anyone who has been involved in a start-up enterprise knows that it takes an enormous amount of personal passion and commitment to overcome the many risks and the endless challenges of building a program from scratch. The absence of staff resources and the pressures of time were unparalleled in our founding of Olin College from scratch. I believe that attitude played a major role in the success of the initial faculty. There just isn't any room for cynicism or self-centered behavior in a start-up. Entrepreneurial thinking and a "whatever-it-takes" attitude are absolutely essential.

DISCUSSION

At this point, Olin College is no longer an early stage, start-up enterprise. It may be better described as an "adolescent" institution. As in the case of humans, the adolescent years may prove to be more challenging than the early years. We are wrestling with a number of issues, including what we want to be when we truly "grow up."

Most of my time is now devoted to worrying about sustainability in one form or another. This is a very worrisome topic (more so than we imagined when we started the institution, given the Foundation's strong commitment to the college). As with other institutions, the past year provided unprecedented challenges to our financial model, causing us to rethink some of our assumptions about the role that our endowment should play in supplying revenue for annual operations. As a result, we decided to reduce the value of our four-year, full-tuition scholarships by half, beginning with students that will arrive in the fall of 2010.

The process of creating a new institution—like the process of teaching a course for the first time—is much more demanding in upfront time and energy than sustaining a successful one. However, inventing an entire institution requires a sustained, intense effort for nearly 10 years, and the potential for burnout among the faculty and staff before even getting to the point of sustainability is substantial. Also, as the nature of the daily activity shifts away from designing from a blank sheet toward sustaining and growing an apparently successful model, some of the most creative people begin to lose interest. They are inherent risk-takers and inventors, and as the risks fade and the opportunity to invent diminishes, it is difficult to hold the attention of the most creative people in the institution.

If Olin College is to achieve its long term objective, it must find a way to develop a culture of continuous innovation and change. It must avoid the natural tendency to become self-satisfied and complacent, and instead embrace the continuous development-and-testing loop that we started with a decade ago in designing the first curriculum. It is vital to embed an ongoing evaluation and redesign of the school into our everyday procedures. I can already detect the seeds of resistance to change at Olin. It will take serious effort here to let go of what we currently believe is essential to enable the next generation to invent a program that is even better. Innovation must remain our central identity.

When I was first appointed president at Olin College, I looked for guidance from others who had attempted something similar. I found Dr. Joseph Platt, the founding president of Harvey Mudd College, and was fortunate enough to spend some time with him. Perhaps the most important observation and advice he gave me was this. He said, "There is no more powerful force for conservatism, than having something to conserve." Obviously, in Olin College's first year, we had nothing to conserve. It was easy to consider any alternative because we had no identity yet, and nothing to lose. But now, only 10 years later, we have begun to establish an identity, and we have begun to convince ourselves that certain of the specific aspects of our learning model are essential to our success. As a result, we are loathe to even discuss sacrificing them for the sake of allowing completely new ideas to surface. Listening to faculty discussions, I can hear echoes of conversations that occurred (and probably still occur) at well-established institutions I served in years past. Many fresh suggestions meet with immediate discouragement on the grounds that something like that was already tried and shown to be ineffective, or it would be too difficult. I suspect that the core value of our institution does not lie within any of our beloved programs, but rather in our willingness to take bold steps to invent new approaches, working together to make Olin College an "exciting, creative, adventurous, rigorous, demanding, and empowering milieu," as Charles Vest suggested. My job now is to make sure we don't forget that.

CHAPTER 8

Starting Up the School of Information Systems at Singapore Management University

Critical Success Factors and Questions of Balance

STEVEN MILLER

Dean and First Employee
School of Information Systems
Singapore Management University

This chapter explores the start up of the School of Information Systems at Singapore Management University (SMU). My goal in the main section is to identify key factors that contributed to the success of this school from my perspective as the leader of the start up as well as the founding dean. The discussion session following the main portion of the chapter delves into complex management and decision-making trade-offs and questions of balance, both professionally and personally.

This story starts on October 17, 2002, when the Singapore Management University received notification from Singapore's Ministry of Education that it had the official go-ahead to establish the fourth school of the university, the School of Information Systems. At this point in time, Singapore Management University was just completing its third year of operation and consisted of a School of Business started in 2000, a School of Accountancy started in 2001, and a School of Economics and Social Sciences started in 2002.

The origins for the School of Information Systems go back to the SMU master planning that was done in the late 1990s, which was also the time of the dot-com boom. SMU was designed to be a niche university centered on "The World of Business, Organizations and Markets." The SMU master planners, including participants from Singapore's Ministry of Education, decided that this new management-centric university would not include engineering, or physical or life sciences. Yet they determined that this new university should also produce bachelor's degree graduates who could deal with the exploding and expanding universe of "infocomm," which is our local way of referring to the areas covered by information and communications technology.

At the beginning stage, there was no specific sense of what this next SMU school, oriented around infocomm in the context of business, should be like. How technology-driven would it be? Would students develop software applications? How would the infocomm bachelor's degree program relate to management? These were wide-open questions. The only constraint was a very general one—a curriculum blueprint for the infocomm program that had been submitted to the Ministry of Education earlier in 2002 that outlined the broad structure of the bachelor's degree program based on the structure being used across the other degree programs in the university: One-third of the courses in the degree's major area, infocomm, and the remaining two-thirds of the courses spread across the SMU common core and management-oriented electives that could be taken in the other existing schools. Also, by this time in late 2002, the dot-com investment bubble had already burst, and business organizations across the world were restraining or stopping the rapid pace of infocomm-related projects and investments that were the drivers for the assumption that more university-trained manpower was needed in this area. This added to the uncertainty of deciding how to shape the new school.

To understand the scale and speed of our School of Information Systems start-up effort, consider the following. In mid-October 2002, SMU was notified to proceed with starting the infocomm-related bachelor's degree program, with an August 2003 target date for the first cohort of 100 students. I joined the university in December 2002 as the first (and only) faculty member in the new School of Information Systems, moving to the university from a Singapore-based position in IBM's e-business consulting group. By August 2003, we had a pioneer intake of 93 freshmen and a handful of faculty. Seven years later, in August 2010, our SMU School of Information Systems had more than 1,000 undergraduate students across all four years, a master's degree program, a PhD program, and more than 40 faculty, plus additional research staff, teaching staff and administrative staff.

This particular start-up effort fits into the overall expansion of the Singapore Management University, incorporated in the year 2000. In August 2003, SMU consisted of four schools, had a total enrollment of 2,163 undergraduates, nearly 111 full-time faculty members, and about 41 part-time master's students. Seven years later, in August 2010, the overall university has grown to six schools, since

Social Science had split from Economics to become the fifth school, and Law was added as the sixth school. There are approximately 6,700 undergraduates, about 290 full-time faculty members, and about 350 full-time post-graduate students (master's and Phd) and 270 part-time post-graduates (master's).

SMU's School of Information Systems is generally regarded by its various peer and stakeholder communities as a successful start-up that has distinguished itself in targeted niche areas across research, education, public service, and outreach. In this chapter, I reflect on some of the things that our school did early on and along the way that we think were important contributors to our ability to start up and progress to our current situation. In retrospect, these are critical success factors that were especially helpful in getting us off the ground, through the initial years of start-up, and into this next phase of our capability development.

CRITICAL SUCCESS FACTORS

Institutional Independence and Support from Central Administration

An important factor in any academic start-up is the relationship between the university's central administration and the individual schools. The university's central administration could play a strong or even dominating role in all the critical design decisions at the school level, such as the vision, selection of faculty, learning model, curriculum design, and so on. Or, the opposite could occur, where all of the critical design decisions are driven at the school level by the dean and faculty. In our case, we benefited from a structure that encouraged our independence, strong support from the central administration and dedicated funding from the government during the start-up period.

We created the School of Information Systems (SIS) within an existing, albeit relatively new, university that had many policies, procedures, and rules already in place. Fortunately, SIS had a great deal of autonomy in terms of the major start-up decisions. From the outset, we were set up as a distinct academic unit with our own dean who reported directly to the provost. I think this institutional arrangement was absolutely critical to achieving our purpose. Given the composition of SMU at that time, the only other organizational option would have been for Information Systems to be set up as a unit within the existing School of Business. I am certain that if we were originally set up as a group or department within the university's existing business school, we could not have taken this new organization where we wanted to take it, as defined by our preferred directions for research areas, faculty competencies, faculty development practices, and attitudes toward learning, teaching, and curriculum. There would have been intractable difficulty fitting in with and accommodating to the norms and evolving practices of our business school.

Most major business schools have faculty and courses in the area of "information systems." If the purpose of the new infocomm-oriented program at SMU was to essentially replicate an existing business-school-based information systems program, perhaps there would have been advantages to setting up within the SMU School of Business. However, from the very outset, this was not what we wanted to do. Instead, we wanted to create a hybrid research and education environment that had three types of elements: 1) selected aspects of information technology (IT) capability and strength found within a computer science school or department, 2) easy access to real world examples of how IT is being used across a variety of private and public sector organizations, and 3) instruction on the type of skills that would enable students to understand and analyze the business and management issues associated with creating and using information systems in organizational settings and to be able to communicate the business value of IT.

Had we set up within our business school, we probably could have addressed the second and third elements above in a way that was similar to what other business schools were doing, but we would have been severely constrained in our ability to pursue the first element. Given that we were creating a new infocomm-oriented school within Singapore Management University, a niche university centered around the world of business, we did not want to create a regular computer science program either, which would consist of an expanded set of the first element but relatively little of the second or third.

While being a stand-alone school gave us tremendous liberty and agility in decision-making, the SMU provost and president also were exceptionally supportive. This high degree of support and trust from the senior administration were the result of several factors. The senior management knew that I was a former Carnegie Mellon faculty member and still had on-going relations with that university. They were well aware that I had spent the prior 13 years in industry working on the interface of IT and business applications, including the most recent few years with IBM in Singapore. While I consulted with the provost and president on all major decisions, they trusted that I could run the school and decide what to do. That trust, and the autonomy that went along with it, made all the difference in the world.

Although we had a great deal of autonomy in our decision making, and our senior management was highly supportive, we nonetheless over prepared for every discussion and presentation to make sure their trust in our directions would continue to grow stronger. I always showed up at president and provost meetings with well-defined plans supported by charts and graphs and visual representations that were much more elaborate and detailed than what the university's senior management were used to seeing at SMU or at any other place they had previously worked.

Since it appeared that I had a clear vision of where to go with the school, and it was evident that we worked up blueprints and detailed execution plans for everything we said we needed to do, SMU senior management would mostly say, "Looks good! Go ahead. Tell us what you need." Also, prior to the end of 2007, the entire university was still operating within an initial eight-year special start-up period where they had access to additional start-up-related support funds from Singapore's Ministry of Education.

From the beginning, we knew we were trying to create a new type of educational program, and while we had a direction and a general sense of where and how to aim, we knew we would be inventing many aspects of the program as we proceeded. We also knew Singapore had an extremely competitive landscape for recruiting undergraduate students. Both the National University of Singapore and the Nanyang Technological University, the two other government-sponsored universities in the country, were larger and more established and offered IT programs in their respective computer science schools as well as in their business schools that would be competing for the some of the same students we would be trying to recruit. In short, we knew we had to very quickly define a niche and move rapidly to differentiate our program. The strong support of the university's senior management, the absence of many constraints, and the availability of funds within the university for start-up initiatives, all made the start-up process easier and allowed us to focus on creating that niche for ourselves and attracting high-quality faculty and students.

Central University Support Services Willing to Customize Services for Individual Schools

The initial SIS staff benefited from the opportunity to work with a number of centralized, university-wide services offices that guided us in developing our operating procedures while giving us flexibility to set our own parameters and make hiring and admission decisions. The university had centralized units for human resources (HR), admissions, career placement, corporate communications, contracts and legal affairs, and some other key university-wide functions, and having these existing capabilities on which to draw was very helpful to us. At the same time, the university had a strong decentralized identity around the individual schools. For example, from the very outset each school hired its own operations staff, with central assistance for doing this staff recruiting and the related HR work. Similarly, there was central support for faculty hiring and for related faculty administration. After I had joined, our very first hires as a new school in early 2003—even before we hired faculty—were two internal operations staff, both of whom still work for us as of 2010. Having strong internal administrative support staff from the outset, even before we brought on faculty, was instrumental to our ability to operate effectively.

The university's Office of Undergraduate Admissions provides a good example of how a central support group with standardized processes was also able to customize its efforts to meet the needs of our new School of Information Systems. The SMU admissions office does the first round of filtering of all the undergraduate applications submitted to each of the respective programs across the university. Then, the admissions office works with each school to arrange follow-up interviews for those who cleared the initial screen. The school determines how it will interview and evaluate these candidates. The school also has the final say on which students it admits, though this involves close coordination and ongoing consultation with the central admissions office.

Having these central support groups working together to support the individual schools was a very good situation for us. Often, the central university resources for admissions, contracts and legal, corporate communications, and information technology would modify and customize their support to meet the specific needs of our new school. This ability for some of the central administration support groups to provide customized services to meet school-specific needs was a great help. The fact that SMU was a niche-type of university and of relatively small size was probably instrumental in making this all work in the way that it did. It might be more difficult to customize operations in a larger, more established university with stronger centralization.

Independent Physical Space

One other aspect that we took for granted was that we were not only an autonomous unit in terms of having our own school, our own program, our own dean, and our own faculty, but from the very outset, we also had our own building. We had a very interesting choice to make right when we started. In early 2003, when the school began planning for the first intake of students, SMU was located on a temporary campus. It was a regular campus in that it was the original location of the University of Singapore dating back to the very early 1900s. However, the campus was temporary in the sense that a new campus was in the process of being built for SMU in the heart of the city, and the university would remain in this temporary setting only until mid-2005, when it would migrate to the new city campus. We had to decide where we would locate the new School of Information Systems within the temporary campus, and this would be our home for our first two and a half years.

Several SMU people familiar with this temporary campus suggested that it would be most convenient for our new school to move into unused space that was right in the center of the complex of buildings on this temporary campus. What we ultimately did was much more on the edge, literally. We took an unused and neglected building on the periphery of the campus that was not physically connected to the other buildings in the complex. The other existing SMU schools did not have interest in this building because it seemed "far away" and also because the building interior was in poor condition and outright ugly, having been unoccupied for a long while. It was all of a seven-minute walk from this "far away" building to the other parts of the campus, which were all interconnected. At any large university, walking 7 or 10 minutes to get to another building seems like nothing. But on that small campus, and in Singapore's always warm and frequently rainy weather, it was like being "way over there," since it was physically set apart and not interconnected with the other buildings on campus.

The university's central facility management group and architecture office were there to help us, and we quickly worked up designs for how to economically refurbish and customize the idle, unused building on the campus periphery to meet our current needs as well as our estimated needs for expansion space over the next 2.5 years until we moved into the new city campus. This facility choice turned out to be a remarkably good decision. Having our own place gave our faculty and staff, as well as our students, their own sense of identity. There was also the mystique of taking space that no one else wanted and turning it into something that was desirable, even cool. And we liked the symbolism, as well as the reality, of being "on the edge" of the university and apart from the mainstream. It was a good way to start. Starting off with our own building enhanced the personalization of the school, which made a huge difference.

We were fortunate that when we moved over to the new campus a few years later, the School of Information Systems also had its own building. Again, that let us customize some things and let our students build a special kind of identity. Our students are always interacting with students and faculty from the other parts of the university, because many of their courses have to be taken outside of the School of Information Systems, requiring them to go to other buildings and work with students from the other schools. But they also have this home with its own physical location and cultural norms. Having autonomous space really made a difference in building our identity and culture.

Guidance from an Experienced and Acclaimed Partner Institution, CMU

In late 2002, barely one week after I started as full-time faculty at the new school, I travelled to Carnegie Mellon University (CMU) to investigate how CMU could assist SMU with the effort to start up our new School of Information Systems. There had already been communication between these two institutions. Two Carnegie Mellon business school faculty had visited SMU in March 2002 to discuss SMU's preliminary proposal for creating a new infocomm-related school with the president and provost. This contact was facilitated by a relatively new (at that time) SMU business school faculty member who had completed a PhD from CMU's Heinz College, joined the SMU faculty in 2001, and ended up heading the SMU committee that drafted the formal request to the Ministry of Education in early 2002 to commence with the infocomm-related school that had been part of the original master blueprint for SMU's expansion.

The relationship progressed very quickly with Carnegie Mellon due to three factors. First, SMU's president and provost already had a few preliminary discussions with Carnegie Mellon faculty regarding the new school in the earlier part of 2002, so our SMU senior administrators were familiar and comfortable with CMU. Secondly, I had a long-standing relationship with CMU as an alumnus and a former full-time faculty member. This gave me rapid access to many key people across the

CMU campus, at all levels. My familiarity with the university made it easy to go back to CMU and informally talk to people across the campus who were in different kinds of information technology programs, including business-related IT, applied informatics, applied IT, and computer science. Third, CMU was deliberately working to strengthening its international presence and to build international partnerships, and Singapore had previously been identified by several key CMU administrators at the school and university levels as one of the more promising foreign countries with which to seek out working relationships. Within a few weeks of that first visit, a formal agreement was signed that set the stage for an initial four years of collaborative activities. While my prior years as a CMU community member facilitated this relationship, the motivation of Carnegie Mellon to be an active partner and to have a diverse set of expertise in their intellectual space was very important.

The nature of this first relationship agreement is important to explain. First, Carnegie Mellon's role was consultative only. The university was to provide us with consultation to support our internal efforts to: 1) design the new school's undergraduate program, 2) hire and develop our new faculty, and 3) identify a few strategic areas of research. The program's owners and decision makers were Singapore Management University and its new School of Information Systems. CMU had no direct responsibility for establishing or delivering the programs for the new SMU school.

CMU's affiliation and involvement with SIS was especially helpful for recruiting research-track faculty—tenure-track assistant professors as well as associate and full professors—during the school's initial four years of start-up. During those early years, all of our SIS faculty candidates for tenure-track assistant professor positions gave job evaluation talks at Carnegie Mellon in addition to going through the evaluation process with our school in Singapore. CMU faculty also were involved in interviewing and evaluating our first three research-track faculty hires at the associate and full professor levels. Although we always made the final decision, the advice and evaluation information from Carnegie Mellon was very important. Also, intensive CMU interactions with our prospective research-track faculty members helped assure those candidates we wanted to hire that we were a good place to work, even though we were a brand new school, and an unconventional one at that.

A second feature of the relationship is that we created a Carnegie Mellon design consulting team composed of faculty from CMU's Tepper School of Business, Heinz College (Information Technology and Public Policy), School of Computer Science, College of Engineering, and College of Humanities and Social Science. We needed faculty representation from all of these different types of CMU information technology programs given the type of school were setting out to create. Carnegie Mellon's ability to easily work across its various colleges and across the corresponding disciplinary boundaries was important for several reasons. First, this ability made it easier for us to interact with selected faculty on a one-on-one basis across these various colleges. Second, when we convened working sessions with our core team of CMU faculty consultants, the faculty from different colleges already knew how to work together on IT-related research, educational, and administrative initiatives. Working with the CMU faculty from these different colleges, representing various points on the spectrum of IT expertise from deep information technology capability to management analysis of information systems impacts, helped SIS build its identity because we also aimed to create an environment spanning various points along the spectrum of IT-related issues and skills.

Our consulting relationship with CMU was very intense during the first four years. Most of the SMU-CMU interactions focused on undergraduate course design and redesign, learning outcomes design and re-design, SIS faculty recruiting, and follow-up professional development coaching for the faculty we recruited, especially our tenure-track assistant professors. We renewed the collaboration agreement for a second four-year term as we approached the end of the fourth year of the first agreement, though the emphasis of the collaboration has shifted over time. From the fifth year onward, there has been less emphasis on undergraduate program issues and more emphasis on faculty-to-faculty research collaboration, working together to create a joint research initiative that we can propose to the Singapore government together, and continuing to develop our faculty.

BUILDING A VISION

Building a vision for SIS was an early first step that would affect all subsequent decisions. Our vision building was a dynamic, cyclical process of creating and testing, and recreating and retesting.

At the very beginning, while there was no clearly articulated vision for the school, a few things were crystal clear to me. One was the difference between the thinking behind the deep theory and some of the deep aspects of analytics that provide the foundation for properly educating a good computer science student versus the types of thinking and problem solving most often required within the various types of real-world business settings to create and apply information technology and related systems solutions to aid, enhance, and transform an organization. These are both important approaches to thinking and problem-solving, but they require different kinds of educational experiences and training.

The second point is that we were very clear we did not want to copy or adapt any of the existing educational models for business school-based information systems programs or for mainstream computer science programs. We knew we wanted to create a new educational program with the following key characteristics: 1) It would allocate substantially more time to designing and creating information systems applications than would be possible in a business-school based program; 2) It would be much more application-oriented than a computer science program, situating IT-related design problems within the context of actual business processes and scenarios; and 3) It still would comply with the university's undergraduate education model, which required a majority of the total courses to be taken outside of the school, including requirements for an SMU common core that had to be taken by students in all four of the schools that existed at that time.

While it was easy to describe ourselves as not wanting to be a business school-based IT program or a regular computer science-based program, it was a lot harder in those early days to describe ourselves in the more positive sense in terms of what we wanted to be as opposed to what we did not want to be. Of course there's a lot of space in the middle of the two types of programs we were making reference to, so we had to first define what kind of hybrid we wanted to become. Starting with that fairly broad notion of a hybrid between these two well-understood reference points for undergraduate IT education, I was able to talk to people in different programs at CMU that reflected these two different approaches, as well as to people from other programs that represented intermediate points between the two. Through these conversations with various CMU faculty, we were able to create a team on their side that was willing to serve as our "kitchen cabinet." That proved to be very important in building the vision. Obviously, an overseas group cannot be the ones who drive something that's here in Singapore. But it turned out to be critical to have experienced university people from another place to reflect off of and to think things through with, especially given that our infocomm-related school was going to be such a different type of entity from the existing SMU schools. We have been fortunate to have long-term continuity with several of the original CMU advisory team members who started consulting with us in December 2002. That continuity in itself has been very helpful.

Before we admitted our first students, Desai Narasimhalu, our first faculty hire, and I did a lot of outreach to the community. We sat down with CIOs, business leaders, and people who were users of technology. Desai had come from a government-supported research lab in Singapore that was doing applied IT research and development, requiring intensive interaction with industry to develop and commercialize new types of IT tools and systems. I had been working with IBM in Singapore for the past several years doing e-business consulting across Asia. Through this consulting work, I was seeing how large organizations were exploring how to use IT software applications and systems to change business-to-business and business-to-consumer type capabilities.

Although Desai and I were coming from different aspects of the IT world, we shared a vision of wanting to build a program that would create students who could actually use IT in the context of business organizations and who could also help to drive both the IT and business aspects of the change, whether related to productivity improvement, new service introduction, or business innovation. The key is that we were focused on creating an educational program centered around designing and applying IT software applications to business-oriented problems and transformations, in contrast to one centered on building better computers, theories, or algorithms.

We received a lot of affirmation about our vision when we spoke with people in industry. We would frequently hear comments similar to, "You guys are brand new on the scene, and it's the first time one of the universities is asking us to sit down and have this conversation about how we create a business-oriented IT professional." Hearing these types of comments from industry IT users and existing providers of IT solutions turned out to be important because it provided us with specific feedback that we could use when we started to interview and interact with our first set of potential students.

In the first few years of interviewing prospective students, they often would say, "You are brand new. Why should I believe this is going to be a good program?" We could respond in compelling ways with great examples from our recent industry interviews. We could quickly rejoin with, "Let us tell you about the conversation that we were having with the head of IT, or the head of operations, just yesterday in this or that kind of organization. Let me tell you the feedback the companies gave us about what we're setting out to do."

We essentially took action to discover the concepts for the vision for the school by going out into the world, interacting, getting feedback from industry, and then shaping and filtering it using our own experiences. During the initial 12 months of SIS development, these industry interaction sessions helped us clarify and improve our way of articulating what the program was going to be about. In real time we were feeding our clarified ideas back to potential student applicants. It just began to snowball. Though the discussion sessions Desai and I were having with industry, through the brainstorming sessions with the CMU advisors, and through our internal efforts to capture, refine, and represent these ideas, we essentially created something from nothing. The vision development was a highly iterative process of creating, interacting, and receiving feedback, followed by ongoing cycles of interacting, reviewing feedback, and re-creating the ways of articulating the vision.

RESEARCH-TRACK AND PRACTICE-TRACK FACULTY

From the outset, SMU aspired to be a well-known, research-oriented university that excelled in its selected areas. At the same time, the very first degree programs at the university were undergraduate programs, and there was a very strong emphasis on highly engaging teaching and professionally relevant curriculum. The way SMU was able to do this quite successfully was to have both practice faculty and tenure-track research faculty.

Research-track faculty include assistant, associate, and full professors on the tenure track who publish in globally recognized, high-quality academic outlets. As with other traditional universities, tenure-track faculty do teach courses but have to spend much more time doing the type of research and writing that leads to academic publications.

In contrast, practice-track faculty are not tenured. They also have ranks of assistant, associate, and full professor and have PhDs in their respective disciplines (or the appropriate terminal degree for Law or Accounting) and industry or professional practice experience. The practice-track faculty maintain their ties with industry and professional practice and use these relationships to bring the outside world into the classroom, as well as to bring the classroom to the outside world. Practice-track faculty do more teaching and service work than the tenure-track faculty and also produce practice-oriented publications.

It takes a long time, often several years, to recruit senior-level tenure-track faculty, especially when they are working overseas. The few senior faculty who were in the other SMU schools in the early years were either part of the original SMU start-up team who had transferred over from the two other universities in Singapore, or had changed jobs and come over to the university within its first year or two. But this was a small number of people. The research faculty that could be added more quickly, in larger numbers, were predominately rookies at the assistant professor level.

In contrast with the difficulty attracting senior-level research professors, it was possible for SMU to hire highly qualified, tremendously experienced practice-track faculty relatively quickly. As a cosmopolitan, business-oriented city with a highly educated workforce, Singapore had an abundance of professionals who had obtained PhDs earlier in their career and who were working in the city. This included Singaporeans who had spent a number of years overseas, either for graduate studies or for work, and who had returned home, as well as expatriates from other countries who were working in Singapore for multinational corporations and decided to remain in the country. The early availability of these more experienced practice-track faculty made it possible to do the "heavy lifting" required to get the under-graduate program going and to rapidly scale it up. This was true across the entire university, not just our new School of Information Systems.

Hiring a few practice faculty at the outset was especially important for SIS. For our undergraduate program, we wanted a strong and clear professional orientation. To have a professional orientation you need people with practice experience. As noted earlier, Desai, my first faculty, had formerly worked in a government-sponsored research institute in Singapore doing information technology related research, and as part of his work he dealt a lot with industry and had many professional contacts. Hiring practice faculty made sense in a professionally oriented program and helped us from the beginning with our curriculum and teaching. The young tenure-track assistant professors we were recruiting in our early years had no previous exposure to the type of professionally oriented IT program that we wanted to put in place and had no idea how to establish such a curriculum. They also lacked the experience required to rapidly engage with industry and other external stakeholders. The experienced practice faculty who joined us early on provided a necessary bridge between industry and the initial group of research-track assistant professors.

STUDENT RECRUITING AND THE INTERVIEW PROCESS

One of the powerful mechanisms by which we were able to directly interact with potential students was through the admissions interview process. I strongly recommend the use of interviews as a means of selection as well as a means of communication and outreach during the early years. Admissions interviews are more than a good mechanism for selecting students. They are an excellent way to communicate the school's expectations and aspirations to these same student applicants. They are also a very important mechanism for orienting and socializing new faculty who come into the organization, since they get to hear directly from potential students about their expectations for the educational program and why they would want to come to our school versus going to other alternatives locally or internationally.

Our university had already established a practice of interviewing all potential applicants who passed the initial screening process conducted by the central admissions office. However, the different schools would do the interviews in different ways. For the first and second year of interviewing, Desai and I worked out an interview protocol that was based on showing students visuals that defined the school's aspirations, vision, curriculum blueprint, and approach toward student-centric learning. We would interact with the students about these types of topics and get the students to talk about their views of learning. This approach turned out to be very useful and effective.

We admitted 93 students to our initial undergraduate class. As one might expect, they were a very energetic and risk-taking batch, as they were choosing to come into the newest program of a relatively new university. We also offered an unusual type of degree that was called a Bachelor of Science (Information Systems Management). None of the applicants knew the meaning of the degree name. During the interviews, they kept asking if it was an engineering degree or a business degree. We had to spend a lot of time explaining that it was neither, but it had elements common to both of these types of degrees.

We also had to spend a lot of time explaining and demonstrating by example our plan for the school. The student interviews provided an especially effective and convenient way to do this. We also did this explaining at outreach events where the SMU central admissions office would arrange for us to go to different high schools and polytechnic schools to tell students what we were trying to do. It helped that we had the ability to convey our recent stories from the many key professionals and executives in industry with whom we had been talking, as those professionals would be likely employers of these students several years later.

From the student interviews and visits, we kept getting feedback about how students responded to both what we were saying and how we were saying it, and we used this feedback in real time to revise the way we would articulate the vision and approach of the school. The interview process and recruiting events thus became an important part of our own learning by doing and were important contributors to our ongoing process of shaping the vision and identity of the institution. The fact that the entire country of Singapore is essentially the same physical size as a city or extended metropolitan area worked to our advantage, because it made it possible for all of our "domestic" applicants to conveniently visit for an interview and also made it easy for us to attend outreach events at schools all over the country.

CURRICULUM—PROCESS AND DESIGN

As we complete our seventh academic year of operation, we have a reasonably well-developed curriculum. To get our degree in the Bachelor of Science (Information Systems Management), a student has to take a minimum of 36 courses, with 14 of those courses taken in the School of Information Systems. Sixteen of the courses are university-wide common courses dealing with leadership, communications, and various aspects of liberal arts. Of the remaining two courses, two are "mandated electives" that build quantitative and numeric skills (e.g., statistics, business modeling with spreadsheets), and the remaining four are what we refer to as "business oriented" electives. They are courses from any of the undergraduate major programs at SMU, which are offered by our schools of Business, Accountancy, Economics, Social Science, and Law.

The Process of Curriculum Change

While the part of the curriculum structure that was outside of the School of Information Systems was essentially defined from the outset and has remained relatively stable, the curriculum structure and courses for the part within our school have evolved continuously. Even now, our curriculum continues to change, though perhaps not at the same rapid rate that it changed over the first five years. Our ability to keep evolving the curriculum and to rapidly make changes while we were executing helped us tremendously. We could not have evolved to the point where we are today if the university or other outside authorities had imposed upon us a cumbersome process for changing course content or curriculum structure for that portion of the curriculum delivered within SIS.

We did have a few strong macro-constraints that we had to work within, given the university-wide structure for all SMU bachelor's degree programs. However, even these high-level structural aspects were changed over time in a way that suited our needs. The early-2002 proposal put forth by the university to create the school outlined a high-level blueprint for our bachelor's curriculum that showed 12 courses being offered within the School of Information Systems and the remaining 24 being composed of non-major-specific courses from across the rest of the university. Toward the end of the second year, we realized we needed a few additional core courses within the school. Between the third and sixth year, the major-related course count within the school increased from 12 to 14 courses. As of this writing, we are working on plans to further increase the number to 15.

Changes of this type, which impact the macro-structure of our university bachelor's programs (i.e., any change in the number of major-related courses) have to go through a formal university-level consultation, review, and approval process, and therefore take a relatively long time to implement, since they impact the basic structure followed by the other bachelor's degree programs. As the university has evolved and become larger and more complex, the university-level review process also has evolved to become more complicated and time consuming. While these types of macro-level structural changes are still possible, they take longer to implement than they did in the first five years of our school's life.

For the major-related courses offered within our own school, we have complete autonomy to put these together and revise them year after year. Each time we want to revise the content or structure for our own major-related courses, which we have done on a somewhat constant basis, we do not have to go through university-level committees and approval processes. Nor is it necessary for the university to go through external approval processes with the Singaporean Ministry of Education since our basic degree structure has already been approved, and we are making changes within that basic structure. This autonomy to make changes in the courses we offer within the school is essential for our success. We learn so much about how to design and deliver our courses with each semester and each academic year of experience that we accumulate, and the only way to make our program better, and to deal with the many design and delivery "bugs" that became evident, is to continuously make changes to curriculum content as we obtain feedback and experience.

One thing that we did not fully understand when we started was the difference—in fact the large gap—between 1) having a workable (though evolving) vision for how to shape the program and for what type of students we wanted to produce and 2) the details of how to actually start the students in a way that they could "climb up the staircase" of capability that we wanted them to develop. While we had a sense of where we wanted the students to end up in terms of a capability set, we did not fully appreciate the most basic things that had to be done in the first and second year to get them moving toward the desired endpoint. We initially underestimated what was required to prepare the freshmen to gradually do the work that would enable them to become the type of business-oriented IT professionals we were aiming to produce. Working backwards to define the details of the first steps the students needed to take in order to develop the capacity to absorb the things we would require them to do in the later years turned out to be the most challenging aspect of our curriculum design and the aspect requiring the most change over the initial years. In fact, we are still working on improving these aspects of the program.

It was surprising to us that some of the seemingly simplest and most mundane aspects turned out to be some of the hardest parts of the curriculum to design.

Had we adopted a standard curriculum blueprint from a business school IT program, or from an applied computer science program, we would not have had this problem to the same extent. But neither would we have had this new and compelling sense of the type of student that we wanted to produce by the end of the program.

One of our earliest missteps was trying to jump too quickly to IT-oriented problem solving in a way that implicitly assumed the students understood how information systems are used in the context of business enterprises. Those of us who designed the initial version of the curriculum did not fully appreciate that when students come out of high school—after learning subjects like math, physics, geography, economics, humanities, and English—they don't have any background to relate to the ways information systems and technology are used within enterprises and across business settings. They don't understand complexity in enterprises, and they have no prior exposure to the study of business processes. Essentially, all that students understand about information technology is what they see and buy at their favorite computer store or online. Pre-college high school students are essentially clueless about the context of what we refer to as "enterprise IT" or IT in the setting of complex work organizations. You can't just tell pre-college students about this world. As one of our faculty members put it, even if you tell them about the business world, they do not have "mental Velcro" where the concepts can stick.

We also underestimated how much time would be required for the "average student" to pick up some of the basic software skills and IT solution design skills that we were requiring. We assumed that we could accelerate the process of exposing the students to higher-level "business solutioning" with software applications, even if they students did not yet have experience with some of the basic aspects of software programming. We had go back and strengthen the way we covered these very first-stage basics, although we did so in the context of where we wanted to take the students. This vision of the end point enabled us to emphasize certain aspects of a regular programming class and omit or de-emphasize others.

Because some of our basic assumptions of how to start the students in year one, and to some extent year two, required revision, our curriculum was constantly evolving over the first three years. This was not easy. A great deal of work was required to address such continual change, which impacted both the practice faculty and research faculty. While the practice faculty played a larger role in addressing these types of issues and getting the work done and implemented, all of our faculty had to invest considerable time in working out the curriculum.

Fortunately, all of the faculty who joined our new school were willing to make this effort. It was part of the culture of this new institution. We just assumed that we were going to put in the effort to invent this approach, and that it would involve a multi-pronged development effort using some content from established curriculum sources, adapting content from other available sources and creating a lot of our own new content. All of our faculty accepted the premise that we were committed to design and redesign the curriculum we needed in an iterative fashion.

At the same time, we continued our frequent conversations and interactions with technology users in the business community in Singapore as well as internationally, and they kept giving us affirmation and encouragement for the type of curriculum and overall educational experience we were aspiring to create. This reinforcement from our external stakeholders was very important. It gave us the confidence to keep moving in the direction we were going, despite the challenges of iteratively working toward the right formula for the curriculum.

The key point is to highlight the critical importance of our ability to rapidly change the curriculum, to keep this body of content evolving and to have total control for doing this within our school. Being a standalone academic unit, trusted by the upper echelons of the university, made this possible.

A related point is that our time-consuming curriculum experimentation was restricted to the major related courses delivered within SIS, which was only about 33 to 40 percent (depending on the year) of the total course requirements for our bachelor's degree. The fact that we were not responsible for creating or revising courses offered outside of the school was an obvious advantage for us, giving the ability to concentrate on the smaller portion of the overall curriculum delivered within school. Also, the fact that the other programs at SMU had started several years in front of us, and that their courses were already further along in their evolution, was enormously helpful to us. Even if we had some rough spots in our major-related courses in those early years, the overall experience of the students was very positive since more than 60 percent of their courses were being taken outside of the new school. Being within the context of a larger and relatively new university, yet having a distinct identity and a lot of autonomy, seemed to work for us.

Curriculum Design

Although we had an evolving design process of explaining our vision for the new school, we still needed to create a specific set of courses that would make us distinctive from other universities in Singapore and other information systems schools in the world. The Carnegie Mellon kitchen cabinet team urged us to make a list of a few key factors that would make our school and our bachelor's program distinctive. When we made this list, two things were especially important. One was the notion of having explicit learning outcomes. Educators have been working with learning outcomes for decades, but only a small percentage of university programs commit themselves to comprehensively integrating learning outcomes into their fabric. From the very outset, we took on the challenge of trying to specify and operationalize learning outcomes for our bachelor's degree program. This turned out to be very important and influenced our initial curriculum design and subsequent redesigns, as well as our conversations about teaching and learning with faculty and students.

Between 2003 and 2007, we created a well-structured learning outcomes framework and a supporting information system. In 2009, we initiated our fourth-generation iteration of deepening and expanding this framework and the supporting information system, and this phase of improvement and implementation will stretch across 2010 and 2011.

If you ask any of our students to name our learning outcomes, the one most often mentioned first is learning to learn. Somehow, the students really pick up on this concept, and it seems to be the most popular one. It is strongly reinforced throughout their undergraduate experience. In their course assignments, they have to fill in a lot of gaps and do a lot of self-learning to figure things out. When they do internships, they get thrown into all types of situations they have never encountered, and they often have to pick up new technical skills that go beyond what we have exposed them to. The same occurs when they do their required upper-year capstone project.

I have found our learning outcomes approach to be exceptionally important and also to be a very strong compass for students, faculty, and staff. It hasn't been an easy journey, though. Faculty question why we should bother with it. Our requirement to map each course to the learning outcomes framework does create extra work for our faculty, and now that we are expanding the framework to include an even more detailed specification of competencies for each course, it requires even more faculty time. Similarly, students have to put in additional work to self assess their learning outcomes. While the self assessments are officially "voluntary," we hound our undergraduates to do them on a regular basis and even require them to complete assessments when and where we can. For example, I will not sign off on any student requests unless they have shown our undergraduate administrators their up-to-date copy of their learning outcomes assessment.

Students naturally question why they have to deal with learning outcomes. Some students have been known to grumble that it is wasting their time since it does not directly help them to get a better grade in a course. But we have persisted in supporting the usage of the system and in educating students about the purposes and long-term benefits. Over time, student acceptance and participation has steadily increased.

Industry has been remarkably supportive of our learning outcomes framework, for a number of reasons. The set of outcomes makes sense to them. The more specific sub-skills are the types of things that are really important to them. And as one industry leader pointed out, when you graduate and start working, you have to do your own skill assessments in order to advance within the company. This IT executive commented that getting our students in the habit of evaluating their own skill portfolios while they are still undergraduates in the program gets them to practice the type of skill-building assessment and planning they will eventually have to do for their own professional development once they are working. Prior to graduating, the students don't realize they will be doing this for the rest of their careers, or they only realize it to some limited extent.

It's been important for us to have the learning outcomes support the evolution of the curriculum. Also, it's clear that without a mandate from the dean, a very strong follow-up effort, and staff support for implementation, the learning outcomes focus would not have been maintained. We have worked hard to make it a bottom-up implementation effort, but the reality is that if there were not a strong motivation and directive from the top, it just would not have endured nor substantially improved over time as it has.

A second way to set SIS apart from other infocomm-related programs was with our three pillars image (see Figure 8.1). The first pillar signified that we were going to have capability and strength in information technology and applications, in addition to the type of information systems management analysis that most existing business schools were doing. The second pillar signified that we would explore the creation and application of information technology and systems and related management analysis in an industry and organizational context. The third column signified that our students would also have exposure to one or more of the disciplines offered in the other SMU schools. The ability for our students to work across these three columns was an important part of our concept of becoming a business IT professional. For the recruiting of our faculty, especially our research-track faculty, this three pillars image signaled that while we want people with classical research depth and capability in one of the areas shown in the first column, they needed to be willing to learn about the other two columns to some reasonable extent in order to teach within our program, and also in order to pursue research that would help define the distinctiveness of the school.

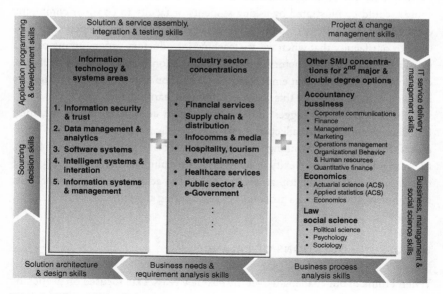

Figure 8.1: Three Pillars of Learning

The three pillars image provided us with a very effective way for interacting with our students during the interview process over the first three years. During the interviews in those initial years, we asked prospective students to select one bulleted item from within each of the three columns and explain how they could combine these three areas into an interesting "package" of study. Interestingly enough, although our potential students had no industry background or experience, especially with respect to the first or second column, they could provide good examples and simple but thoughtful scenarios (e.g., how they might study the management of data in the retail industry and combine that with marketing studies.) As helpful as the use of this three pillars image was in our interviewing in those initial years, its usage might also have misled us, as we assumed that potential students who could verbalize simple combinations of interests and problem-solving across the three pillars would catch on very quickly to designing and applying IT solutions in the often complex way they are used within industry sectors. As noted earlier, it was much more difficult than originally anticipated to prepare the students to do deeper problem solving within the first pillar, and across the first and second pillar, not to mention across all three of the pillars. Even so, this three pillars visualization turned out to be very important. It continues to help us articulate the high-level concept of our curriculum design to our new faculty, and it also helps us to communicate to our students by example what we were aiming for when we say we are trying to create a business IT professional.

Our learning outcomes and our three pillars image were created independently of one another, but in parallel. Given they were both motivated by the same vision and were both artifacts used to articulate that vision, there is commonality in the content, though the content may be expressed in different ways. For example, our learning outcome of integrating business and information technology in a sector context could be illustrated by asking students or faculty to consider combining elements across the three columns in the three pillar image. This helped us to reinforce to our faculty that when we are teaching introductory programming or data management, or an introductory course on information systems, we need to choose examples and exercises that emphasize the integration of business and technology in a sector context because this is one of our stated learning outcomes.

What has made the biggest difference for us in curriculum design includes: (1) developing some intellectual tools (i.e., the learning outcomes and three pillars) from the very beginning; (2) using these tools to guide our specific focus; (3) recognizing the complexity in building a curriculum and creating support for that curriculum from the top and bottom; and (4) acknowledging our changing environment and building a process of experimenting and redesign.

DISCUSSION: QUESTIONS OF BALANCE

When I think of our challenges over the next few years, I am focused on deepening students' experiences and our school's quality, rather than starting new things from scratch. We have many new things coming, but these are strategically planned to enhance overall experience and quality. For example, we are expanding the master's degree program within our school with a new track, but it is not the same as starting from scratch. Also, we are about to launch a "Living Analytics" research center, a collaboration with Carnegie Mellon, that will be a seven-year commitment. It is a major new effort, but it's building on the base of an established research capability and working relationship between our institutions. I view it as quality deepening as opposed to starting anew. Similarly, with our educational programs: They are there, they are running, and they are "quite okay," which is a Singaporean way of saying pretty good. But we see and sense ways to make the bachelor's program richer in terms of being even more of an immersive experience that provides better ways to learn.

Challenges

With all of the pride and satisfaction of what we have accomplished to date, there is this lurking fear I have that we can easily lose that edge, that we can calcify, that we stop adapting and become routinized. Of course, you need stability and routinization to some degree within an institution of higher learning, which are important parts of building a quality base. And yet, placing an emphasis on stability and routinization for its own sake kills the special spirit of a relatively new and evolving organization.

Every organization struggles with the inherent dynamic tensions between stability and continuous innovation. It's a balancing act with no easy answers. Now that we have more happening and more infrastructure and legacy, it gets more complicated to balance the need to constantly evolve against the need for stability. In this next phase of our evolution, we need to focus on the consistency and the persistence of steady change versus the very rapid responsiveness we experienced during our start-up phase. When we took in our first batch of undergraduates in August 2003, a great deal of raw speed and agility were required as we were experimenting to find what would really work.

Now we are steering a bigger and more complex system, yet one that is also much more capable in terms of what it can do and what it can offer across education and research. There are too many interdependencies to just switch it around from one day to the next. Now I spend more time probing and experimenting with how to keep our school in a state of continuous change, but in a more measured and evolutionary type of way. In essence, we are moving from an initial phase where our survival and success were dependent on our ability to create and execute discontinuous change, to a new phase where growth and improvement must be in the form of more evolutionary change. The evolutionary biologist Stephen Jay Gould and colleagues elaborated on the phenomenon of "punctuated equilibrium," special short periods of very rapid change within a much longer and more gradual evolutionary cycle. I refer to this to allow for the contingency that we may well need brief periods of rapid and discontinuous shifts even as we move forward into longer and steadier evolutionary trajectories.

I think the biggest challenge for our school is maintaining this spirit that there is something really special happening here, especially as we eventually transition into the second and third generation of leadership. Years from now, it would be a delight to get confirmation that this sense of a unique and special type of place was still alive and thriving. However, it may go differently in those future years, beyond my administration, than I might have wanted it to go. That is easy to say, but I am sure it will pain me in my heart if and when it happens.

The educational landscape continues to change rapidly in Singapore. The government is bringing up a fourth university, which will attract a lot of good students. This new institution will be in the technology and design arena, so of all the schools at Singapore Management University, the greatest degree of competitive overlap will be with our School of Information Systems. That's a competitive threat that we need to think through and respond to appropriately. That is one of the reasons why, to some extent, I am so anxious to move quickly and steadily to deepen the quality of students' experiences across our educational programs. There are changes I want to accomplish in the near term, perhaps faster than the overall university environment will let us. I am focusing more on the strategy and persistence required to continue executing change efforts to strengthen our curriculum.

Another challenge is getting the presence and name of the school to be more visible. We do good work in the niches where we have chosen to focus, yet it takes persistent effort over extended periods of time to gain solid recognition and acceptance. You can only make so much headway toward legitimate recognition through marketing and external communication campaigns. Realistically, one has to acknowledge that building deep capability and gaining serious recognition require at least 5 to 10 year, and that's only with respect to a few selected "niche" areas across research and education. At the same time, you have to keep making substantial improvements in the quality of education and research content on a yearly basis to stay competitive. There is this duality of simultaneous short-cycle and long-cycle development processes that one has to balance.

After spending so much time and effort as the dean of a start-up institution, transitioning to thinking and behaving in terms of longer-term, multi-year capability development cycles is a big role change. It is more of a steering role, in contrast to the role of earlier years where I had to get right in there with our faculty and staff, lift heavy rocks myself, and push them up a hill to get anything done. A personal challenge for me is in adjusting the way in which I work with people to advance the ever-evolving development blueprint.

Planning for the inevitable leadership succession is, of course, another vexing challenge. I was the first employee of the new school. Everyone knows how hard it is for the founding entrepreneur to learn to let go, and it certainly is a challenge for me. As the founding dean, it is hard to really let go of being the main one to drive new initiatives and oversee regular operations, even while recognizing that unless I gradually let go of this control, the school cannot grow beyond the things that I might have been limited to imagine.

Are any of these challenges easy to overcome? Are there any clear answers for how to do this? The answer to both questions is "no." Is there a lot of trial and error? Of course. A lot of this give-and-take can be worked out through personal relationships and informal conversation, but it will take more than personal relationships for SIS to continue to thrive and grow. There has to be a shared sense of how to frame and think through the choices related to the school's ongoing evolution. Fortunately, several of the administrative staff, practice faculty, and research faculty who came in toward the beginning and in the early start-up phase are still part of our organization. This high degree of continuity has been enormously helpful, providing links and guidance to the next generation of the school's leadership.

Personal Reflections on Learning

The creation and expansion of our School of Information Systems has been a large experiment in change. We created a new type of school in the information technology space within the context of a management-oriented university that was distinctively different from any other information technology school that previously existed in this country.

The development and implementation of SIS has been a massive "realization process." The term "realization" is one that I emphasized when we shaped our undergraduate educational program, because we wanted our students to know how to contribute to the realization of IT solutions. I lived through large realization processes in my professional career prior to coming here. I have always worked on the boundary of technology systems and large organizational systems. But this has certainly been the longest and fullest realization process that I have been through, moving all the way from a single-page letter authorizing the creation of a new info-comm school to where we are now over an eight-year time frame. In some ways, this experience has only reinforced the excitement I have always felt about being part of complex real-world realization processes. My understanding of seeding, cultivating, and growing a "learning-based" organization have grown tremendously.

On an intellectual level, I have really come to appreciate a simple phrase— "capacity building." Now I understand the term, especially as it is a process, not something that occurs overnight. It takes time to build real, meaningful capacity. One of the big mistakes I made in the early phases was to assume we could just put something into place—such as announcing and launching a new program or course—without taking the time to build deep capacity on the part of our faculty, staff, and students. It always seems to take us several years of practice to build the real capacity to execute any new educational or program initiatives. It is incredibly important to appreciate the difference between the earlier iterations of realization, where the motions are happening but the understanding is shallow, versus later iterations built on a real, deep capacity to produce the experience and the outcomes that are desired.

The dilemma, of course, is that anything new and really different has to start from the beginning, before one can have "real capacity" to deliver, and real capacity can only be built through iteration and experience. The important thing, therefore, is to figure out how to position and start a new educational program in such a way that even the earliest iterations, which are bound by inherent limitations in experience and necessarily superficial in many aspects, are still good enough to launch in a reasonably competitive fashion and to get you though the critical initial cycles of sensing, learning and changing that iteratively lead toward real capacity for ongoing, effective delivery of an educational program.

In the very personal realm, the past eight years have been a sacrifice in the sense that I spend a tremendous amount of time absorbed in work while at the office and at home. Large-scale realization efforts such as the development of SIS require a constant and unrelenting push over long periods. Because time is finite, you must spend less time in one area to do more elsewhere; by and large, that is what has happened with my family. We do a lot of family things, but there has always been a tension in terms of work/life balance. A challenge with launching the school, as well as with pursuing my whole career, has been living with the tension caused by the zero-sum tradeoffs across devotion to the professionally related realization efforts at work, and the time needed to sustain quality relationships with my wife and family members.

Work/life balance is a classic and enduring challenge, and naturally these challenges become especially acute in non-steady-state situations such as organizational start-ups. Those in such a situation must try to balance opposing mindsets, one being, "It's not perfect, it's not where we want to be, but it is good enough for now," versus the opposite perspective characterized by Andrew Grove, former CEO of Intel, who described his compulsion and drive as "only the paranoid survive," where there is no "good enough" reprieve that allows you to lighten up for a while, turn down the intensity, and resume pushing ahead later. For others who struggle with this, my personal learning may give some perspective on this subtle balance. One of the recognitions that has emerged from my years of working in start-up and rapidly evolving organizational settings, including this project, is you can never outwork the work. There is no such thing as working harder and being able to clear it all, because in complex and evolving organizational settings, the more you work, the more things there are to follow up on. It is an interesting paradox: The more stuff you get done, the more stuff comes your way to do. Also, the operational aspects of any organizational system, including university programs, practically, if not necessarily, co-produce "issues and problems" along with producing their primary service or product outputs. This seems to be a natural law of large-scale and complex operations, even those with the finest quality-control and improvement practices.

The way to survive a long organizational start-up, and to make progress with respect to work/life balance tensions, is to learn when certain types of things can wait. Even this is a subtle and complex balance. The trick is to selectively wait, which in practice usually means refraining from pressing forward with something you know needs to be done to improve the school, but in a way that does not at all dampen the organization's perceived sense of the leadership's passion and enthusiasm for seeing the environment we have created play itself out to its full potential.

Living outside the United States for nearly 13 years of my professional life has been a learning experience in and of itself. In particular, one of the great things about living in parts of Asia is the cultural comfort with the "yin-yang" world view, meaning that there can be opposing and quite often contradictory forces coexisting at the same time. Accepting that it's okay for this to happen, and perhaps even natural and good, has its own special logic. This type of viewpoint is very helpful for sustaining energy and motivation through a long start-up experience.

CHAPTER 9
Design Issues

The purpose of this chapter is to identify critical design issues that are likely to arise during the establishment of new colleges and universities. Design represents the process of planning and discovery, which leads to the development of a product or system. In our case, the end product is an innovative educational system. This chapter differs from chapters 1 through 6, which are primarily about the OLC concept, differences in OLCs across schools, and the implications of these differences on student expectations, attitudes, and learning outcomes. In chapters 7 and 8 we wanted to present the perspectives of people who run these institutions. Those chapters captured the learning involved in the start-up and operation of new universities, providing practical advice to others seeking to do the same thing. This chapter extends chapters 7 and 8, identifying a number of practical considerations for the designers of new colleges. We will consider questions such as: What are the conditions that indicate whether a designer should or should not engage in the development of a new educational project, what are the relevant decision criteria necessary to build a successful design team and what are some approaches for designing an OLC, curriculum courses, and non-course learning activities? This chapter is organized around these questions.

Typically there will be two principal role-players in the development of a new institution—the owner and the designer. The owner is the person or organization that has the resources to initiate a new institution and holds the final authority on the institution's operation. There could be a third party which is the initial source of the resources. As an example (see chapter 8), the Singapore government commissioned one of its universities to start a new college. The government provided the resources and the university selected the dean of the new college and had final say on the college's operations. In this case, the owner role was the university. The university then selected an independent design team to work with the dean to design the new college. The dean would manage the institution, within the constraints established by the university.

Typically, the design role is different. While the designer contributes heavily to the architecture of the new institution, he or she typically does not run or operate the institution. Although one might think of the designer as a consultant of sorts, this is probably too limited a viewpoint. There are some similarities, but a consultant usually has special knowledge about only one aspect of the institution (e.g., its financial process or admissions process). The designer in our context is involved in the whole planning process for the new system. Also, since it is a start-up, the task is not providing advice about an existing system, but rather how to build a new system. We see the designer as more architect than consultant.

Note that the owner is an important player in the design process. Involving the owner in the design of the institution is a way to create a realistic preview of the challenges and potential outcomes of the new institution. We have been relatively successful in our start-ups when the owner was engaged. In one case, the start-up of a new educational institution in Latin America, we were successful in the design phase but were not able to implement the design, and the project was abandoned. The owner was not engaged except for the decision to set up this institution. In another case, we (the designers) were approached by a larger institution to set up a new college. Because of this, we were able to influence the selection of the dean of this college, which helped result in the selection of someone with high capabilities and strong personal ties with the designers.

MY ROLE IN DESIGN

Most of my life has been spent doing field research in organizations about topics such as change in organizations, teams, and effectiveness. Chapters 1 through 6 reflect that orientation. However, for the last 20 years I have worked on global initiatives for the provost of Carnegie Mellon University (CMU). These projects represent a range of initiatives related to research and, in particular, to education. One set of activities deals with expanding existing Carnegie Mellon programs. For example, we set up a cooperative PhD program between our university and a university in another country. I label this as an existing initiative because it is an extension of an ongoing Carnegie Mellon educational program. Students from the other country still need to meet our PhD requirements in order to get a Carnegie Mellon degree. They pay tuition and other expenses when they are on our campus.

Another set of initiatives are more in the spirit of this book. They represent educational start-ups. There are two kinds. The first kind follows the structure of Colleges A and B. They represent the start-up of new four-year educational institutions in Latin America and Asia. The other start-ups are educational networks—groups of universities that work together to achieve some learning objective.

Typically, these networks focus on serving disadvantaged populations. For example, a network called RELATED (Red Latinoamericana de Tecnologia Educativa), located across five Latin American countries, is focused on using technology-enhanced learning to improve math skills in public schools. RELATED has been sustainable for at least 12 years. Its target population typically has been grades 7 through 9. This concept of a network might at first glance seem to be very different from what happened in Colleges A and B and to bear little relation to the central OLC concept. Our position is that while a network like RELATED is different from a four-year college, it is a start-up in the sense that the network did not exist before, and it will offer a new educational service. In terms of an OLC, there is a learning outcome, improving skills in algebra, and there is a new learning environment, the use of cognitive algebra tutors. Also, to introduce and sustain the technology, a set of system mechanisms needs to be in place to reorient how algebra is taught in the classrooms. The network I have worked with in India, called NPTEL (National Programme on Technology Enhanced Learning), also represents a new type of collaboration of the elite Indian institutions (the IITs and IISc) with a focus on improving the quality of regional engineering colleges. Quality is measured by the number of new and updated courses in the curriculum of the regional colleges. Both of these networks are designed to deal with deficiencies in the educational system in their respective countries and to find new ways to resolve inequality in education.

In all of these examples, there was a design team. I served as the lead coordinator for each of these teams. In most cases, the design team worked on the planning process for at least one year. Three of the four start-ups (i.e., both the networks and one new institution) have continued their work for 7 to 12 years. That is, they continue to be sustainable, a measure of effectiveness, and have continued funding. In this chapter we will focus on design issues in these new start-ups as well as Colleges A and B. The new start-ups include two new colleges (Latin America and Asia) and two new networks (Latin America and India). In the final chapter, we will address redesign issues for both new and existing institutions.

AGREEMENT TO PARTICIPATE IN DESIGN

The agreement to participate in the design process is a fundamental decision. It represents, in most cases, a major investment in both time and resources for multiple people. It is not merely consulting for a day. Most of my design work lasted over a year. The purpose of this section is not to tell anyone whether they and others should participate in a design process, but rather to outline the basic parameters for making this decision. We will explore (1) the nature of the opportunity, (2) the form of the relationship between the designer and owner, (3) financial issues, and (4) how the opportunity fits into some broader strategic plan.

Opportunity

What is the new institution supposed to look like? How will it be different from other institutions of higher education? What are the goals of the person or organization proposing the new school? These are relevant questions for exploring the opportunity and a basic consideration in the decision to go forth with the design phase. We have seen a set of different scenarios. One, I would call a traditional request. In this case, the proposer wants to set up a new institution. The motivation is often a reaction to large public universities (outside the United States) where students can get a degree, but the quality of teaching and learning is questionable. The motivation to set up a new university is noble in that the "owner" wants a better educational setting. The fundamental OLC is the same as the large public universities, but class sizes and attention to students is better. I have observed this phenomenon in Latin America. Another example mirrors a recent request to set up a joint university (between Carnegie Mellon and another institution) in a country where the need or demand for college graduates far exceeds the supply. Again, the model is to create an institution that represents parts of existing universities. There is no focus on creating an entirely new, innovative institution.

Another scenario is where there is a strong motivation to set up a fundamentally different kind of institution, such as the aspirations behind Colleges A and B. Here the question is: If you were going to start from the beginning with no constraints, how would you design an institution of higher education? In many ways, this was the question driving all four start-ups I have mentioned in this chapter, as well as Colleges A and B. The huge advantage for a designer in this case is a relatively open-ended proposal. It is a setting that encourages innovation and creativity.

A third scenario is characterized by more ambiguity. The "owner" or proposer wants to start up a new educational institution, but the "what" and "how" are very unclear. This represents a dilemma for the designer. One can invest time to clarify or at least identify the boundaries of the new institutions. On the other hand, this exploration represents a time commitment that may ultimately lead to a decision (on the part of the designer) not to participate in the start-up.

Of course there are many other scenarios, including various combinations of the above. We have experienced all of the three scenarios. Most of the design work has been in the innovative scenario. We also have rejected proposals to participate.

Relationships

Another relevant dimension is the nature of the relationship between the designer and the owner. The designer is involved in the whole planning process of developing a new educational institution. In many cases someone—an individual or an institution—has approached us to design and build a new institution. They are the owners in the sense that they have final say over funding, who would lead the new institution, and the general parameters of the new institution. The "owner" also could be a designer. For example, in the Latin American educational network, RELATED, I had set up a partnership with a Mexican university (Instituto Tecnológico y de Estudios Superiores de Monterrey, ITESM) and my university. Over time, my counterpart in ITESM decided to extend the basic idea of our relationship, the use of technology-enhanced learning, to other countries in Latin America. We then built a partnership with the Ford Foundation and the process of creating the network began. In this case, the roles of the designer and owner merged. That is, my Mexican counterpart, the Ford Foundation officer, and I served as both the designers and owners of this new network. The Foundation, for example, provided funding, but also was involved in the effort.

Given the complexity and investment in starting up a new institution, the quality of relationships is critical in the decision to participate. The bottom line for me was developing a relationship that featured high commitment to the goals of the proposed institution, high degrees of trust, and good methods for conflict resolution. Basically, I wanted to build a personal, ongoing relationship versus a shorter-term, arm's length transactional relationship. In some cases, as with the Mexican university and CMU, there is a prior relationship that provides the designer some predictability about the interactions that can be expected during the design project. If we are talking about entirely new ties, I would recommend some kind of honeymoon or other process to assess relationships before committing to design.

Some examples might help. As mentioned above in the Latin American network, we started with two universities, ITESM and Carnegie Mellon. Over a 3 to 5 year period, we had built good relationships and wanted to expand. We found another partner in the Mexican office of the Ford Foundation. Our vision was to build a network to improve public education (focusing on grades 7 through 9) by using technology-enhanced learning (TEL). To build the relationships we needed to broaden our original relationship, we visited many Latin American universities. But an hour visit with a rector (i.e., president) does not build a relationship. What followed was a series of high-level workshops on TEL applications that took place over a two-year period. Only rectors were invited. After the third workshop, there was energy within the group of around 30 universities to move toward putting what they had learned about into practice. The workshops served both as an educational intervention and as a selection mechanism. A smaller subset of institutions emerged, which formed the basis of the network. Given the strong support of the rectors, a critical feature in Latin American institutions, we were on our way to building the network. With this support, we were able to develop a highly committed set of representatives who were quite open, shared information (i.e., had developed trust with one another), and were able to find integrative solutions. This network has now been in operation for more than 12 years. I think its success is highly tied to the form of relationships among the members. Note that the network has collected assessment data showing positive changes in public schools we worked with in Latin America. But the key was a year and one half of visits, workshops, and commitment from some key institutions before the network ever got started.

In contrast, we did not build a sustainable relationship in another start-up with which I was involved. We were asked by a CEO of a large multinational firm to design a new management educational institution in his country (also a Latin American country). We had a long-standing, positive relationship with this CEO and his corporation and accepted the proposal to design a new institution. He connected us to a local educational institution, which became our design partner. The design process was collaborative and creative. However, given the nature of the CEO's job, he was not highly involved in the process of designing the school or in the development of ongoing funding sources for the start up and operation of the new institution. As the design process was coming to an end, there was some political turmoil in the country. Given these factors, the project came to a close. Despite a great opportunity, a strong relationship with our design partner, and a creative design, this institution did not become operational. We did not anticipate the effect of the political turmoil or the difficulty of engaging the CEO in the funding part of the project.

Financial

Designing a new educational institution represents a significant investment in time and other costs (e.g., travel, administration). In the four examples discussed above, the time for design lasted at least one year and sometimes longer. The prospective designer should carefully think through the financial parameters. The financial issues can be sorted into several categories. The first category includes the direct (e.g., salary, travel, communication) and indirect costs. In the projects that we were involved in, we generally agreed up front on an amount to cover the direct costs. Note that in the beginning of a project there is a tendency to underestimate direct costs. Covering indirect or overhead costs may or may not be problematic. The major foundations may contribute to indirect costs but not at the U.S. government-approved rates. We did not receive full overhead reimbursements in any of the four start-ups mentioned above. This may be the norm for global projects, but it leads to fewer resources to do other exploratory projects.

The second category concerns funding over time; that is, for the design, start-up, and operating phases. The question is whether there is a commitment to fund only one phase (e.g., design) or all the phases. In the example of setting up the new management school in a Latin American country, the commitment from our CEO partner was to fund the design phase and seek funding for the start-up and operational phases. As the design phase was coming to an end, however, there was political and economic turmoil in the country. While there was $3 to $5 million in the bank, it was not a sufficient amount, given the problems in the country, to successfully launch the new school. This project stopped after the design phase. In the example of the other college start-up in Asia, the government is the primary funder, and we have an eight-year-plus commitment.

The Latin American network provides a different example of how funding sources can change dramatically over time. While the network was initially funded by the Ford Foundation, we knew we could not count on the foundation to continue funding the project forever. So the other partners and I approached the Hewlett Foundation and received further funding. When the Hewlett Foundation funding expired, there was a time where the member universities continued the network activities in the public schools without external funding. More recently, the InterAmerican Development Bank funded new activities to improve math skills through cognitive tutor technology. The key idea in this example is that the designers and owners are merged, and the responsibility for continuous funding during the operational phase rests on network members.

Finally, the other educational network we helped start up is in India. The primary source of funding comes from the central government. This network—NPTEL—recently received a substantial commitment of resources for the next five years.

Some of the lessons on this financial discussion include the following: First, you should be able to cover direct expenses, but be careful about reflecting all the direct costs. Second, it would be desirable to get some contributions to overhead, though as we experienced this can be difficult in an international start-up. Third, you should really think of the phases for design, start-up, and operation *ex ante*. Designing an institution may be an interesting intellectual experience, but if there is no guarantee of a new institution at the end of the day, one might wonder about the feasibility of doing the design phase at all. Fourth, be aware of the potential for spinoff activities that bring funding along with them. In a country where we did set up a new college, unexpected educational opportunities have arisen at the doctoral and master's levels, changing the financial picture in a positive way. While I would not decide to participate in a design project solely based on the hope of these unexpected activities, I would consciously explore them during the design phase. Presence in another location can make a difference.

Strategic Considerations

A fourth issue pertains to how the decision to compete fits into the broader strategic considerations of the designer and his or her organization. In my context, creating global alliances, there may be an overriding strategy about what geographical areas should be stressed. However, even if one were focusing solely on the United States, there might be strategic geographical areas in which to locate, or strategic types of initiatives. For example, Carnegie Mellon has a campus in the Silicon Valley that reflects our strategic interests in both information technology and "edutainment" technology. These should affect the decision to participate in a new design venture.

Some institutions enter into the design and operation of an educational program with a clear understanding that they will lose money, but other strategic considerations outweigh that fact. For example, their fees for tuition may be substantially lower than U.S. fees, but the fact that they want to have a presence in a particular country (e.g., China) dominates their decision making. While I think strategic considerations must be factored into the decision to participate, the nature of the opportunity, form of the relationship, and financial considerations probably dominate the decision. Each of these criteria is dominant in its own right; a proper balance must be struck. Obtaining lots of funding but not creating a challenging opportunity or viable relationship, for instance, will probably not lead to a sustainable relationship.

THE DESIGNER'S JOB

An early design decision is defining the job of the designer. The basic question is what is the designer to contribute, what are the specific activities to be done? This is different from the earlier discussion of relationships mentioned under the decision to participate with the owner, which really focused on how the relationship between owner and designer would unfold: Was there evidence that high levels of commitment, trust, and good conflict resolution mechanisms could be put in place? In one sense, these questions are different from *what* the designer would do, which is our current focus. In reality, there often is a merging between the *how* and *what* questions.

The simplest way to define the designer's job is in terms of the major phases—design, start-up, and operation. In the design phase, activities could range from framing the basic OLC to curriculum, course design, designing learning environments, and so on. During the pre-start-up phase the designer could be involved in selecting faculty, students, and administrators and in all the socialization activities we discussed as being necessary to the development of strong OLCs. In the actual start-up or implementation phase, designers could help launch individual courses or learning environments, assist faculty in the transition, and so on. In the ongoing operational phase, there could be a major emphasis on assessment and redesign as well as regular activities such as hiring new faculty and creating new programs.

A designer might be involved in one, two, or all three of these phases. To illustrate the potential variation, in setting up the network in India the designers were limited to a preliminary design phase. Most of the early design activities centered on building a consensus among multiple institutions about the basic model of the network and its goals. After that, all of the subsequent activities (including detailed design of the network, start-up, and operational matters) have been run by the owners. The designers have continued to communicate with the owners, but we have no involvement in decision making. In contrast, with one of the new colleges we helped set up, the designers have been involved in all aspects of the institution (i.e., design, start-up, operations) for more than 7 years. Basically, most of the faculty for the new college gave their job talks at Carnegie Mellon. We provided a hire-no-hire recommendation, with the owner having a final say. The OLC, curriculum, and specific courses were created by the design team and local participants. Mechanisms to reinforce the learning outcomes and learning environments were created by the design team and local faculty. We had deep involvement through year four and saw a gradual decline in our activities in years five through seven. This was a very different level of designer involvement than with the Indian example.

In discussing what the designer will do, I pointed out the evolving nature of the role. It is hard to define the complete details of the role in the beginning. However, at the meta-level, there should be some initial understanding whether the designer will be involved in design, start up, and operation, only one phase or some combination of phases. The specific activities will naturally evolve over time. The more explicit one can be, and the sooner one can identify defining elements in the role, the better. The other qualification is to revisit the designer's role periodically and see how it may evolve. Flexibility on both sides helps. Also, we have no position on whether it is better to work only on the design phase or all three phases. In the Indian network, we played an important role in the initial design phase, though our ongoing participation was limited; in the end, this network became a viable, effective, and sustainable institution with a multi-year commitment of government funding.

DESIGN TEAM SELECTION

After choosing a designer and defining at least the broad parameters of his or her job, the next step is to choose the members of the design team. We have identified three potential phases that might involve the design team—design, start-up, and operations. Within the design phase we may need expertise ranging from creating an innovative OLC to curriculum and course development to designing socialization, assessment, and redesign mechanisms. The start-up phase puts a high premium on change and implementation, while the operational phase focuses on reinventing the socialization, assessment, and redesign processes. Each of these sets of tasks could involve one or more people with varying skill sets. The challenge, therefore, is to select team members consistent with the task requirements.

As mentioned above, it is important to engage the owner as a member of the design team to the greatest extent feasible. Other needed skills dictate the inclusion of other team members; note that some may be core members of the team throughout the design and implementation of the institution, while others may participate only as needed. If we were to build a new liberal arts college versus an engineering college, for example, a different set of disciplinary-required skills would be needed in each case. Similarly, a new institution has an important administrative component dealing with topics such as recruiting, admissions, finances, student services, and so on. There are few people who can bridge the academic and administrative sides of a new institution. The important idea in selecting design team members, other than the owner, rests on the task demands.

Some examples might sharpen this issue of team composition. In the Latin American educational network, the key universities emerged after more than a year of workshops, which were designed to improve the understanding of technology-enhanced learning. Some of the universities wanted to take the workshop ideas and put them into action; these universities contributed staff to the design team. The representatives of each university were people experienced in technology applied to education, held visible positions in their universities (e.g., CIOs) and had access to their rectors. In the Indian network, where the designers helped in the initial design only, team members included disciplinary people involved in technology-enhanced learning (TEL) activities as well as very senior and internationally known academics at Carnegie Mellon who had strong ties to India. In the design phase for both new colleges we had senior university personnel; some had strong interests in building technology-enhanced learning systems, others had strong administrative experiences, while others reflected the disciplinary diversity of the proposed educational institution.

In addition to the consideration about who to place on the team, a basic idea discussed in the section on deciding to participate holds for the design team, as well: Relationships that are based on respect, trust, and commitment are critical. In most cases, the design team does not exist during the initial decision to participate. But relationships are a major predictor of sustainability. The Latin American network is made up of a design-owner team that has been together for more than 12 years. There is a strong level of trust and respect among members. Conflicts are approached in an integrative way. The fact that there has been stability with the group is an important factor for its sustainability. The new college in Asia enjoys similar orientation and stability among design team members during the design, start up, and initial operation process.

What can we learn from this discussion on selecting the design team? First, including the owner as an integral part of the design team is important. Second, the design team may play a role in one, two, or all three of the phases of a start-up. It is difficult to know at the beginning if you will be involved in all three phases, but giving this some consideration is important because the skills required in each phase will be different. Designing a curriculum or a course is very different from implementing a total system (start-up phase). The basic take away is to designate a core design team but maintain sufficient flexibility to change the team's composition as the task demands change through the phases. Finally, it is important to build relationships among design team members that are based on respect, trust, and commitment, just as with the decision to participate in the first place.

In discussing these three decisions (the decision to participate, the designer's job, and the design team selection), we have treated these as independent decisions. They are obviously interdependent in terms of decision making and time.

An important early design task is to develop the OLC. This means specifying the learning outcomes, learning environments, and system mechanisms for the new educational institution. Key design features of a strong OLC are that it is explicitly stated, it is shared among the relevant constituencies, and the necessary mechanisms (i.e., socialization, assessment, and redesign) are in place to sustain the OLC over time.

Two qualifications are necessary. First, this design process is quite different from exploring the potential opportunities in the decision to participate. In that early process there would be a general understanding of the direction of the new institution, but not the level of detail found in "designing the OLC." Building a shared understanding among relevant constituencies is a very different task.

The second qualification is that the OLC can be quite complex or relatively simple. The OLC in College A had multiple learning outcomes, learning environments, and systems. In the Latin American educational network there is one learning outcome (improving algebra skills) and one major learning environment (i.e., the cognitive tutor). Implementing this technology in public school systems is no trivial task. It requires teachers to teach differently (e.g., two days each week the students work alone on computers, while the teacher serves as a coach). In both of these cases, there is an explicit OLC that needs to be shared. But the complexity of the dimensions and the level of involvement are different than those in College A.

Designing an OLC is a challenging task. Although we have provided some examples here (e.g., Colleges A, B, and C), each OLC is unique and should fit the strategic intent of the institution and the expertise in the design team. Our experience is that this takes considerable time. In the cases of the Latin American and Indian networks, more than a year had passed before the OLC or model of the institution emerged. In the case of the two new colleges, more than a year elapsed before learning outcomes and learning environments emerged.

What is more challenging is ensuring that the OLC is both understood and shared among relevant constituencies. To be shared means each constituency member understands the contract and knows that other relevant constituencies understand and accept the OLC. It is a property of the institution, not just a belief shared by some.

How does this shared understanding come about? Identifying the components of a learning contract is one means. We pointed out how in many cases that task required multiple workshops and meetings taking place over a year or longer. This level of joint work leads to shared understanding among the design team and newly hired faculty. We have argued that strong OLCs in new higher-level institutions come from continuous socialization mechanisms beginning during recruitment (pre-college) to the end of the four years on campus. These mechanisms likely would be created by the design team. The actual enactment of different learning environments targeted to specific outcomes is another facilitator of shared understanding among faculty, students, and staff. The process of assessing whether learning outcomes are improving as a function of the effectiveness of different environments represents another mechanism that can be built into the design process of the OLC. Multiple mechanisms (i.e., socialization, assessment, and redesign) over multiple periods (e.g., initial design, start-up, and operation) seem to be key ingredients for building a strong OLC.

We can look at the components of an OLC to get other insights into its creation. Different institutions will focus on different learning outcomes. Guidance might come from accreditation agencies. Another source is the strategic focus of the new institution. How does it want to differentiate itself from existing institutions? This is a strong theme in chapter 8, regarding the School of Information Systems. It is clear the knowledge and expertise of the design team will shape some of the outcomes.

There are at least three lessons from our experience in addition to the points above. First, it is preferable to identify the major sub-skills within any learning outcome. Identifying "team skills" is too general. We need to know the specific sub-skills. Second, we need to operationalize these measures in order to determine if there has been any change in the desired outcomes. This, of course, would drive the redesign mechanism. Third, we need to be sure the outcomes are linked to learning environments. For example, College B selected global awareness as an outcome but there were no formal learning experiences to enhance this outcome.

Similarly, exploring learning environments would be a key part of the OLC design process. We all are familiar with a few, such as lecture, discussion, and labs. But there are many others, such as peer teaching, the studio, and a variety of non-course learning experiences. One challenge for both the design team and the relevant constituencies is to expand their knowledge of different environments. One can learn about these by reading, though a more powerful source might be seeing them in action. For example, the studio is an environment used in architecture education. However, it has been extended to other disciplines such as physics and chemistry (Wilson, 2001). In architecture, we can visualize students building models. But how does it work in physics? We think seeing multiple learning environments can open new windows into applying those environments in various disciplines.

Underlying our knowledge about learning environments is our experience and belief about learning. Something that was not done in Colleges A or B or in any of the four institutions I have been involved with is to turn to the learning literature. What do we know? How does it fit in with our strategic intents? What are the relevant meta-analyses? How can we design with evidence from this literature? So far this has been a lost opportunity.

The design team also needs to build the system components. In many ways, they drive the shared understanding and the viability of the new system over time. We already have discussed the need for multiple socialization mechanisms over time. Good assessment over time is a necessary condition for redesign. Without redesign, it is unlikely the OLC will be shared. It is highly likely that the initial design will be changed. Over time, learning environments will require redesign. Redesign will be the basis of sustainability and effectiveness.

College A has employed various mechanisms such as curriculum reviews, retreats with faculty, and student involvement to assess and redesign the system. College B has used some IT systems to assess changes in learning outcomes and has asked students to be involved in the redesign of courses. The Latin American network has used multiple methods (e.g., surveys, interviews, case studies) to assess its effectiveness and to stimulate redesign. The Indian network has not done extensive assessment, at least in the formal sense of assessment and redesign. It has informally evolved and has convinced the government to continue its funding. The new college start-up in Asia has used many of the mechanisms discussed above. Again, early in the design phase, one needs to build a strong OLC. "Strong" means it is explicit, shared, and supported by multiple socialization, assessment, and redesign mechanisms. One can create this model from considering the three specific elements of the OLC. We have suggested some sources or procedures to accomplish this.

DESIGNING THE CURRICULUM

Once the OLC is in place, another design team task is to sketch out the curriculum. The identified learning outcomes should drive the curriculum design. During the four years of learning experiences, you want to see changes in these outcomes. One ingredient is the selection of learning environments. These environments have different impacts on the outcomes. For example, project-based team projects versus a lecture will have a stronger effect on shaping team skills. Or, a laboratory setting is a more powerful environment to create skills in designing and analyzing experiments. A useful design exercise is to create a matrix of learning environments and learning outcomes, and draw the strong ties between these two components. That is, which environments create the greatest changes in which learning outcomes. Another ingredient is the specific courses. It is the combination of learning environments integrated into courses that will lead to changes in learning outcomes. The matrix idea mentioned earlier can be used to match courses and outcomes. There would be a matrix for each of the four years. Table 1.1 illustrates a matrix for a new educational institution in Latin America. It includes outcomes relevant for a management school and corresponding courses plus environments for two quarters. A review of this particular matrix shows multiple learning environments for a specific outcome and different combinations of courses and environments for different outcomes.

The matrices help *ex ante* by identifying missing opportunities. We mentioned in College B they had selected global awareness as an educational outcome. But an analysis during the design phase showed no educational interventions in the global awareness space. That finding generated reflective discussion and some solutions.

An important issue is whether to assess at the course or a broader level. Assessing at the course level will depend on what outcomes are relevant for that specific course. If there are multiple courses or educational interventions targeted to a particular outcome, which is our basic argument, one should design an assessment of learning outcomes at a cross-course level. All of these are design team activities.

DESIGNING COURSES

Designing courses is a more specific task than the broad development of a curriculum. It requires defining a syllabus, readings, problem sets, etc., all of which are guided by the learning outcomes and incorporate the appropriate learning environments. My interest is not to talk about the specifics of a particular course but to identify some overarching issues to consider when designing courses generally.

First, as this is a more specific task, the design team may provide guidance but a number of other options are available. New faculty represent a key source of course design. Part of the recruitment process is providing a realistic preview of the OLC and expectations about the form that learning will take in the new school. Each new faculty member is therefore a source of new courses following the OLC concept. Another way to create courses is from institutions represented on the design team. Members of the team, with permission from their institutions, could provide existing course materials to use as the basis for courses at the new institution. Another source is having PhD candidates or faculty who are familiar with a particular course present that course in the new institution and mentor a new faculty member to take it over. A fourth option is to have faculty members from the new institution come to an institution represented by a design team member and sit in a course both for content and teaching perspectives. All these options need to reflect the explicit OLC of the new institution.

Throughout this book, we have discussed the importance of assessment and redesign. This typically happens at formal periods such as the end of a semester or academic year. For brand new start-ups, however, we recommend real-time monitoring for all courses in year one and possibly year two. A new institution is very vulnerable. It does not have a stable reputation; major mistakes can substantially affect the school's initial reputation and ability to attract new students. From our observation, these mistakes will often be defined in terms of poor courses or course "failures" such as those experienced in College B. Basically, one needs an early warning system to identify troubled courses and manage a resolution of the problem.

DESIGNING NON-COURSE EXPERIENCES

An important part of learning occurs outside the classroom in other formal or informal activities. The design team should be involved in at least the conceptualization of these activities. The actual creation of these non-course learning experiences would be done by others (faculty, staff) with input from the students. As with other elements of the learning environment, the OLC guides the creation of these activities.

Student organizations represent settings for practicing leadership, team, and communication skills. Institutions valuing community service create venues for students to practice those activities. These represent non-course activities found in most schools, but more can be done. In Colleges A and B as well as some of the institutions where I have served as a designer, we find students much more involved in the governance of the college and redesigning the curriculum and courses. These activities can enhance decision-making and communication skills, at the same time creating higher levels of involvement and identification with the institution. There have been other non-course innovations. College A has formal presentations at the end of the academic year for faculty and company personnel. The presentations are targeted to specific learning outcomes. Everyone participates in these activities. College B built an IT system and organization to focus on learning outcomes. The IT system included a self-rating system for all the outcomes. Basically, students could assess their own development. But IT systems often do not work by themselves. So with a faculty leader, the college identified a set of learning outcome "champions." Each champion had responsibility for 10 other students. Their job was to encourage other students to use the IT system and focus attention on their development of the learning outcome. This is clearly a non-course option to create changes in learning. There are many possible examples. The role of the design team is to legitimize non-course learning and to develop creative options for these types of activities.

DISCUSSION

The process of creating a new educational institution features a number of interdependent decisions. The basic decision of whether to get involved in the design of a new institution is clearly fundamental. Participating in the design is a potentially long-term commitment that requires time and resources. A set of dimensions (e.g., financial, strategic) were laid out to facilitate this decision. In most cases, the designer's role is not solely in the design phase. Often, to really implement the new design of an institution, participation in the start-up and operational phases also is necessary. What is important is to recognize the three phases and initially negotiate what phases you can work on. At the same time, one must remember this is a dynamic situation; how long one participates, and in what manner, may change over time.

The composition of the design team also is critical. One challenge is that the basic task through design, start-up, and operational phases is changing. To some extent, that means the composition of the team will change. The dilemma on one hand is that you need to change the team composition over time and, simultaneously, you need to build strong personal ties among the team members. Our approach has been to have a stable core team and add people to the team as needed. The design of the OLC, curriculum, courses, and non-course activities are guided by the central concepts in this book on learning outcomes, learning environments, and system mechanisms.

This chapter has been oriented toward the creation of new educational institutions, but the basic design processes would be the same for an existing institution that wanted to redesign an existing college or program. One still needs to consider the decision to participate, the designer's role, the design team composition and so on. Clearly, one needs to understand the constraints provided by the existing institution, which will place limits on the design. However, the processes we discussed would be much the same for a new start-up or a redesign.

In writing this chapter, I wondered whether the design of educational systems (rather than a tangible product) leads to a different perspective on design. To explore this, I talked to designers who were both professors and practitioners. It seems many of the early processes are similar for designing an educational system or a new product. You still have to do an assessment of whether to participate. You need to form a relationship with the owner or client that will help sharpen what you are going to do and why. Your initial design role should be specified, but both the designer and client need to recognize that the role will evolve over time. The basic considerations regarding the composition of the team are important for both kinds of design efforts. Obviously, the latter categories in this chapter (designing the OLC, curriculum, etc.) are unique to educational systems.

What are some lessons that our design team learned? First, it is very difficult to predict how the process will really unfold. The chapter provides an organized, linear way to think about the design process, but it rarely works that way. There are multiple iterations and obstacles, all embedded in uncertainty. As a participant in this dynamic process, you need all your sensors to be fine-tuned and to maintain a strong orientation toward flexibility. We are talking about designing new educational systems, which inherently have lots of uncertainty. The designers may need to demonstrate this flexibility over a long time period.

This suggests the importance of instilling a process to periodically assess how the design process is going in real time, receive feedback, and identify changes that might make the project better. Just as continuous assessment and redesign is necessary with the OLC, so, too, is it needed when designing a new institution. For example, in our start-up institution in Latin America, funding turned out to be a key issue. Although we participated in the effort to secure funding for the implementation and operation of the institution, it was really the responsibility of the owner, the CEO, to obtain the necessary ongoing funding. Our focus was on the educational side, not primarily acquiring funds. Probably more importantly, we were not measuring the timelines for the college to start up and obtain funds. If we had engaged in assessment, feedback, and redesign in our own design process, we might have learned earlier about whether we would be able to launch this institution. Another example is that our partner in the educational design process also required funding from some of the same sources as the new proposed school. Although he made presentations on behalf of the new college, he was in a conflict of interest position. Although others in the design team knew about this, there was no formal assessment of the problem or redesign of our process in an attempt to address the issue.

Another issue is to be more aware of context, meaning the institutions and environment outside of your design project that may influence your work. Continuing the example of the new college in Latin America, when the design team started there was no discussion of the national election that would occur toward the end of the design process. Later on, this election proved to be full of conflict, which created political turmoil within the country. Businesses were very apprehensive about the results of the election, and capital moved out of the country. This clearly affected the funding prospects for the proposed new college. A different and slightly more extreme example of context is the following: We had been involved for more than six years in the initiation of an Arab-Jewish leadership program in Israel focused on collaboration and social change. During this time period there have been several wars. When these events have occurred, although they are independent of our project both in terms of content and geographical location, they have stopped our program in its tracks. The basic idea is although *ex post* we acknowledge the role of external forces, most of the time they are not explicit in the design process. We did not pay attention to the context.

The goal of this chapter was to outline some of the critical design decisions in setting up a new educational institution. We tried to delineate the major decisions and share some lessons learned. Now we move to the final chapter to review the basic findings about the OLC and its implications for the future of higher education.

CHAPTER 10
Conclusion and Future Issues

This final chapter examines the development and sustainability of strong organizational learning contracts. We first discuss our findings in studying the OLCs in three institutions, including two start-up institutions and one well-established one. Next, we turn to the implications of OLCs for people managing new start-ups as well as existing educational institutions. We then discuss some key issues raised throughout the book, and finally we offer some thoughts for administrators of both new and existing institutions hoping to create OLCs, especially as it relates to the potentially substantial changes in approach and attitude necessary within faculty, staff, students, and alumni to successfully establish a strong contract.

WHAT WE HAVE LEARNED

We have presented a number of findings regarding the organizational learning contract, this book's core construct. We have explored its dimensionality, how to operationalize it, and, most importantly, its impact on effectiveness indicators for both students and their institutions. Strong OLCs create expanded student learning, positive attitudes about that learning, and strong identification with the institution. An institution with a strong OLC is able to attract very high-quality students and faculty, differentiate itself from other institutions, and build a loyal set of alumni. In institutions with weak OLCs, students are less aware about what they should learn, exhibit less transfer of learning, and are less committed to the institution.

Components of the OLC

The OLC has three central elements—learning outcomes, learning environments, and system components. Specifying learning outcomes, or what students are supposed to learn, is essential for focusing the students' and faculty's attention on what is to be learned. Targeted outcomes provide a critical frame to guide the design of a new school or the redesign of an existing institution. One cannot build a contract without stating the outcomes, and being as specific as possible with the outcomes is essential. For example, "Learning how to learn" on your own or after college is stated by the institutions in our sample, as well as many others, as a learning outcome. Although this is an important skill to acquire, we pointed out that it is too general. We need to look at sub-skills within the broad category of learning how to learn (e.g., doing high-quality and efficient information searches) and develop operational measures of these sub-skills. The key processes are to assess learning on the sub-skills, provide feedback, and, as needed, redesign the learning environment to enhance the development of these skills.

The learning environments deal with how students learn. In this study, the new institutions we examined used a variety of different environments. Their focus tended toward learning environments that actively engaged students in learning (e.g., project work) as opposed to more traditional passive modes, such as the lecture. The objective is to facilitate learning by using distinctive yet complementary learning environments. For example, improvements in communication skills can be enhanced by project work, learning on your own, peer teaching, mentoring, and the studio. The key assumption is that employing an array of appropriate learning environments enhances the acquisition of skills as opposed to working with just one learning method.

The system component of the OLC also is inherent in the contract. Without effective mechanisms to back it up, the contract is merely words. For the contract to "take" among students, faculty, and staff, there need to be multiple socialization mechanisms, measurement systems to assess whether the contract is being enacted, and some feedback and redesign mechanisms. All of these mechanisms need to be in effect for the development of a fully operational contract that can evolve as needed over time. Creating socialization mechanisms without any redesign mechanism, for example, will lead to failure.

In a strong OLC, there is a shared understanding about what, how, when, and where learning will occur. The college is the unit of analysis, and its faculty, students, and administrators/staff are parties to the agreement. Explicit in the OLC is that the contract expectations come from the college rather than from other institutions such as family, high school, etc. We found that strong OLCs, such as those exhibited in the newer institutions we studied, were created by the institutions rather than general socialization sources (e.g., peers). Also, the contract expectations were more differentiated and consistent over time in the newer institutions.

Findings and Impacts of the OLC

Our data reflected institutional differences among the colleges in our sample. Some of the differences reflected differences in the strength of the institutions' respective OLCs.

For example, Colleges A and B were focused more on active learning environments (e.g., project teams) than the traditional College C. At the same time, the quality of professors, close contact with professors, and the overall quality of teaching was higher at College A than the other two. We noted that College A was a stand-alone institution, while students in College B took many courses outside of their college and experienced different learning approaches. College A's learning experiences also were more homogenous across students. In terms of personal models of learning (chapter 5), there were parallels between Colleges A and B in their emphasis on learning from others from freshman year on. During the first two years in College C, students are exposed to a lecture environment that discourages learning from others. College A, in terms of the strategic part of their personal model of learning, has a more complex mapping compared to Colleges B or C. Using a variety of indicators, the strongest OLC (i.e., more explicit, more dimensions) was in College A, then College B, and then College C.

We explored the impacts of different OLCs by investigating changes in inputs, processes, and outcomes at the three colleges. All three were able to attract high-quality students over time. This, of course, was more challenging for Colleges A and B because they were new. Any significant failures in the early years would have made subsequent recruitment harder. College C, which is well-established and highly ranked, also is able to attract good students due in part to its reputation. Quality of students remained high over multiple years for all three institutions. We also looked at the quality of faculty as an input. All three colleges attracted good faculty over time. The absolute scores for A and C are somewhat higher than B. In terms of overall indicators (e.g., high-quality, challenging environment) or more specific indicators (e.g., closeness with faculty), College A dominates. In terms of other process indicators such as student involvement in design of the institution, College A and College B were the strongest initially, but over time as the institution stabilized, involvement in design of the college dropped. This is predictable given the initial activity surrounding a start-up, but is something for the colleges to be aware of and monitor given that they use student involvement in curriculum development as a selling point.

In terms of final outcomes, College A demonstrates stronger transfer of learning to a work setting. College B reports more changes in learning outcomes over time (Chapter 5). In terms of job placement or retention rates, there were no notable differences among institutions or over time. In terms of overall rating of the institution, College A's students reported the strongest level of institutional identification.

Each institution will have its own OLC that is unique to its leaders, goals, culture, and history. In terms of content, there is no prescription in this book for the "best" OLC. There is no ideal number of learning outcomes. In some institutions, such as traditional institutions trying to change their OLC, the initial focus may be on one outcome. In other cases, the upper limit may be determined by what people can typically remember (e.g., 6 ± 2). Similarly, there is no optimal number or mix of learning environments. We do know that multiple learning environments are needed to develop any learning outcome in a lasting way.

Our focus has been on building the three elements of the contract. All three elements should reflect the context of an institution. They all need to be explicitly stated. Multiple forms of socialization are necessary to build an explicit shared understanding, and forms of assessment and redesign will be necessary for sustainable growth.

A final word about context. Although the colleges we studied offer courses in the same disciplinary area, these three institutions have very different organizational contexts. College A is a stand-alone institution. Although it has ties to other institutions, the primary learning experiences are on campus. This is in contrast to College B, which sits within a university. Students take courses within the college, but also within other parts of the university. Although there is a strong OLC in College B, its efforts are diluted by these other learning experiences. Also, in this college's start-up phase, there were a few courses that failed, which is not uncommon in new institutions (though College A did not have the same experience). These failures were very visible to the students, faculty, and staff at College B and affected the opinions that some had of the college. College C, the more traditional institution, is a well-established institution. College C was good at certain things. It attracted high-quality students. This college also had a good record at student job placement, which was acknowledged by the students. This is not surprising, given their high reputation and many years of placement experience. It is the nature of the OLCs in these institutions, plus their context, which accounts for differences and similarities in the data.

ISSUES

In chapter 2, we outlined a number of issues whose resolution is integral to building OLCs. One topic was defining the appropriate level of analysis (e.g., college, university) for the "contract." The basic goal is to build a shared understanding about the specific OLC. This task is complicated by the fact that there are multiple groups—students, faculty, administration, and staff—and players within each of those groups. Without a shared understanding among and within the groups, however, the OLC cannot come into being or be sustained over time. Shared understanding does not mean people have 100 percent identical expectations about, say, learning outcomes, but it does mean the students and faculty could name most of the outcomes in the OLC and discuss the learning environments that exist to ensure those outcomes are learned. There would be a variety of socialization mechanisms before and during college, reinforcing these learning outcomes as part of the college's contract. If the students know the outcomes but the professors do not enact them, nothing will happen. To assert these learning outcomes are *shared* is to say that they are *understood*. Shared meaning does not imply necessarily using the same language, listing outcomes in the same order, or even knowing all the expected outcomes. Table 4.7 illustrates that the outcomes are shared more in College A than in Colleges B and C.

Given the complexity of building a shared understanding among the different players, we argued for the OLC at the college versus university level. A driving factor was the likelihood of greater homogeneity within a science college than across, say, the science, fine arts, and liberal arts colleges. Homogeneity refers to both the similarity of what is to be learned and the learning environments used. Designing an experiment or doing quantitative analysis, for example, are skills more likely to be developed in a science college than a fine arts college. Even if the OLC is most appropriately developed at the college level, it does not mean that each college's OLC should be an island unto itself. Some university-wide outcomes can be included in the OLC. For example, teaching students good communication or presentation skills seems to be important whether you are in a science, liberal arts, or fine arts college. However, given the complexity of building a shared understanding among multiple roles and people, our primary focus is at the college level.

Another issue raised was generalizability. To build comparability within our sample, we chose colleges operating in the same discipline and placing students in comparable jobs or graduate schools. However, the basic ideas of the OLC are generalizable to different disciplines. Of course, the outcomes will be different (e.g., learning the experimental method in a science college) as would be the learning environments (e.g., learning in the lab in a science college). As long as the three central components—learning outcomes, learning environments, and system mechanisms—are in place, the OLC should be applicable to different disciplines. Of course, the content of the OLC needs to be adapted to the specific discipline.

Although the OLC is generalizable to different disciplines, it is not generalizable to different forms of higher education. We are focusing on a face-to-face, multiple-year, full-involvement institution. Colleges running primarily via distributed technology or with a lot of part-time students would have difficulty building a strong OLC environment. Throughout this book we have emphasized the importance of building a shared understanding of the OLC components across all the relevant constituencies. This is more viable when all the players are in the same place and more deeply involved in the institution over time.

Although we have focused on undergraduate education, we think the OLC could be helpful in graduate education, particularly if it is a full-time, face-to-face experience. It might be easier to implement in full-time professional master's programs, which have a more structured set of courses set in a specific college. The challenge of defining learning outcomes, learning environments, and system components would be the same.

NEW ISSUES—CREATING CHANGE

The fundamental challenge for utilizing the organizational learning contract is the issue of creating effective organizational change. At this point, the reader should have a good understanding of the OLC, some ways to measure it, and the fact that we can explain OLC differences and impacts across institutions. But the critical challenge is whether it can be successfully introduced and sustained. This meta-change issue can be separated into sub-issues including:

- Motivating the need for OLC
- Creating an effective design/planning phase
- Implementing an OLC
- Sustaining an OLC

Our view is that the first and last issues pose the greatest challenge. Below, we examine these issues in the context of a new and an existing institution.

Motivating the Need for an OLC

Colleges and universities are slow-moving institutions. They are not fast moving or agile. Although there are many forces for change such as economic competition (virtual universities), changing composition of the college population, emergence of high-quality international universities, and so on, there are many forces for the status quo. These forces come in the form of regulation at the federal and state levels, the role of accrediting agencies, faculty members more interested in research than education, and so on. We do not want to suggest that colleges and universities do not change at all. But moving to a strong OLC environment represents a major change. Whether new or existing universities will engage in such a change is problematic. One goal in this chapter is to provide a realistic preview of whether this is possible and how. In new institutions, at least, the opportunity to launch an OLC environment is there. The leaders of this effort have a clean slate. They are asking, "If we were to start from the beginning, how would we design the educational environment for a college or university?" But having the opportunity and capitalizing on it are two different things. There are a number of examples where new colleges with private financial support have come into being as a reaction to large, traditional institutions. However, these new institutions were not substantially different from the traditional college with the exception of smaller class sizes and perhaps better facilities. The point being, starting from the beginning has some inherent advantages, but it does not necessarily lead to new, innovative educational environments or institutions with clear OLCs.

The new institution has the opportunity. There is less baggage from prior practices, institutions, agreements, and so on. But there needs to be more. In the case of a start-up, motivated leaders need to carefully choose other administrators, faculty and even students with the idea of developing an OLC in mind. In chapter 7, we learned the Olin School was created especially to find new forms of engineering education. As the initial leaders of this school were brought in, they were able to select administrators who wanted to be part of a new start-up. The vision of these initial leaders helped facilitate the selection of faculty with strong motivation to build a new form of education. The faculty selection ratio was 1,500 applicants to eight positions. From such a pool of applicants, it should not be hard to find eight motivated faculty members with new ideas about higher education. The selection of students had a similar effect. A small group was asked to come for a year to help design a new school without earning any credit. Again, the kind of student who would select this option versus going to a good traditional school demonstrates a strong motivational commitment. In the School of Information Systems (Chapter 8), there also was a strong force to be part of a new institution. In addition, SIS was trying to create a new type of IT professional. These factors similarly aided in the selection of faculty and students who wanted to be part of a new institution. This selection advantage in start-ups represents a powerful set of motivated resources to launch a new college.

In existing institutions, motivating the need for an OLC environment is more difficult. There is an existing curriculum, courses, and teaching experiences; both professors and students have reached some equilibrium. In most cases, there is not a major crisis or a visible demand for change. Also, although there are regular reviews of curricula, accreditation visits or reviews of a college, most of these do not examine in detail the fundamental educational experience. Also, these reviews typically evaluate schools on fairly traditional dimensions. They do not delve into the nature of the OLC or its components.

In an existing school, there are few opportunities for change or redesign. This does not mean that the OLC concept is not applicable to existing institutions. However, the motivation to redesign an existing college differs from the new institution. First, we need someone inside the institution who has a vision about new forms of education and some source of formal power. Ideally, that leader would recruit a small coalition of respected faculty, administrators, and students who might help. Second, creating a total OLC transformation seems very unlikely in an existing institution. Our view is to start with one key outcome. The selection of the outcome is important. It should be something that would be endorsed by all faculty, administrators, and students, whether one is in chemistry, engineering, or English literature. Selecting one outcome that is accepted makes the change problem more manageable. Demonstrating the successful implementation of one outcome would lead the way to others.

Another focused approach to change in an existing institution would examine the difference between the school's stated expectations and actual behaviors. A dean from a college once told me all faculty, students, and administrators knew the eight critical learning outcomes required by their college. Nonetheless, a majority of students knew none or only one or two of these learning outcomes. That gap in shared understanding is another stimulus for motivating change. However, when I presented data counter to the expectations, the dean argued the data collection was not accurate. Although this example seems counter to the suggestion of collecting data on differences between expectations and actual behavior, the general idea is still viable. If, in this case, the dean and his staff had collected the data, the reaction might have been different. He would have "owned" the data and it would have been harder to dismiss. This example shows that change can be difficult to motivate from outside the institution. Despite the reaction I got from this particular dean, presenting data on expectations and actual behavior—especially when those data have been collected by one or more people from within the organizations—can motivate change.

Another alternative is to introduce the OLC into a new program such as an honors college or a new educational program. This new setting produces an opportunity for reflection and change without the same kind of resistance that one might encounter from entrenched faculty or administrators in an existing college setting.

Creating an Effective Design-planning Phase

A second change challenge is to manage an effective design phase. This is true for new or traditional institutions. In a new institution, one would build a total OLC from the ground up, while in the traditional institution the focus may be targeted to one outcome or to gaps between expectations (by administrators) and reality, what students and/or faculty understand. Although the scope of design may be broader in the new institutions, the same difficulties can be encountered.

In chapter 9, we outlined some issues from the designer's point of view. These included considering the criteria (financial, strategic forms of relationships) for engaging in a start-up, the nature or composition of the design team, the role for design team involvement (i.e., in design-planning, implementation, sustainability) and so on. Other considerations are pertinent to the design phase in start-up institutions as well as in existing institutions that want to develop or redesign an OLC. First, it is important to identify the relevant constituencies. In this book, we primarily focus on students, faculty, staff, and administrators, but there are others. Alumni, in particular, are an important group. In the newer institutions they are a source of information, which is important in recruiting. In an existing institution they could tell a new story about the college and the emerging OLC. If outcomes such as life-long learning are part of the change effort, involving alumni either as students or teachers is another way to reinforce this outcome and strengthen the relationship with outside constituencies. Other constituencies exist beyond alumni, however. For new and existing institutions, building and maintaining ties with industry leaders facilitates job placement, another benefit of broadening the constituencies. In new start-ups this tie is critical, and in existing institutions these relationships provide an opportunity to talk about proposed critical changes in the institutions' OLCs. Providing class projects or teaching cases is another benefit of engaging industry counterparts in the institution. The traditional functions of alumni giving or firms providing internships or jobs are always there. Engaging them in the OLC—in the life and change of the institution—has benefits, as well.

Another issue in the design phase is matching the social and technical systems of an institution—in other words, does the physical environment facilitate the learning environment? A well-developed literature (cf. Emery & Trist, 1969) discusses the importance of matching these systems. A lesson from this research is that one should not try to optimize on one of the systems but rather think about how both systems need to work together. In chapter 7, Rick Miller provided a wonderful discussion of the dilemma of linking the technological system with the social learning system in a new institution. Olin's administrators had to start building classrooms and offices (the technological system) before they had designed the learning environments (the social system). The physical setting could have served to either constrain or enhance the learning system, but it was difficult to connect the systems because these two activities were being initiated at different times. Note that this issue of social versus technical systems is not unique to start-ups. If the redesigners of existing institutions want to change the model of learning to more group work, studios, peer teaching, etc., this needs a compatible physical environment (e.g., space, computers, specialty equipment), and existing buildings might not support these new modes of learning.

A different perspective on matching social and technical systems appears in chapter 8. In chapter 8, Steve Miller talked about using physical space (i.e., the building) in a different way. By physically isolating his school in a temporary building and then having his own building in the current setting, he was able to create an environment where students could develop the identity of SIS and collaboratively build a unique culture.

Implementation

The third critical change issue is putting the model created in the design phase into action. There is an extensive literature on implementation (cf. Goodman, 2001). Many of the existing reports are about *failures* and how to learn from these experiences. In this section we highlight some processes critical to a *successful* implementation of an OLC. It is important to distinguish implementation from sustainability. In our context, implementation deals with taking the OLC design and putting it into practice. Sustainability deals with maintaining the basic features of the OLC over time. These are two distinct processes. A successful implementation is necessary before sustainability can take place.

The challenges in new and existing institutions are fundamentally different. In new institutions, initially, there is a powerful selection effect. That is, the opportunity to be involved in the design and start-up of a new institution of higher education is very attractive to many people. In College A and College B, we saw this for both faculty and students. In its recruitment, both colleges were very explicit that there were opportunities to create new forms of higher education and the students and faculty who joined the institution would be involved in the creation process.

The motivation and commitment to the design and implementation processes were in place due to the selection process. At the same time there were obstacles and risks. These were start-up schools with no track records. It would have been easy to make mistakes in curriculum, learning environments or the implementation of a specific course. These consequences would have offset the benefits of selecting a highly committed team. As we have said, new start-ups have no reputation and no evidence they can produce a better product. Early failures would be very disruptive. In year two and after, student or faculty applicants would like to know about the initial results. We mentioned that College B had a few courses that failed. This was widely discussed and had a negative effect on students in our sample and probably on future applicants. So in the start-ups we have the benefits of a selection effect, offset by initial risks of failure.

In an existing institution, one has a different problem. The organization has reached some equilibrium—there are rehearsed teaching practices that seem appropriate; they work. Now there is an effort to create or change the OLC. There is bound to be resistance to change that will impede the implementation. We view the words "resistance to change" in neutral terms, not in evaluative terms. Resistance naturally occurs because (cf. Goodman, 2001):

- Gains and losses are subjectively understood
- Losses are more powerful than gains are good
- With change, losses often precede gains
- Losses affect other dimensions such as commitment, learning, and motivation

One implication is that implementation may be somewhat easier in new institutions, where there are not entrenched processes, assuming there are no significant failures. Implementation obstacles will be stronger in existing institutions. The only offset for these institutions will be to focus on a smaller set of changes and to start with changes that are attractive to the majority of the constituencies.

Given this characterization of start-ups and traditional institutions, it is a very real challenge to successfully implement a new or redesigned OLC. There are four key processes, which mirror processes we have discussed elsewhere:

- Socialization
- Commitment
- Motivation
- Redesign

Throughout this book, we have talked about the importance of socialization. Creating a shared understanding among multiple constituencies is a non-trivial task. Our argument is that we need multiple socialization mechanisms over different time periods. For the new institutions we begin before students, faculty, or staff enter the institution. In an existing institution, socialization can begin when the change in OLC is first conceptualized. The idea of building multiple socialization mechanisms is very important. It could be in recruiting materials, observing an OLC in a different institution, looking at data about your own institution, and so on. The other principle is that socialization must continue over time. Chapters 7 and 8 both discuss institutions that deployed different socialization interventions at different times.

Commitment means psychologically attaching yourself to a new OLC. This, too, is easier done in start-ups. The selection advantage we discussed previously draws people voluntarily and publicly into the implementation process. Evoking commitment in an existing institution is more difficult. One would probably have to identify a small set of committed faculty members and use them as a model for others. In my own university, I have observed very eminent faculty members leading a change effort. Their prestige and perseverance drew others into their change effort.

Creating motivational value for the participants is another key process. Building a new kind of educational institution has both intrinsic and extrinsic value. However, as we have noted, people are generally more sensitive to losses than they are to gains. In many change efforts, losses tend to come earlier. Therefore, strong initial commitment can be an offset to early losses. At the same time, there need to be rewards (e.g., involvement in building a new institution, recognition), which motivate all the participants engaged in the implementation process.

Finally, as we have stated, no change will work without an effective feedback and redesign mechanism. Any effort to implement change will most likely manifest gaps between what the implementers desire and what actually occurs. The socialization process is supposed to create knowledge about the learning outcomes and learning environments, but students might have little understanding about learning outcomes. Faculty members may not use the new proposed learning environments. A new course might get started, but the initial results are poor. These situations are very detrimental to creating a new OLC. In this context we need a good measurement system to capture the discrepancies, and some organizational mechanism to remedy the situation. As we have noted, failures in the initial years can be very harmful. Still, there will potentially be failures in any change implementation process. The basic idea is that there needs to be sensitive, real-time measurement of the changes as they are implemented and a redesign mechanism to put any wayward changes back on track. This idea of a continuous cycle of experimenting, testing, and redesign is a persistent theme in chapter 8. This is true for the new start-up or an existing institution moving toward a new learning contract.

Sustainability

A fourth change challenge is institutional sustainability of any change effort. The implementation question is how to translate concepts into actionable behavior. The second question is the sustainability or institutionalization of change over time.

Both are critical elements in any change strategy. There is probably more literature on implementation.

The sustainability challenge is important for both new and existing institutions. New institutions often start out with a highly committed group of people who want to build a new institution. Since these institutions are start-ups, they are more at risk of failure in the form of not meeting expectations or creating unsuccessful courses, which could affect sustainability in early years. In addition, over time they become more regularized institutions. The energy that was dominant in the beginning may start to subside in the mid-term. We pointed out there is much inertia in existing institutions and implementing new OLCs is a very difficult undertaking. If an OLC is successfully implemented, many of the forces against changing the OLC will likely be still in place. This would work against institutionalization. In addition, similar to the new colleges, existing institutions have devoted a lot of energy at the time of change. Whether this persists over time is questionable. The implications for sustainability are clear.

Given that the concept of sustainability is relevant and similar in nature across both new and traditional institutions, we will examine some common factors that affect institutionalization. In this analysis we will consider two questions: First, does the relevant process continue over time? Second, does the process evolve over time? We look at these questions for the processes of socialization, commitment, and recommitment to the OLC; whether supporting the OLC is viewed as rewarding; feedback and redesign of the contract; and, finally, the extent to which the school's efforts are understood and viewed positively outside the institution.

First, socialization is a key process in both implementation and institutionalization. The major difference with respect to institutionalizing change is that we want to know whether socialization continues and whether its form changes over time. To learn more about this process, we did informal interviews with new faculty in College A in years three and four. One of our findings was that the newer faculty had a less differentiated understanding of the college's OLC than the original professors in year one and the intensity of socialization was less. For example, if I apply as a faculty member to one of the colleges with strong OLCs, I could learn about the OLC through recruiting materials, during a recruiting visit, and when I join the faculty. Other forms of learning how the OLC works could come from observing other faculty members, joint teaching, and getting feedback on my classes from students. These all represent different ways to learn about the OLC. The fundamental questions are whether socialization actually continues over time and different forms of socialization (e.g., reading versus observing) evolve over time. One finding from the research on change in work organizations (Goodman, 1979; Goodman and Griffiths, 1991) is that the intensity of socialization declines over time, which contributes to lower levels of institutionalization.

The reader should note that these meta-processes of implementation and institutionalization are similar. Socialization is important in both. The benefit is that this simplifies the theoretical processes underlying both. At the same time, the specific processes are different. For the socialization process to be effective it must both persist over time and evolve in its form.

Another process relevant to both implementation and sustainability is commitment. For sustainability, the basic question is: Do people recommit themselves over time to the new OLC environment? Again, commitment is a voluntary public act to do something. In research on a specific labor-management cooperative program, everyone votes each year about whether to continue the labor-management program. This is a clear form (public in nature) of recommitment over time. We are not proposing that faculty, students, and staff should vote each year on maintaining the OLC, but we do think recommitment is an important process for institutionalization of the contract. It could come in the form of current faculty mentoring new faculty on the OLC experience in their college. Similarly, current students could be actively involved in socializing new students. In both examples, people voluntarily accept new roles that represent recommitments to the broader vision of the OLC. Other examples might include involvement in redesign committees to improve the function of the college.

A third relevant process is the extent to which the participation in the OLC experience remains rewarding. We can think of rewards directed to individuals, groups, and the organization. Also, there are different types of rewards. As with the other processes, we are looking at the fundamental question for sustainability: whether the rewards remain relevant and evolve over time. For many of the early participants in places such as Colleges A or B, there was an attraction about building a new institution. This is an individual-level, intrinsic reward. Will this continue to be a powerful reward over time for the initial participants or the latter entrants to the college? That is, once the college is up and running and students are graduating, is an incentive that was powerful in the initial years still an important motivator?

A different set of incentives might come into being when the new college becomes accredited or its reputation as a leader is recognized by others in their field. This type of external recognition is a different type of incentive directed at the institution itself. But as a student, faculty, or staff member, their identification of this recognition generalizes to them. The picture then is evolving types of rewards, appearing at different levels of analysis, all playing a role in sustaining the OLC over time.

Another process that is critical for stability is feedback and redesign. The focus here is not just on the traditional areas of course design and results. The focus should be on all aspects of the system. If there is a designated learning outcome, such as group skills, can we measure and, if needed, redesign the learning environments that deliver that skill? If recruiting is an important part of the socialization process, we need to assess over time whether the recruiting process is declining, staying the same or improving. Redesign mechanisms should be implemented where needed.

As mentioned, there is a big push to socialize the initial entrants, but this level of socialization drops over time. For example, we mentioned College A's professors, interviewed in years three to four, seemed to have a less differentiated view of the OLC compared to the original entrants. The point is that collecting data on learning outcomes or learning environments is pretty obvious given the OLC. But assessing the perceptions of recent faculty (or students) is not that obvious. The central idea is that the OLC is a system and it exists over time; it is not stagnant or locked into its original structure. The dynamics in year one cannot be the same as year five. The point then is how to devise a feedback and redesign system that is system focused and dynamic over time. This means what you are measuring and changing in year one will not be the same as in year five.

The interview was the major data collection instrument in our study. It was semi-structured so it had a formal set of areas, but the questions were open ended. We wanted to capture the respondents' perceptions and not prime their answers. In creating feedback and design mechanisms, the interview is an appropriate tool. If we wanted to assess the recruiting process, we might interview prospective students on what they learned about the college. One might repeat our questions on how knowledgeable students are about learning outcomes and learning environments. Other methods, such as observation (in the classroom or non-classroom environments), student diaries, analyzing course syllabi, and so on, also could be used over time.

There is one additional process that should be considered for institutionalization. This is the diffusion of the principle underlying the change to other institutions. Let's say College A has been very successful in demonstrating a new approach to higher education. A question is whether the ideas from this institution have had effects on other institutions or to the overall profession or discipline. This is important because we all operate in an environment where external forces matter. If professional organizations or accrediting institutions or other colleges adopt these ideas, then there are stronger legitimating forces for College A. The opposite could be true. If accrediting agencies do not give their approval to the new approach, this would affect the recruiting of faculty and students, which, in turn, would affect the institution. For new institutions, diffusing their ideas and gaining external legitimacy is another way to sustain the OLC and, by extension, the institution.

Failure to diffuse can have negative effects on the change effort. This is more likely in existing institutions. Here the focus of attention is on surrounding organizational arrangements. What our research (Goodman, 1979) experience suggests is that changes in the OLC can be affected by other institutional arrangements. For example, if one or two elements of the OLC are changed in an existing college but the rest of the college remains in a traditional format, there could be challenges to the sustainability of the new elements from forces operating within the more traditional mode. Or if the college is a part of a larger university and selected changes occur at the college but not in the larger institution, this could create countervailing forces against the change. Diffusion is a source of legitimization. Failure to diffuse a new approach like the OLC can undermine the sustainability of the change by leaving the change isolated from its surrounding environment.

GETTING STARTED

In this book we have tried to link theory, data, and practice for the researcher and administrator. How could one take ideas from this book and implement them in a real educational setting? In doing so, the first key task would be developing an organizational learning contract. Remember that we are operating at the college level, not at the curriculum or course levels. The goal is to chart out a shared vision. In a change context, the vision is a compelling picture of where you want to go. It is not a one liner such as "treat students well" or "create well-educated people." Rather, it is a map of the institution in two or three years. This map is not complete, but it provides enough detail about what the institution might look like (e.g., learning outcomes, environments) and how you will get there and perhaps when. In getting started, we should explore some basic questions:

- Why should we do this in the first place?
- What would be the setting or context for this change?
- Who should lead the development of a new model of learning?
- How do we go about creating this new model?
- What specific elements should be in our OLC?

Why Should I Do This?

An administrator might say, "I am running a good university, we get good-quality students, they get well placed in the job market or graduate school, so why disrupt this equilibrium?" One response is to look outside the institution, in the changing environment of higher education. There is an increasing growth in high-quality global institutions (U.S. News and World Report, 2008) that would draw on the population of possible students. Many U.S. universities have dominated this market, but they probably will not be able to do so in the future. Increasing financial pressures will close down some institutions and create new challenges for existing institutions. Changes in technology will provide new forms of competition and new ways for existing universities to operate. That is, the physical setting of a university may become less important and new forms of distributed learning and research may be more prevalent. Although these external forces are real, they may not support the rationale for building a new form of higher education. In addition, the external forces, which are quite real, do not often lead to dramatic changes for a specific institution. We rarely see dramatic short-term changes in revenue or market share in an educational setting to motivate change. Despite these countervailing forces, external factors could motivate change.

Another argument about why one should engage in developing an OLC, either as part of a start-up institution or an existing one, stems from the data in this book and other research on higher education. If one looks at the data on institutions with strong OLCs, they represent a good model of an institution I would want to run. The students have incredibly high identification with the institution. Their level of affect is off the charts (Table 6.9). They rate the educational environment as outstanding. They have a more differentiated model about how to apply what they have learned and continue learning on their own as they move from college to a complex work environment. These and other attributes create a new, innovative institution. Should one simply replicate an institution such as College A? Absolutely not. Could one do that? Probably not. But it does illustrate that people who want to explore new forms of higher education can be successful in creating exciting, effective institutions.

The above discussion really focuses on evidence as a motivator, but is that enough? We have a theory (i.e., the OLC); it becomes actualized in a real setting and produces positive results. One line of reasoning is that evidence should guide our decision-making. The problem with that line of reasoning is that it emphasizes intellect versus attitudes and values. Many years ago, I wrote a book on organizational change (Goodman, 1979). The focus was on new organizational forms that would create new models of organizational effectiveness. The results confirmed the positive effect of the organizational innovation on various effectiveness indicators. The results were disseminated in talks, conferences and papers. However, all of this created little change in other organizations. One of the reasons is that the change (which was primarily about control, authority, and decision-making systems) was highly tied to strong attitudes and values. Many of the leaders in this particular industry had attitudes and values that ran counter to the results. Over time, the results of this and other studies became more influential, but not in the near term. This illustrates that more is likely needed within an institution to spur change than some data or research alone.

What Is the Setting for This Change?

The setting or context is important because it sets the constraints for educational innovation. One possible setting is a stand-alone institution. Olin College (chapter 7), for example, was expressly set up to develop new forms of engineering education. There are other stand-alone institutions with a mandate to make improvements in education, but the changes are incremental, not fundamental. Other settings include new institutions that are developed within a university context. The initial goal of developing a new school inside an existing university may or may not be to create an innovative OLC; regardless, the situation does lend itself to creation of a contract with the students, faculty, and staff of this new institution. A critical contextual variable is the degree of independence between the new college and the existing university. In chapter 8, recall that an important contributor to the start-up's success was the intellectual and physical independence of the School of Information Systems from the rest of the university where it was housed, but at the same time it could draw on customized central services (e.g., the university's admissions department). A different and predominant setting is an existing institution that wants to create change in its current educational model (rather than creating some entirely new setting for learning). In this situation, the key issue is the degree of innovation under consideration. These different settings are another starting point for setting up a new OLC and innovative approaches to learning. There are both similarities and important differences in getting started in each of these settings.

Who Should Craft the Vision?

There needs to be a small group of people who see the changing environment and acknowledge the implications for their institution. Yet more importantly, these people must have the values and compelling foresight for redesigning their educational setting. As we saw in chapter 7, after Rick Miller was selected as president of Olin College, a few other senior administrators were hired. Then, in a timely fashion, the first of the new faculty members were hired (eight professors). At this point there were at least two options: Evolve the model from the top down, or the bottom up. In the case of Olin College, the latter route was chosen. Miller was hired to create a new form of engineering education. He and the other senior administrators understood this charge and had been developing a vision. Yet, they stepped aside and charged the new faculty they had hired with the task of defining the new vision. The advantage of this approach is that the faculty became the owners of the new vision, representing the major mechanism for its implementation. The risks were that the senior administrators were experienced in higher education and had already done some thinking about what Olin College should look like, and their vision might have been at odds with that of the faculty. In the School of Information Systems (chapter 8), a more top-down approach was taken. The dean and another faculty member spent lots of time interacting with senior industry people in crafting a vision. In addition, they talked with prospective students. These interactions over time created the basic elements of the School's vision. They also had an independent design partner who contributed to this evolution of the vision.

There are obvious tradeoffs between the bottom-up or top-down approach. The defining features for me are in the *selection* of the senior administrators and faculty with a similar vision and motivation to build a new institution. The ties to industry, prospective students, and a design partner are critical elements in forming a vision. Also, the key feature of an OLC is building a shared understanding. If the faculty members are not highly committed to a new form of OLC, there will be no shared understanding and hence no contract. Faculty involvement in design is an important mechanism in creating a shared understanding. In a sense, involving both leadership of the institution and those "in the trenches" in a hybrid approach might be the most preferable.

How Do We Go about Creating a New Model of Learning?

Now that you have chosen some people to help create a vision, the next question is *how* to do it. Gathering information on what has been done elsewhere and what you might do in your institution is key. This book is one obvious source. Chapter 9, in particular, outlines many of the design issues and processes. A range of other books (cf. Duderstadt, 2003) charts out issues and processes in designing a new learning model.

Another option is visiting some of the new start-ups. Two are mentioned in this book (chapters 7 and 8), but of course there are others. Visiting is a powerful way to learn. You can see college life in action from a variety of perspectives. It is a strong forum for both explicit and implicit learning. Note that one short visit is a bit superficial. Instead, stay for several days, go to classes, eat in the dining hall, observe student presentations, and so on.

One dilemma with visits is that the observers often leave saying, "Well, this was an interesting visit, but College X is very different from mine." This happens because at one level the new start-ups are different from most institutions. College A and College C attracted very good students and faculty, but differed on a lot of dimensions. The real question is what you want to learn. My recommendation would be to learn more about meta-processes used in designing and sustaining the OLC at the institution(s) you visit, rather than the details or specifics. The key thing to learn would be *how* the start-up built a shared understanding around an OLC, not what was in the OLC. Also, knowing how one institution did it is not enough. You want to see variation in OLC design and implementation, and then pull features from these processes that suit your institution. In addition, you will want to find out the lessons these institutions learned—not only what they did well, but what they did not so well—that you could use in creating your setting's own shared understanding about the organizational learning contract.

As the initial parameters of the OLC become defined, interacting with your constituencies can be very helpful. This is best illustrated in chapter 8. One of the dean's initial goals was to define their desired output—IT professionals. They spent considerable time defining what that meant. There was a process of talking with industry leaders, refining, talking with other leaders, and refining that created their vision of the school. A lot of the legitimization for their focus on a specific set of learning outcomes and learning environments came from these discussions with leaders.

There are other ways to learn about how to build an OLC. Most universities have teaching centers. In some cases, people in these centers are up to date about new approaches to higher education. Whether you are designing a start-up or new institution, or a new model in an existing institution, the teaching centers could be a resource. Another source would be psychology departments. Although psychology departments were not used by any of the three colleges we studied, they are the source for research on learning. It should be relatively straightforward to identify experts in learning who are conducting research in the higher educational context.

An interesting observation in chapter 5 about learning is that most of the students' personal models of learning were not informed by current psychological research on learning. Their own inductive experiences framed how they thought about learning.

What Specific Elements Should Be in the OLC?

As we said earlier, there is not a single "best" OLC; the elements of a contract will differ from one institution to the next. We have pointed out ways and sources of discovering what should be in the OLC. The question should be more about some of the meta features of the OLC, not the specific content. With respect to specifying learning outcomes, I recently talked to a rector of an international university who was setting up a new honors college. In response to my question about the distinctive features of the new honors college, he pointed to leadership and global awareness. In addition, in response to another question, he pointed out leadership would come from a course on leadership and global awareness from going abroad to study. In our discussions about learning outcomes, our recommendation has been to take a general outcome, explicitly identify the sub-skills related to this outcome, and then create operational measures. Both of these factors are integral to stating learning outcomes. Leadership is a valuable, but very broad, construct. There are many forms of leadership. What forms would be most relevant for a person graduating from college and going to work in a specific industry or field? One might think of team leadership and, less likely, building transformational skills for running a large organization. If it were building skills to lead a team, then the capabilities of creating a strategic focus for the team, managing time, and facilitating conflict resolution would be pertinent.

Thinking through the learning outcomes you want to achieve on a deeper level, as we just did with the concept of leadership, is important. Developing specific sub-skills such as time management and conflict resolution and measuring progress on these sub-skills is a much more viable way to build leadership than having someone take a leadership course. Similarly, global awareness might be facilitated by going abroad. But, following the same argument, we want to break down global awareness into specific sub-skills. Learning a new language would be an example. In addition, achieving this skill is pretty operational. If we think back to chapters 4 through 6 in this book, there is evidence some colleges were able to create visible learning outcomes. However, even in the best examples (e.g., College A) the outcomes were stated in a very general way and there could have been a more detailed focus on measurement.

In identifying learning environments, we provided one list. Our expectation is that this list will evolve over time through new innovations. For example, the concept of the studio was on our list. However, 10 years ago that might have only appeared in an architecture course. Some people (cf. Wilson, 2001) took that concept, which is built around doing and mentoring from professors and peers, and translated it into learning in the sciences (physics, chemistry, etc.). Our expectation is that new forms of learning, particularly distributed collaborative learning, will become more prominent in the future on the list of learning environment options.

Our main position on learning environments is that you need to link compatible but different learning environments to specific learning outcomes. If we went back to the leadership skill, we would want to create a variety of learning environments. Students could take a course, or practice leadership in a group, or practice follower-ship in a class project, or manage a group in the community, or "shadow" a leader in a work setting. To build any of the learning outcomes discussed in this book or other sources, the key is to design multiple different learning environments that will enhance the relevant sub-skills and to identify new innovative environments.

In terms of what should be in the system component, we know there need to be multiple socialization, measurement, and redesign mechanisms. In terms of social-ization we know there need to be multiple different mechanisms over time. The colleges in our study used different mechanisms. The ones that built stronger OLCs had explicit multiple mechanisms before and during the student's stay at the college. In one college, the measurement system captured both the course grade but also the learning objectives that were relevant for the course. Another college built the learning outcome evaluation into an IT system that was filled out by the students. Another example was having students report on project work that high-lighted a few learning outcomes. Assessment came from teachers and invited industry people. The last and equally important mechanism is redesign. We have said many times that building a shared understanding is a very difficult task. There will almost certainly be gaps between the expected OLC and the actual experience. A redesign mechanism is critical both for implementation and sustainability. Therefore, it is an important element in the design process. Typical curriculum reviews are not particularly timely. To launch an OLC and to sustain it, one needs fairly timely measurement and redesign. I would recommend multiple measure-ments and opportunities for redesign during the early semesters of a launch. This needs to be part of the design of the system component. Perhaps as the OLC becomes institutionalized the measurement and redesign may become less fre-quent. However, I would see these system-component mechanisms being imple-mented multiple times during the academic year. Also, I would see this linked, but independent of curriculum or accreditation reviews.

FUTURE

We have tried to paint some realistic scenarios for higher education. Some are quite positive. Institutions with strong OLCs seem to be able to attract very high quality students, and such students find the learning environments to be challenging and stimulating. In terms of outcomes, they report positive changes and development of new skills and express high positive affect toward their college. We assume most administrators of higher education would be excited to be a part of the creation and management of such an institution. At the same time, we pointed out that the start-up of new innovative colleges—at least in the United States—is not a frequent event. It probably is more likely to happen outside of the United States as countries invest in higher education. The principles in this book are not U.S.-centric. The basic ideas in the OLC are relevant in other countries, although they would be shaped by the cultural context.

We also acknowledged that creating an OLC in an existing institution is a non-trivial task. There are many forces working against substantive change. Creating a spin-off gets closer to the "stand-alone" institution and makes substantive change more possible. But the opportunity for these new educational ventures is often not affordable. Building an OLC in an existing institution is quite difficult, although we have suggested some options.

Two fundamental questions are: Do we expect to see significant changes in higher education, and would the concepts of this book help frame that change? There are at least two approaches to answering these questions: one intellectual and one more affective-based.

The intellectual approach looks to changes in the environment of higher education. One change is in the level of competition and the development of new forms of competition. From a U.S. perspective, the country has had a leadership role in higher education. There is some evidence that is changing. Improvements in the quality of higher education in the world have important implications for all institutions of higher education, not just for colleges in the United States. Part of this globalization of higher education is characterized by new forms of education, particularly at the masters and PhD levels. Traditional universities are providing their degrees in other countries or in collaboration with universities located outside the United States. Underlying these new forms is rapidly changing technology, which facilitates the connectivity and forms of technology-enhanced learning. The technology also gives rise to new institutions providing learning within a country in a distributed way. All of these changing forms of competitions are challenges to existing institutions that are defined by having their faculty and students located in a specific physical location. They are all calls for change.

The economics of higher education is another force. The focus is not solely on the current economic crisis, although that has real consequences in terms of federal or state governments funding higher education. Also, the consequences of government intervention in this crisis will have implications partly because of the affect of accumulated debt on future funding opportunities. But independent of the crisis, there continue to be increases in tuition and other fees that affect the ability of certain economic groups to access higher education. There continue to be increases in the costs of running a college or university. These economic conditions and their consequences are another call for rethinking how we design and manage higher-education institutions.

A third factor that has become more important is the question of accountability. In the future, accountability is likely to be even more important. The call for accountability will come from multiple sources, including the federal and state governments who contribute to higher education, accrediting bodies or professional associations (e.g., ABET in engineering) and, eventually, the consumers will become more of a force. At a private institution one can pay more than $200,000 for a four-year education when counting tuition, fees, and expenses. Obviously, the cost is much less in public universities, but they are subsidized by the states, which in many cases have serious financial problems. One real dilemma in assessing accountability is agreeing on a set of metrics. If you invest $200,000 in the market, you will get a rate of return, which can be compared to other relevant indices. If you buy a car there are a variety of metrics (driving enjoyment, service costs, resale value, etc.) that you can use to assess your car investment. At an institution of higher education it is more complex to identify some clear metrics. Some widely used metrics do exist, such as job or graduate school placements, but they do not speak to directly what capabilities have been developed and which have not. One benefit of the OLC is that it explicitly deals with accountability. That is, the college says "in the contract" what you will learn (learning outcomes), how you will learn (learning environments), as well as why, where, and when. The student and faculty understand the contract and engage in behaviors to fulfill the contract.

This intellectual perspective makes it clear that we do expect significant change in higher education. The forces that I mentioned as well as others have driven and will continue to drive change. These forces can stimulate the start up of new colleges such as College A and College B. I expect these types of start-ups to be initiated throughout the world of higher education. Also, we expect new forms of global collaborations using technology-enhanced learning to emerge more frequently in the near term.

Although we have argued that there will be forces for changes and some institutions will either react to or be proactive about these forces, there are lots of reasons to believe many institutions will not change. Intellectual arguments are important, but often they do not change behavior. What this book is about requires substantial change in behavior, which leads us to the affective-based argument for the relevance of the OLC concept.

One of the underlying lessons in this book is the selection advantage inherent in the development of a new institution. You propose to build a new college that will represent a new learning environment. In chapter 7, we learned that 1,500 faculty applied for just eight positions in such a college. It is not difficult in that setting to select some highly creative and committed individuals. Both "Millers" in chapters 7 and 8 were high-energy, visionary leaders who helped start up new institutions. Both are now managing existing institutions, but their focus on continuous innovation speaks to the ability to sustain the OLC and lead continuous change in both institutions over time. This emotional commitment was also true for students and staff, not just the people at the top. It is this strong commitment, or collective attachment to the new institution, that made a difference. The basic idea is that intellectual understanding is important, but affective commitment generates the set of behaviors that are critical for lasting educational change.

A fair question is that although selection advantage can work for a start-up, is it likely to be the driver in an existing institution? The answer is no. The institution already has an existing set of faculty, students, and staff. In a steady state, it is unlikely such an institution would have a selection advantage. The challenge is to find another way. One way to get this emotional commitment in an existing institution is to select a leader from within the university community. Consider the following example: Dick Cyert was president at Carnegie Mellon University for 19 years. He changed the university from a regional institution to a highly regarded national institution. He had an idea about a new computing environment for the university. In 1980, he asked Alan Newell, a highly regarded computer scientist, to take the lead. Alan was one of the founders of artificial intelligence and a very prestigious faculty member in the university community. He led a group that created one of the first distributed computing environments, in partnership with IBM. Alan invested huge amounts of energy and high involvement with other faculty. This example is the same as the one about the "Millers." One identifies a leader with high energy and vision, with a sense of involving others, to create substantial change—whether the organization is new or old. As with many organizational changes, ongoing emotional commitments from the institution's leadership and groups of faculty are critical for real change to occur and be sustained over time.

A strong organizational learning contract represents one form of organizational change. We have presented what it is, how it can be designed, how it can be implemented and sustained and some of its consequences for the institution. It is a complex change effort, not a simple one. When done properly, the final outcomes are beneficial to faculty, students, staff, alumni, and the employees who work with the school to hire interns and employ its graduates. In a start-up or spin-off institution, the OLC serves as a powerful guide. In existing institutions, it points to ways to reinvent oneself. The intellectual forces on higher education justify its use.

Given understanding of the intellectual forces and strong emotional commitment, opportunities for educational change exist. This book can drive some of this change. We have argued throughout the book that the OLC is a strong framework for designing new forms of educational change. Chapters 4 to 6 speak to the role of the OLC in creating effective institutions of higher education. Chapters 7 and 8 provide personal accounts in creating effective institutions of higher education. Our intention is to link theory, data, and practice. In this chapter we identified some of the change issues as well as some specific steps on how to get started building a new OLC. Recognizing contextual differences (new versus existing institutions) has been a central theme throughout the book.

BIBLIOGRAPHY

CHAPTER 1 REFERENCES

Belanger, C., Mount, J., & Wilson, M. (2002). Institutional retention and image." *Tertiary Education and Management, 8*(3), 217–30.

Braxton, J. M., Vesper, N., & Hossler, D. (1995). Expectations for college and student persistence. *Research in Higher Education, 36*(5), 595–611.

Cruz Limon, C. (2001). The virtual university: Customized education in a nutshell. In P. Goodman (Ed.), *Technology enhanced learning: Opportunities for change.* (pp. 183–202). Mahwah, NJ: Lawrence Erlbaum.

Duderstadt, J. (2000). *A university for the 21st century.* Ann Arbor: University of Michigan Press.

Goodman, P.S. (1982). *Change in organizations.* San Francisco: Jossey-Bass, Inc.

Goodman, P.S. (2001). *Technology enhanced learning: Opportunities for change.* Mahwah, NJ: Lawrence Erlbaum, Inc.

Kraatz, M. S. & Zajac, E. J. (1996). Exploring the limits of the new institutionalism: The causes and consequences of illegitimate organizational change. *American Sociological Review, 61,* 812–36.

Kuh, G. D., Gonyea, R. M., & Williams, J. M. (2005). What students expect from college and what they get. In T. E. Miller, B. E. Bender, J. H. Shub & Associates (Eds.), *Promoting reasonable expectations: Aligning student and institutional views of the college experience.* (pp. 34–64). San Francisco: Jossey-Bass.

Levine, J. (2001). The remaking of the American university. *Innovative Higher Education, 25*(4), 253–67.

Pike, G. R., Kuh, G. D., & Gonyea, R. M. (2003). The relationship between institutional mission and students' involvement and educational outcomes. *Research in Higher Education, 44*(2), 241–61.

Rhodes, F. (2004). Reinventing the university. In L. Weber & J. Duderstadt (Eds.), *Reinventing the research university* (pp. 3–14). London, Paris, Geneva: Economica.

Rousseau, D. M. (1995). *Psychological contracts in organizations.* Thousand Oaks, CA: Sage Publications.

Sax, L. J., Lindholm, J. A., Astin, A.W., Korn, W.S., & Mahoney, K.M. (2001). The American freshman: National norms for fall 2002. UCLA Higher Education Research Institute (HERI) 37th Annual Report.

Zemsky, R. & Duderstadt, J. (2004). Reinventing the research university: An American perspective. In L. Weber & J. Duderstadt (Eds.), *Reinventing the research university* (pp. 15–28). London, Paris, Geneva: Economica.

Zhao, H., Wayne, S. J., Glibkowski, B. C., & Bravo, J. (2007). The impact of psychological contract breach on work-related outcomes: A meta-analysis. *Personnel Psychology, 60*(3), 647–80.

CHAPTER 2 REFERENCES

Anderson, J. R. (2000). *Learning and memory: An integrated approach.* New York: Wiley.

Barnett, S. M. & Ceci, S. J. (2002) When and where do we apply what we learn? A taxonomy for far transfer. *Psychological Bulletin, 128*(4), 612–37.

Gersick, C. J. G. (1988). Time and transition in work teams: Toward a new model of group development. *Academy of Management Journal, 31,* 9–41.

Gersick, C. J. G. (1989). Marking time: Predictable transitions in task groups. *Academy of Management Journal, 32,* 274–308.

Jackson, S. E. & Schuler, R. S. (1985). A meta-analysis and conceptual critique of research on role ambiguity and role conflict in work settings. *Organizational Behavior and Human Decision Processes, 36*(1), 16–78.

Kahn, R. L., Wolfe, D. M., Quinn, R. P., Snoek, J. D. & Rosenthal, R. A. (1964). *Organizational stress: Studies in role conflict and ambiguity.* New York: John Wiley & Sons.

Rousseau, D. (1995). *Psychological contracts in organizations: Understanding written and unwritten agreements.* California: SAGE Publications.

Tubre, T. C. & Collins, J. M. (2000). A meta-analysis of the relationships between role ambiguity, role conflict, and job performance. *Journal of Management, 26,* 155–69.

CHAPTER 3 REFERENCES

Best Colleges 2010 [Electronic Version]. *U.S. News and World Report,* Accessed Mar. 2010.

Braxton, J. M., Vesper, N., & Hossler, D. (1995). Expectations for college and student persistence. *Research in Higher Education, 36*(5), 595–611.

Kuh, G. D., Gonyea, R. M., & Williams, J. M. (2005). What students expect from college and what they get. In T. E. Miller, B. E. Bender, J. H. Schub & Associates (Eds.), *Promoting reasonable expectations: Aligning student and institutional views of the college experience* (pp. 34–64). San Francisco: Jossey-Bass.

Light, R. (2001). *Making the most of college: Students speak their minds.* Cambridge, MA: Harvard University Press.

Miles, M. B. & Huberman, A. M. (1994). *Qualitative data analysis: An expanded sourcebook.* California: SAGE Publications.

Pike, G. R. & Kuh, G. D. (2005). A typology of student engagement for American colleges and universities. *Research in Higher Education, 46,* 185–209.

CHAPTER 4 REFERENCES

Baker, R. W., McNeil, O. V., & Siryk, B. (1985). Expectation and reality in freshman adjustment to college. *Journal of Counseling Psychology, 32,* 94–103.

Bandura, A. (1997). *Self-efficacy: The exercise of control.* USA: W.H. Freeman and Company.

Bean, J. P. (1983). The application of a model of turnover in work organizations to the student attrition process. *Review of Higher Education, 6*(2), 129–48.

Berger, J. B. & Braxton, J. M. (1998). Revising Tinto's interactionalist theory of student departure through theory elaboration: Examining the role of organizational attributes in the persistence process. *Research in Higher Education, 39*(2), 103–119.

Braxton, J. M. & Brier, E. M. (1989). Melding organizational and interactional theories of student attrition: A path analytic study. *Review of Higher Education, 13*(1), 47–61.

Darlaston-Jones, D., Pike, L., Cohen, L., Young, A., Haunold, S., & Drew, N. (2003). Are they being served? Student expectations of higher education. *Issues in Educational Research, 13*(1), 13–52.

Desrochers, L. A. (2007). A fragile birth. *New Directions for Higher Education: Special issue on the founding of the University of California, Merced, 139,* 13–26.

Dweck, C. S. & Legett, E. L. (1988). A social-cognitive approach to motivation and personality. *A Psychological Review, 95*(2), 256–73.

Ehrenberg, R. G. (2005). Method or Madness? Inside the U.S. News & World Report College Rankings. *Journal of College Admission, 189,* 29–35.

Ewell, P. T. & Jones, D. P. (1993). Actions matter: The case for indirect measures in as-sessing higher education's progress on the national education goals. *Journal of General Education, 42,* 123–48.

Feldman, D. C. (1981). The multiple socialization of organization members. *The Academy of Management Review, 6*(2), 309–318.

Helland, P. A., Stallings, H. J., & Braxton, J. M. (2001–2002). The fulfillment of expectations for college and student departure decisions. *Journal of College Student Retention: Research, Theory, and Practice, 3*(4), 381–96.

Howard, J. A. (2005). Why should we care about student expectations? In T.E. Miller, B.E. Bender, J.H. Schub and Associates (Eds.), *Promoting reasonable expectations: Aligning student and institutional views of the college experience* (pp. 10–23). San Francisco: Jossey-Bass.

Kuh, G. D. (1995). The other curriculum: Out-of-class experiences associated with student learning and personal development. *The Journal of Higher Education, 66*(2), 123–55.

Kuh, G. D. (1999). How are we doing? Tracking the quality of the undergraduate experience, 1960s to the present. *The Review of Higher Education, 22,* 99–119.

Kuh, G. D. (2001). Assessing what really matters to student learning: Inside the National Survey of Student Engagement. *Change, 33,* 10–17.

Kuh, G. D. (2005). Student engagement in the first year of college. In L. M. Upcraft, J. N. Gardner, & B.O. Barefoot (Eds.), *Challenging and supporting the first year student: A handbook for improving the first year of college* (pp. 86–107). San Francisco: Jossey-Bass.

Kuh, G. D., Gonyea, R. M., & Williams, J. M. (2005). What students expect from college and what they get. In T. E. Miller, B. E. Bender, J. H. Schub and Associates (Eds.), *Promoting reasonable expectations: Aligning student and institutional views of the college experience* (pp. 34–64). San Francisco: Jossey-Bass.

Kuh, G. D., Lyons, J., Miller, T., & Trow, J. (2003). *Reasonable expectations: Renewing the educational compact between institutions and students.* Washington, DC: NASPA.

Lipsky, S. (2003). *College study: The essential ingredients.* Upper Saddle River, NJ: Pearson/Prentice Hall.

Longden, B. (2006). An institutional response to changing student expectations and their impact on retention rates. *Journal of Higher Education Policy and Management, 28*(2), 173–87.

Miller, T., Kuh, G. D., & Paine, D. (2006). Taking student expectations seriously: A guide for campus applications. *NASPA–Student Affairs Administrators in Higher Education.*

Olsen, D., Kuh, G. D., Schilling, K. M., Schilling, K., Connolly, M., Simmons, A., et al. (1998). Great expectations: What first-year students say they will do and what they actually do. Annual Meeting of the Association for the Study of Higher Education, Miami, FL.

Pike, G. R. & Kuh, G. D. (2005). A typology of student engagement for American colleges and universities. *Research in Higher Education, 46,* 185–209.

Rousseau, D. M. (1995). *Psychological contracts in organizations.* Thousand Oaks, CA: Sage Publications.

Stern, G. G. (1966). Myth and reality in the American college. *AAUP Bulletin, 52,* 408–414.

Tinto, V. (1997). Classrooms as communities: Exploring the educational character of student persistence. *Journal of Higher Education, 68*(6), 599–623.

Tinto, V. (1987). *Leaving College: Rethinking the causes and cures of student attrition.* Chicago, IL: University of Chicago Press.

Vroom, V. H. (1964). *Work and motivation.* New York: John Wiley & Sons.

Win, R. & Miller, P. W. (2005). The effects of individual and school factors on university students' academic performance. *Australian Economic Review, 38*(1), 1–18.

Yorges, S., Bloom, S. L., DiFonzo, A. J., & Chando, E. M. (2005). Great expectations? Student reactions when courses don't measure up. *Psychology and Education: An Interdisciplinary Journal, 44,* 18–29.

Zhao, H., Wayne, S. J., Glibkowski, B. C., & Bravo, J. (2007). The impact of psychological contract breach on work-related outcomes: A meta-analysis. *Personnel Psychology, 60*(3), 647–80.

CHAPTER 5 REFERENCES

Berger, J. B. & Braxton, J. M. (1998). Revising Tinto's interactionalist theory of student departure through theory elaboration: Examining the role of organizational attributes in the persistence process. *Research in Higher Education, 39*(2), 103–119.

Flanagan, J. C. (1954). The critical incident technique. *Psychological Bulletin, 51,* 327–58.

Garcia, T. & Pintrich, P. R. (1994). Regulating motivation and cognition in the classroom: The role of self-schemas and self-regulatory strategies. In D. H. Schuck and B. J. Zimmerman (Eds.), *Self-regulation of learning and performance: Issues and educational applications* (pp. 127–54). London: Taylor & Francis.

Kuh, G. D. (2001). Assessing what really matters to student learning: Inside the National Survey of Student Engagement. *Change, 33,* 10–17.

Kuh, G. D., Gonyea, R. M., & Williams, J. M. (2005). What students expect from college and what they get. In T. E. Miller, B. E. Bender, J. H. Schub & Associates (Eds.), *Promoting reasonable expectations: Aligning student and institutional views of the college experience* (pp. 34–64). San Francisco: Jossey-Bass.

Lambert, A. D., Terenzini, P. T., & Lattuca, L. R. (2007). More than meets the eye: Curricular and programmatic effects on student learning. *Research in Higher Education, 48*(2), 141–68.

Light, R. (2001). *Making the most of college: Students speak their minds.* Cambridge, MA: Harvard University Press.

Pascarella, E. T., Edison, M. I., Nora, A. Hagedorn, L. S., & Terenzini, P. T. (1996). Influences on students' openness to diversity and challenge in the first year of college. *Journal of Higher Education, 67*(2), 174–95.

Wilson, Jack M. (2001). The development of the studio classroom. In P. S. Goodman (Ed.), *Technology-enhanced learning: Opportunities for change* (pp. 265–88). Mahwah, NJ: Lawrence Erlbaum Associates.

CHAPTER 6 REFERENCES

Allen, N. J. & Meyer, J. P. (1990). The measurement and antecedents of affective, continuance, and normative commitment to organization. *Journal of Occupational Psychology, 63,* 1–18.

Ancona, D. G., Goodman, P. S., Lawrence, B. S., & Tushman, M. L. (2001). Time: A new research lens. *Special Topic Forum on Time and Organizational Research, Academy of Management Review, 26,* 645–63.

Best Colleges 2010 [Electronic version]. *U.S. News and World Report,* 2010. Accessed Mar. 2010.

Best Colleges 2008. *U.S. News and World Report,* 2008.

Birnbaum, R. (1988). *How colleges work: The cybernetics of academic organization and leadership.* San Francisco, CA: Jossey-Bass.

Cameron, K. S. (1981). Domains of organizational effectiveness in colleges and universities. *Academy of Management Journal, 24*, 25–47.

Duderstadt, J. (2000). *A university for the 21st century.* Ann Arbor: University of Michigan Press.

Goodman, P. S. & Pennings, J. (1977). *New perspectives on organizational effectiveness.* San Francisco: Jossey-Bass.

Goodman, P. S. (1979). *Assessing organizational change: The Rushton quality of work experiment.* New York: Wiley-Interscience.

Goodman, P. S. (2001). *Technology enhanced learning: Opportunities for change.* Mahwah, NJ: Lawrence Erlbaum.

Lawler, E. E. & Worley, C. G. (2006). *Built to change: How to achieve sustained organizational effectiveness.* San Francisco: Jossey-Bass.

Rhodes, F. (2004). Reinventing the university. In L. Weber and J. Duderstadt (Eds.), *Reinventing the research university* (pp. 3–13). London, Paris, Geneva: Economica.

Schneider, B. & Bowen, D. E. (1995). *Winning the service game.* Boston: Harvard Business School Press.

Zammuto, R. (1982). *Assessing organizational effectiveness: Systems change, adaptation, and strategy.* Albany, NY: State University of New York.

Zemsky, R. & Duderstadt, J. (2004). Reinventing the university: An American perspective. In L. Weber and J. Duderstadt (Eds.), *Reinventing the research university* (pp. 15–28). London, Paris, Geneva: Economica.

CHAPTER 7 REFERENCES

Greis, G. P. (2009). *From the ground up: The founding and early history of the Franklin W. Olin College of Engineering, a bold experiment in engineering education.* Needham, MA: Olin College.

Honan, W. H. (1997, June 6). $200 Million, largest gift ever, endows new engineering college. *New York Times.*

Miller, R. K. (2000). Invention, 2000. Olin College. n.d. Web. 12 Jan. 2010. [http://www.olin.edu/about_olin/invention2kf.asp].

Somerville, M., Anderson, D., Berbeco, H., Bourne, J., Crisman, J., Dabby, D., et al. (2005). The Olin curriculum: Thinking toward the future. *IEEE Transactions on Education, 48*(1), 198–205.

CHAPTER 8 REFERENCE

Ducrot, J., Miller, S., & Goodman, P. (2008). Learning outcomes for a business information systems undergraduate program. *Communications of the Association for Information Systems, 23*, 95–122.

CHAPTER 9 REFERENCE

Wilson, J. (2001). The development of the studio classroom. In P. Goodman (Ed.), *Technology enhanced learning: Opportunities for change.* Mahwah, NJ: Lawrence Erlbaum.

CHAPTER 10 REFERENCES

Best Colleges 2008 [electronic version]. *U.S. News and World Report.* n.d. Web. Jan. 2009.

Duderstadt, J. (2003). *The future of the public university in America.* Baltimore: The Johns Hopkins University Press.

Emery, F. E. & Trist, E. (1969). Socio-technical systems. In F. E. Emery (Ed.), *Systems thinking* (pp. 21–32). Harmondsworth, England: Penguin.

Goodman, P. S. (1979). *Assessing organizational change: The Rushton quality of work experiment.* New York: Wiley-Interscience.

Goodman, P. S. (2001). *Technology enhanced learning: Opportunities for change.* Mahwah, NJ: Lawrence Erlbaum, Inc.

Goodman, P. S. & Griffiths, T. (1991). A process approach to the implementation of new technology. *Journal of Engineering and Technology Management, 8,* 261–85.

Wilson, J. M. (2001). The development of the studio classroom. In P. S. Goodman (Ed.), *Technology enhanced learning: Opportunities for change* (pp. 265–88). Mahwah, NJ: Lawrence Erlbaum Associates.

APPENDIX 1

Wave 1 Questionnaire

Learning Contract

Date:

1.0. Demographics
Name:
Class:
Major:
Prior to (College A) where did you go to school?
Where else did you apply to college?
Probe: You were accepted by:
Why did you select (College A)?

2.0. Introduction
When you came to (College A) in _____ (year) there was a "contract."
(College A) was going to provide you a set of educational experiences and
there were a set of activities and responsibilities you were going to do. We
want to explore these expectations.

2.1. When you first came to (College A) (in the first semester), what were the expec-
tations or promises of what they were going to do for you—educationally?
Probe: What were other expectations you had with respect to (College A)?
Probe others

2.2. You have listed the following expectations. How did you learn about these? In some cases you learn by direct communication or experience, and there are other things you learn more implicitly. How did you learn about _____
Expectation:
Probe:
Expectation:
Probe:
Expectation:
Expectation:
Expectation:

2.3. In any relationship expectations can be met, exceeded or not met. Let's review the expectations you specified.

2.3.1. Expectation. You mentioned _____

2.3.2. Would you say this expectation has been:
(Note – tense might change)
Expectation not met_____
Expectation met_____
Expectation exceeded_____
Why did you select this answer?

> Note: If expectations unmet, how did you feel?

2.3.3. Expectation. You mentioned _____
Would you say this expectation has been:
Expectation not met_____
Expectation met_____
Expectation exceeded_____
Why did you select this answer?

2.3.4. Expectation. You mentioned _____
Would you say this expectation has been:
Expectation not met_____
Expectation met_____
Expectation exceeded_____
Why did you select this answer?
Probe:
Expectation:

2.3.5. Expectation. You mentioned _____
Would you say this expectation has been:

Expectation not met_____
Expectation met_____
Expectation exceeded_____
Why did you select this answer?

2.3.6. Let me ask a different question. Were there any other expectations that you had that were not met? If yes, what expectations were not met?
Probe: How did you feel about that (for each unmet expectation)?

2.4. Let's change our focus from when you arrived as a freshman to today as a _____ (year in program). What are your current expectations about (College A) (pause), what they are going to do for you educationally? (Not relevant for Freshman - Go to 3.0)

2.4.1. You have listed the following expectations. How did you learn about
Expectation
Expectation
Expectation
Expectation
Expectation

2.4.2. We have been talking about your expectations about _____. Let's switch this around and ask what expectations (College A) has about what you should do?
Probe: What other expectations do they have with respect to you?
Probe:
Probe others

3.0. Competencies
I want to focus our discussion on competencies (e.g., knowledge, skills, abilities) that one should develop in this institution.

3.1. Is there a list of competencies? ____ Yes ____ No
3.1.1. If no, is there a general understanding about the competencies one should develop?

3.2. If yes, can you list the competencies?
Competency   Meaning
Competency   Meaning
Competency   Meaning

| Note: There could be a competency not on the list. |

Probe: Anything else? — then go to meaning.

3.3. Ratings.

    3.3.1. Here's a list of competencies at (College A). Some students focus on some of these, other students focus on others. Select 3 that are most important to you and 3 that are least important.

Most Important   Least Important

_____   _____

_____   _____

_____   _____

        3.3.3.1. (P) Why did you select _____ as most important?
        3.3.3.2. (P) Why did you select _____ as most important?
        3.3.3.3. (P) Why did you select _____ as most important?

3.3.2. We want to know how you would rate yourself on the competencies you mentioned (most and least important).

    3.3.2.1. How would you rate your level of (competency) using a scale? (F = first came, N = now)

1   2   3   4   5   6   7
Poor   Average   Excellent
F=
N=
Why did you select this rating? (Rating now)

    3.3.2.2. How would you rate your level of (competency) using a scale? (F = first came, N = now)

1   2   3   4   5   6   7
Poor   Average   Excellent
F=
N=
Why did you select this rating?

    3.3.2.3. How would you rate your level of (competency) using a scale? (F = first came, N = now)

1   2   3   4   5   6   7
Poor   Average   Excellent
F=
N=
Why did you select this rating?

3.3.2.4. How would you rate your level of (competency) using a scale?
    (F = first came, N = now)
1   2   3   4   5   6   7
Poor   Average   Excellent
F=
N=
Why did you select this rating?

3.3.2.5. How would you rate your level of (competency) using a scale?
    (F = first came, N = now)
1   2   3   4   5   6   7
Poor   Average   Excellent
F=
N=
Why did you select this rating?

3.3.2.6. How would you rate your level of (competency) using a scale?
    (F = first came, N = now)
1   2   3   4   5   6   7
Poor   Average   Excellent
F=
N=
Why did you select this rating?

4.0. Major Incident/Event
If you think about the time you spent at (College A), can you think of 1 or 2 incidents or events that greatly shaped how you think about this place?
4.1. Incident 1
Probe: Description
Probe: How did it affect how you think about (College A)?
4.2. Incident 2
Probe: Description
Probe: How did it affect how you think about (College A)?
5.0. Learning Environments
In institutions of higher education there are many different environments to create learning. Below is a list:

5.1. What % of your total course time (all the time you spend in the classroom and out of the classroom to complete a course) is allocated to any of these learning environments? _____

Environments	% Total Formal Course Time	% Total Learning Time
—Lecture/discussion	_____	_____
—Lab work	_____	_____
—Group project work	_____	_____
—Peer teaching	_____	_____
—Learning on your own	_____	_____
—Mentoring	_____	_____
—Internships	_____	_____
—Research project	_____	_____
—Studio	_____	_____
—Student clubs	_____	_____
—Other	_____	_____
	100%	100%

5.2. What % of your total learning time (all of the time you are involved in learning in course and non-course activities) is allocated to these different environments? _____

5.3. I am interested in how you would map the relationship between the learning environments you used and the competencies. Let's focus on the top 3 and bottom 3 competencies (interviewer cross out other competencies).

Draw lines between the environments which have had the *greatest* impact on the development of your competencies

Environments	Competencies
Lecture	Quantitative
Group discussion	Qualitative
Lab work	Diagnosis
Group project work	Team work skills
Peer teaching	Life long learning
Learning on your own	Communication
Mentoring	Contextual/analyses
Internships	Design
Studio	Assessing/pursuing opportunities
Student clubs	Other

6.0. Activities

At (College A) there are a variety of activities that you find may or may not impact on your learning.

6.1. Have you participated in _____? Yes ____ No ____

   6.1.1. How would you evaluate this experience?<Unnumbered table 3>

1	2	3	4	5	6
very dissatisfied	dissatisfied	slightly dissatisfied	slightly satisfied	satisfied	very satisfied

   6.1.2. Why did you select _____?

6.2. Writing an annual report

   6.2.1. Have you written an annual report? Yes ____ No ____

   6.2.2. How would you evaluate this experience?

1	2	3	4	5	6
very dissatisfied	dissatisfied	slightly dissatisfied	slightly satisfied	satisfied	very satisfied

   6.2.3. Why did you select _____?

7.0. (Adjacent College)

7.1. Have you been involved in any relationships with (Adjacent College)?
Yes ____ No ____
If yes, what, why?
Probe:
If no, why?

8.0. Any questions?

9.0. We plan to return next year and would like to talk with you at your convenience. Would that be ok? Yes ____ No ____

APPENDIX 2

Wave 1 Coding Sheet
CONTRACT DIMENSIONS
(School Expectations)

1.0 Why Attend (College A)?
    10 People positive
    11 Students
    12 Faculty–Student connections
    13 Staff
    14 Candidates week
    15 Community

    20 Education
    21 Focus learning, education focus
    22 Variety—multidisciplinary
    23 Project based
    24 Undergrad focus
    25 Innovative—curriculum, American education
    26 Entrepreneurial
    27 IT/Bus
    28 Content, engineering, computer, fit my interest

Note: Instructional notes and comments to the coders are not included in this form.

30 Financial

40 Institution
41 Contrast—other schools
42 Build new college
43 Facilities
44 Size
45 Prestige, ranking

50 Other
51 Location, city

2.1 When you *first* came to (College A) (in the first semester), what were the expectations or promises of what they were going to do for you— educationally? (2)

Academic environment

10 <u>EDUCATION</u>
Code:

11 Challenging academic environment, hard work
Good solid high quality engineering education comparable
12 Innovative education—mentions different learning environments
13 Project-based work, teams, learn, others
14 Learning by doing real work. Problem based in real world
15 Teach how to learn
16 Interdisciplinary
17 Mixing Arts/Education, IT Business, Cross Culture
18 Freedom/flexibility course structure, minor, double major, other schools
19 Small classes, participation, seminar
20 Outside of class learning, extra curricula, sports
21 Other unique—entrepreneurship, research, soft skills
22 PROFESSORS
Code:
23 Best, high quality
24 Close contact, support
30 <u>STUDENTS</u>
Code:
31 Make friends
32 High quality
33 Diverse

40 <u>INSTITUTION</u>
    Code:
        41 Strong support system
             Strong mentoring, we are a community, fun
        42 Trust, respect, honor, open
        43 Feedback and change, innovation, different place
        44 Accent diversity
        45 Prestige, reputation
        46 Help me marketable, graduate school work, internship, outside ties
        47 Facilities, technology, resources
        48 Service within, outside
        49 Other (accredit)
50 <u>ENVIRONMENT</u>
    Code:
        51 Cultural sports in city
        52 Networking
        53 City preferred location

2.2 HOW LEARN EXPECTATIONS

How did you learn about these expectations? In some cases you learn by direct communication or experience, and there are other things you learn more implicitly.

10 <u>UNIVERSITY</u>
        11 Mailings, brochures, printed materials, website, catalogues
        12 Visits to (College A)—students, professors, administration
        13 Candidates' week—students, professors, administration, sleeping bags
        14 Admission—interview
        15 (College A) students—not at (College A)
        16 (College A) visits to high school
20 <u>OTHERS</u>
        21 HS advisory teacher
        22 HS alums at (College A)
        23 Friends—other universities
        24 Princeton Review
        25 Other materials
        26 Other
30 <u>REFERENCES</u>
        31 Actual being student
        32 Prior beliefs
Note: Need to match up code in 2.1 with 2.2. Ex. 11-12

2.3 Expectations Met, Exceeded, Not Met

01-02   Code Expectation (from: see 2.1, 2.2)

3   Code: Contract status—Time - Freshman
                 Exceeded = 1
                 Met = 2
                 Not met = 3
                 Can't code = 4

4   Code: Direction
                 1 = Positive
                 2 = Negative
                 3 = Neutral
                 4 = Can't code

5   Code: Contract status—Interview Time (later)
                 Exceeded = 1
                 Met = 2
                 Not met = 3
                 Can't code = 4

6   Code: Direction
                 1 = Positive
                 2 = Negative
                 3 = Neutral
                 4 = Can't code

2.3.6 –UNMET EXPECTATIONS (2)

10 INSTITUTION
   Code:
   11 Bubble, isolated location.
   12 Not well rounded, narrow. Not college full life
   13 Culture
        - anti competitive
        - more flexibility
   14 Building school, innovate, change, receptive change
   15 Student body—more diversity
   16 Student body—too small

17 (College A)/(Adjacent College) link other schools

18 (College A)—Other schools link (Colleges B, C)

19 Other—Postgrad, Jobs, Resources, Facilities

20 EDUCATION

Code:

21 Course demands vs. other interests (see 25)

22 Course content, learning environments, changing (see 28)

23 Majors

24 Non course education (e.g., passionate pursuits)

25 Exhausted, free time—work time, balance (see 21)

26 Performance, faculty, staff

27 Advice, guidance, support

28 Course broad/not enough depth (see 22)

29 Other

30 COMMUNITY

31 Among students

32 Among faculty

33 Outside University

40 NO UNMET EXPECTATIONS

Code Freshman Time

1 = Positive

2 = Negative

3 = Neutral

4 = Can't code

Code Time Interview

1 = Positive

2 = Negative

3 = Neutral

4 = Can't code

2.4.1 –EXPECTATIONS NEW

10 EDUCATION

Code:

11 Challenging, good solid, high quality, top faculty.

12 Innovative.

13 Project, scope.

14 Learning by doing—real work.

15 Interdisciplinary, triangle.

16 Freedom, flexibility.

17 Small classes.

18 Outside, class learning.

19 Other.

20 CAREER EXPECTATIONS
Code:
21 Help support for career.
22 Help support for graduate school.
23 Help support for internships.
24 Skills helping job—communication.

30 INSTITUTION
Code:
31 Strong support, mentoring.
32 Honor, trust, respect.
33 Change—innovation.
34 Accept diversity.
35 Innovative, different.
36 Help me work, grad, marketable.
37 Facilities.
38 Community.
39 Other.

2.4.2 COLLEGE EXPECTATIONS OF YOU

10 EDUCATION

11 Do best academically, succeed, handle work well, diligent, work hard, stretch, participate

12 Learn what know, don't know. Learn to learn, learn why things wrong. Learning continuum.

13 Try new things, innovate, differentiate

14 Go outside of engineering (double major)

15 Balance work and self, academic and non-academic (not working) (see 14)

16 Entrepreneurship.

17 Stay, not leave.

18 Build competencies—leadership, communication, interact.

19 Other—multidisciplinary, diversity, research.

20 OTHER—COMMUNITY

2.1 Build Colleges A, B, C feedback, help, change (Note 13)

2.2 Build Colleges A, B, C community, participate. Active involvement (Note 15)

2.3 Be (Colleges A, B, C) ambassador, reflect positively, don't embarrass

2.4 Honor Code—be good, trust, respect, integrity.

2.5 Care, help others, mentor

2.6 Seek help, advice for you, learn with other

2.7 Other

30 BEYOND INTITUTION

    3.1 Maintain and do good internship work; as a graduate: contribute, high performer (Note 23)

    3.2 Community service, society

    3.3 Financial support

    3.4 Network

    3.5 Give back time, $

2.4.2

Pretty straight forward.

Distinguish build College A vs. build community.

Will be categories when there is no code—(e.g., express yourself).

Don't code repeats.

X = unusual answer.

Coding 3 **COMPETENCIES**

3.1.1	1 = yes	2 = no	3 = no answer
3.1.2	1 = yes	2 = no	3 = no answer

3.2 - Knowledge of competencies

- Read competencies
- Only include competencies on college list
- If there is ambiguity, read 2.3 answers. This may help the rating if competency is understood
- Ratings

    1. Did they list competencies from the school list = number

    2. Did they understand competencies from school list?

    3. I would put in codes for competencies understood. Competencies with X are not understood–Numbers should match #2.

3.3 Most important/Least important

    1. I would assign each competency a number. Note these differ by college.

    2. For most important and least important, I would enter the codes (competencies).

    3. For the ratings, I would first enter code for competency and then two spaces for first came and now.

College A

Quan	1
Qual	2
Diagnosis	3
Team	4
LCC	5
Comm	6
Context	7
Design	8
Opportunity	9

College B

Design	1
Quantitative	2
Project Management Skills	3
Learn-to-Learn	4
Collaboration	5
Change Management	6
Across Countries	7
Communication Skills	8

College C

Scientific Methods	1
Scientific Knowledge	2
Problem Solving	3
Teamwork	4
Lifelong Learning	5
Communication	6
Design	7
Context	8

4.0 - Major Incident/Event

If you think about the time you spent at (College A, B, C), can you think of 1 or 2 incidents or events that greatly shaped how you think about this place?

SETTINGS   Meanings

FORMAL

10 EDUCATION

  Code:

    11 Course, course work

12 Project course.

13 Extra course.

14 Professors, staff

15 Other students (see 31)

20 FORMAL ACTIVITY IN INSTITUTION

    21 _____

    22 Roles—RA

    23 Student Government, committees

    24 Candidates week, school function, orientation

    25 Clubs, sports.

INFORMAL

30 INFORMAL

Code:

    31 Quasi school, within school (see 15)

    32 Meet alumni

    33 Meet others

40 OTHER WORK/Activities

    41 Internship

    42 Research

    43 Start up, entrepreneurial activity

    44 Exchange

IMPACT

50 INDIVIDUAL

Code:

    51 Learning, fun learning, I'm capable, new skills

    52 Setting priorities, study, play hard

    53 Success, failure, competencies about myself, concept of self

    54 Experiencing success in an activity

    55 Learning and frustrations, how to learn

    56 IT/Bus intersection/multidiscipline

    57 Rel faculty, quality, attractiveness

    58 Rel students, quality

60 INSTITUTION

Code:

    61 Not care, involved.

    62 "(College A)"—Community, personal support or not

    63 People, quality, excitement, fun

    64 "(College A)"—Different institution, unique or not contributions for learning, different learning environment or not, educational problem

    65 Improvement, continuous, takes feedback or not

    66 Honor code—respect, integrity, trust

    67 Enhance reputation

        68 Strong work, pressure, drive
        69 Broader community, outside institution
  70 OTHER
        Code:
            Positive
            Negative

5.0 Learning Environments

5.1 Calculate what % of students' *total learning time* (all of the time involved in learning in course and non-course activities) is allocated to each of these different environments

Lecture/discussion	___
Lab work	___
Group project work	___
Peer teaching	___
Learning on your own	___
Mentoring	___
Internships	___
Research project	___
Studio	___
Student clubs	___
Other	___

5.2 Relationship between the learning environments student used and the competencies. Focus on the top 3 and bottom 3 competencies–

	Quant	Qual	Diag	Team	LLL	Comm.	Contx	Des	Opportunity
Lecture									
Gp dis									
Lab									
Gp pjt work									
Peer tch									
Self lrn									
Ment									
Intern									
Studio									
Clubs									
Other									

6.0 Activities (College A)

At (College A) there are a variety of activities that the student find that may or may not impact on his learning.

    6.1.1 Has the student participated in _____?

    6.1.2 If yes, how did the student evaluate this experience?

            1= very dissatisfied

            2 = dissatisfied

            3 = slightly dissatisfied

            4 = slightly satisfied

            5 = satisfied

            6 = very satisfied

    6.1.3 Why did the student select _____?

6.2 - Writing an annual report

    6.2.1 - How did the student evaluate this experience?

            1= very dissatisfied

            2 = dissatisfied

            3 = slightly dissatisfied

            4 = slightly satisfied

            5 = satisfied

            6 = very satisfied

6.0 Activities (College B)

Has the student been involved with any relationships outside of (College B) but within the university that are not required universities (e.g. courses)?

    Yes = 1

    No = 2

If yes, what?

If yes, why?

10 ACADEMIC (not required)

    Code: 11 Courses

            12 Research Assistant/TA

20 NEW ACADEMIC

    Code: 21 Clubs

            22 Sports

            23 School activities, movies, newspapers

            24 Peer help mentoring - student focused

            25 Business, entrepreneurial

            26 Student government

6.0 Activities (College C)

Has the student been involved in any relationships outside of (department) but within (College C) that are not required activities (e.g. courses)? Has the student taken other courses?

    Yes = 1

    No = 2

If yes, what?

If yes, why?

10 ACADEMIC (not required)

    Code: 11 Courses

           12 Research Assistant/TA

20 NEW ACADEMIC

    Code: 21 Clubs

           22 Sports

           23 School activities, movies, newspapers

           24 Peer help mentoring - student focused

           25 Business, entrepreneurial

           26 Student government

If no why?

Coding for 7.0 - Relationship with (Adjacent College)

College A - Has the student been involved in any relationships with (Adjacent College)? Has the student taken courses at (Adjacent College)?

    Yes = 1

    No = 2

Of all the activities (College A) students engaged in at (Adjacent College), what % was positive, negative, or neutral?

Wave 2 Dimensions Survey

1.0 Core values

In many universities there are some core values. In some there is lots of agreement and support from students, faculty, administrators, and in others, there is less agreement and support. We would like you to rate the extent to which there is agreement and support on following dimensions at (COLLEGE).

   (Please use scale below)

   1 = to a very great extent
   2 = to a great extent
   3 = to some extent
   4 = to a little extent
   5 = not at all

1.1 _____ Quality and continuous improvement at (COLLEGE)
1.2 _____ Student learning and development
1.3 _____ Institutional integrity and community
1.4 _____ Institutional agility and entrepreneurism
1.5 _____ Stewardship and service within and outside (COLLEGE)

2.0 Organizational processes—1

You are part of a college. These questions are about your views about the *college* rather than some courses. Please rate your satisfaction with the following dimensions using the satisfaction scale below:

   1 = very dissatisfied
   2 = dissatisfied
   3 = slightly dissatisfied
   4 = slightly satisfied

5 = satisfied
6 = very satisfied
7 = don't know

2.1 _____ Quality of communications about important events and activities at (COLLEGE).
2.2 _____ Quality of decision making/problem solving at (COLLEGE).
2.3 _____ Speed of decision making at (COLLEGE).
2.4 _____ Level of innovation at (COLLEGE).
2.5 _____ Recognition and rewards for performance at (COLLEGE).
2.6 _____ Level of collaboration within (COLLEGE).
2.7 _____ Quality of faculty hired at (COLLEGE).
2.8 _____ Quality of students brought in to (COLLEGE).
2.9 _____ Processes for conflict resolution at (COLLEGE).

3.0 Organizational Processes–2

These are some other questions about your views of (COLLEGE).
Using the following scale:
1 = very effective
2 = effective
3 = slightly effective
4 = slightly ineffective
5 = ineffective
6 = very ineffective

How would you rate:
3.1 _____ Overall effectiveness of teaching at (COLLEGE).
3.2 _____ Relationship with other institutions for you.
3.3 _____ Opportunities to get internships at (COLLEGE).
3.4 _____ Opportunities and assistance for your career planning at (COLLEGE).
3.5 _____ Opportunities for job or graduate school placement at (COLLEGE).
3.6 Overall, would you say the quality of teaching in your college compared to last year is
_____ Much better than last year
_____ Better
_____ Same
_____ Worse
_____ Much worse than last year

4.0 Expectations—Academic

As a student at (COLLEGE) you developed certain expectations about what the school would do for you academically.

To what extent have the following expectations been met about:
Using this scale:

    1 = to a very great extent
    2 = to a great extent
    3 = to some extent
    4 = to a little extent
    5 = not at all

4.1 _____ Challenging high-quality engineering education
4.2 _____ Innovative learning environments
4.3 _____ Learning in project based teams
4.4 _____ Opportunities to learn how to learn on your own.
4.5 _____ Flexibility in selecting the courses you want
4.6 _____ Interdisciplinary education
4.7 _____ Small classes
4.8 _____ Learning outside of the classroom
4.9 _____ Having excellent professors
4.10 _____ Close contact with the professors

5.0 Expectations—Institution

As a student at _____ you developed certain expectations about what the school would be like for you.

To what extent have the following expectations been met about
    Using this scale:

        1 = to a very great extent
        2 = to a great extent
        3 = to some extent
        4 = to a little extent
        5 = not at all

5.1 _____ a place with strong mentoring
5.2 _____ a place with a strong support system
5.3 _____ a place that values trust and integrity
5.4 _____ a place that is constantly innovating
5.5 _____ a place that has good resources/facilities
5.6 _____ a place that will help you be marketable for jobs/grad school
5.7 _____ a place where I have made strong friendships

6.0 The following are some questions about your relationship to (COLLEGE)?
Please use the following scale to describe your feelings:

    1 = strongly agree
    2 = agree
    3 = slightly agree

4 = slightly disagree
5 = disagree
6 = strongly disagree

6.1 _____ I feel a strong sense of belonging to (COLLEGE).
6.2 _____ This organization has a great deal of personal meaning to me.
6.3 _____ I enjoy discussing (COLLEGE) with people outside of this institution.

INDEX

Implementation, of OLCs, 5, 8, 25, 28, 189–91
Implicit OLCs, explicit *vs.*, 4
Independent variables, 70
India, 166, 170–74, 176
"Infocomm," 140. *See also* School of Information Systems
Information sources
    expectations from school-initiated sources, 53, 54–55, 54*f*, 65
    types of, 54, 54*f*
Information systems, 141–42
Information technology (IT), 10, 97, 142. *See also* School of Information Systems
Innovative institutions, 12–13. *See also* New institutions
Input-process-outcome model, 46, 97–98
Inputs, 98–102
    defined, 97
    discussion of, 101–2
    examples of, 97
    faculty inputs, 100–101, 100*t*
    student inputs, 98–100, 99*t*
    subjective measures of, 101, 102
Institutionalization, of OLCs, 5, 8, 104, 192–94
Institutions of higher education. *See also specific types*
    aligned, 33
    comparisons among, 44–45
    forces challenging viability of, 10, 13, 97
    image, culture, and mission of, 5
    types of, 26
Instituto Tecnológico y de Estudios Superiores de Monterrey (ITESM), 168
Instruments, and research, 42–44
Intellectual origins, of OLCs, 4–5
InterAmerican Development Bank, 170
Interdisciplinary learning, 90
    expectations of, 55–56, 56*t*–57*t*, 60, 67
International universities, 10, 100, 100*t*, 199
Internships, 17, 72, 105, 107*t*, 108, 114
Intersender conflict, 31
Interviewers, 43
Interviews
    in research, 35–36, 41–44, 41*t*, 116, 194
    student recruiting and interview process at SIS, 143, 149, 151–52, 158
    surveys *vs.*, 71

"Invention 2000," 123, 130n3
IT. *See* Information technology
ITESM. *See* Instituto Tecnológico y de Estudios Superiores de Monterrey

Job placement, 111–13, 112*f*, 112*t*–113*t*, 114, 183

Kerns, David V., Jr., 134, 136
Kerns, Sherra E., 134
Kuh, G. D., 49, 70

Lambert, A. D., 70
Latin America, 6, 165–70, 173–74, 176, 179, 180
Lattuca, L. R., 70
Leadership, 199–200
Learning, 69–95. *See also* Personal models of learning; *specific types*
    active, 12–13, 21, 52, 71, 73
    creating new model of, 198–99
    critical incidents and, 71, 80–86
    defined, 18
    discussion of, 93–95
    to learn, 29, 182
    literature on, 69–72
    personal reflections on, 161–63
    psychology of, 91
    systemic approach to, 69–71
    on your own, 21, 73, 84
Learning climate, 91–93
    learning climate impacts–antecedents to education experiences % of responses, 92*f*
    learning climate impacts–personal affiliation, 114*t*
    learning climate impacts–teaching, 86*t*
Learning environments, 18*f*, 20–22, 72–73. *See also* Learning environments and outcomes, relationship between; Learning models; *specific environments*
    basic assumptions underlying, 20
    collaborative skills linked to, 20
    in College A, 38, 52, 60, 71, 72–73, 72*f*, 74*f*
    in College B, 38, 52, 60, 71, 72–73, 72*f*, 74*f*
    in College C, 38, 52, 60, 71, 72–73, 72*f*, 74*f*
    defined, 8, 20